AN ELEMENTARY TEXTBOOK
OF PSYCHOANALYSIS

AN ELEMENTARY TEXTBOOK

OF PSYCHOANALYSIS

CHARLES BRENNER, M.D.

Past President, American Psychoanalytic Association
Past President, New York Psychoanalytic Society
Instructor, New York Psychoanalytic Institute
Lecturer in Psychiatry, Yale University Medical School

Revised Edition

INTERNATIONAL UNIVERSITIES PRESS, INC.

New York

To
MY WIFE

CONTENTS

FOREWORD TO THE SECOND EDITION xi

INTRODUCTION xiii

CHAPTER I *Two Fundamental Hypotheses* . . . 1

Psychoanalysis and general psychology—psychic determinism: definition, importance, examples—unconscious mental processes: relation to psychic determinism, methods of study—development of the psychoanalytic method—survey of sources of evidence for existence of unconscious mental processes.

CHAPTER II *The Drives* 16

Link with biology—nomenclature and definition—psychic energy and cathexis—classification of drives—fusion of drives—genetic development of erotic drive: oral, anal, phallic phases of infantile sexuality—libidinal progression, fixation and regression—development of aggressive drive—drive discharge and pleasure.

CHAPTER III *The Psychic Apparatus* 34

Historical development of structural theory—differentiation of ego from id—ego as executant for drives—basic ego functions: perception, memory, affects, thought—factors in ego development: maturation, experience—experiential factors: relation to own body, identification with objects of environment—types of identification—modes of functioning of psychic apparatus: primary and secondary process, primary and secondary process thinking—neutralization of drive energy.

CHAPTER IV *The Psychic Apparatus (continued)* 62

Ego adaptation to and mastery of outer world (environment)—function of reality testing—conflict or opposition between ego and inner world (id)—ego as inhibitor

CONTENTS

or master of drives—pleasure principle—theory of anxiety
—roles of anxiety and pleasure principle in conflicts between ego and id—defensive operations of ego—defense
mechanisms of ego.

CHAPTER V *The Psychic Apparatus (concluded)*　　106

Object relations: definition, importance of early relations
—narcissism—stages of preoedipal object relations: inter-
mittent, continuing, part and whole objects, ambivalence,
identification with object—object relations and drives—
crucial significance of oedipal phase of object relations—
description of oedipus complex—oedipus complex and
superego—superego formation: internalization; relation
to anxiety; identification with parental ideals, prohibitions, and superegos; transformation of object cathexes
to narcissistic ones; internalization of aggression and
severity of superego—superego functions: guilt, inferiority feelings, virtue, *lex talionis*, magical equation of
wish and deed, unconscious need for punishment—defenses against superego—superego and group psychology.

CHAPTER VI *Parapraxes and Wit* .　.　.　.　.　138

Definition of parapraxes—causes of parapraxes with examples: unconscious defensive activity of ego, unconscious id derivative, unconscious superego activity—
"intelligible" vs. "unintelligible" slips—summary of psychoanalytic theory of parapraxes—technique of wit:
primary process thinking, ego regression—content of
wit: repressed, sexual and/or hostile impulses—laughter
as consequence of saving in psychic energy—similarities
and differences between parapraxes and wit.

CHAPTER VII *Dreams* .　.　.　.　.　.　.　162

Importance of dreams—manifest dream, latent dream
content, dream work—constituents of latent content—
relative importance of constituents—relation between
latent and manifest dream content: early childhood
dreams, manifest dream as wish-fulfilling fantasy—un-
intelligibility of manifest dream due to dream work:
translation of latent content elements into preverbal,
primary process thinking; ego defenses—manifest dream
as compromise formation—examples of compromise for-

mations—anxiety dreams—punishment dreams—emergence of "the repressed" and diminution of defenses in sleep—secondary elaboration in dream work—predominance of visual, sensory elements in manifest dream—sense of reality in dreams.

CHAPTER VIII *Psychopathology* 186

Freud's earliest views on psychic disorders: hysteria, actual neuroses, etiological vs. descriptive approach—psychic conflict and psychoneurotic symptoms—defense neuropsychoses—role of childhood sexual experiences—infantile sexuality—normality, neurosis, and perversion—neurotic symptom as meaningful compromise formation—mental disorders as evidence of malfunctioning of psychic apparatus—continuum between "normal" and "neurotic" functioning—character disorders—neurotic symptoms and failure of defense; examples—primary and secondary gain—regression—ego-alien vs. ego-syntonic malfunctioning or symptoms.

CHAPTER IX *Psychic Conflict and Normal
                Mental Functioning* 210

Character traits—mannerisms—hobbies and avocational interests—choice of vocation—choice of sexual partner—fairy tales—myths and legends—religion—religious practices—individual and group morality—politics—magic and superstition—conflict between generations; the generation gap—revolution and revolutionaries—daydreams—artistic creativity—artistic enjoyment.

CHAPTER X *Psychoanalysis Today* 259

Psychoanalysis a challenge—broader horizons: the psychoanalytic image of man—future prospects—psychoanalysis and psychiatry—psychoanalysis and child observation—conclusion.

REFERENCES 271
INDEX 275

CHAPTER I

TWO FUNDAMENTAL HYPOTHESES

Psychoanalysis is a scientic discipline which was begun by Sigmund Freud and which is still indissolubly associated with his name. Its beginning cannot be dated precisely, since it extended over a period of several years. By 1895, however, the evolution of psychoanalysis was well under way. Like any other scientific discipline, psychoanalysis has given rise to certain theories which are derived from its observational data and which attempt to order and explain those data. What we call psychoanalytic theory, therefore, is a body of hypotheses concerning mental functioning and development in man. It is a part of general psychology and it comprises what are by far the most important contributions that have been made to human psychology to date.

It is important to realize that psychoanalytic theory is concerned with normal as well as with pathological mental functioning. It is by no means merely a theory of psychopathology. It is true that the *practice* of psychoanalysis consists of the treatment of people who are mentally ill or disturbed, but the theories of psychoanalysis have to do with the normal as well as the abnormal even though they have been derived principally from the study and treatment of the abnormal.

As in any scientific discipline, the various hypotheses of psychoanalytic theory are mutually related. Some are naturally more fundamental than others, some are better established than others, and some have received so much

1

confirmation and appear to be so fundamental in their significance that we are inclined to view them as established laws of the mind.

Two such fundamental hypotheses, which have been abundantly confirmed, are the principle of psychic determinism, or causality, and the proposition that consciousness is an exceptional rather than a regular attribute of psychic processes. To put the latter proposition in somewhat different words, we may say that, according to psychoanalytic theory, unconscious mental processes are of very great frequency and significance in normal as well as in abnormal mental functioning. This first chapter will be devoted to a consideration of these two fundamental hypotheses, which are mutually related, as we shall see.

Let us start with the principle of psychic determinism. The sense of this principle is that in the mind, as in physical nature about us, nothing happens by chance, or in a random way. Each psychic event is determined by the ones which preceded it. Events in our mental lives that may seem to be random and unrelated to what went on before are only apparently so. In fact, mental phenomena are no more capable of such a lack of causal connection with what preceded them than are physical ones. Discontinuity in this sense does not exist in mental life.

The understanding and application of this principle is essential for a proper orientation in the study of human psychology as well in its normal as in its pathological aspects. If we do understand and apply it correctly, we shall never dismiss any psychic phenomenon as meaningless or accidental. We shall always ask ourselves, in relation to any such phenomenon in which we are interested: "What caused it? Why did it happen so?" We ask ourselves these questions because we are confident that an answer to them exists. Whether we can discover the answer quickly and easily is another matter, to be sure, but we know that the answer is there.

An example of this approach to psychic phenomena is the following. It is a common experience of everyday life to forget or mislay something. The usual view of such an occurrence is that it is "an accident," that it "just happened." Yet a thorough investigation of many such "accidents" during the past seventy-five years by psychoanalysts, beginning with the studies by Freud himself, has shown that they are by no means as accidental as popular judgment considers them to be. On the contrary, each such "accident" can be shown to have been caused by a wish or intent of the person involved, in strict conformity with the principle of mental functioning which we have been discussing.

To take another example from the realm of everyday life, Freud discovered, and the analysts who followed him have confirmed, that the common, yet remarkable and mysterious phenomena of sleep which we call dreams follow the same principle of psychic determinism. Each dream, indeed each image in each dream, is the consequence of other psychic events, and each stands in a coherent and meaningful relationship to the rest of the dreamer's psychic life.

The reader must realize that such a view of dreams, a subject which we shall discuss at some length in Chapter VII, is quite different, for example, from that which was current among scientifically trained psychologists seventy years ago. They considered dreams to be due to the random or incoordinated activity of various parts of the brain during sleep, a view that is directly at variance with our law of psychic determinism.

If we turn now to the phenomena of psychopathology, we shall expect the same principle to apply, and indeed psychoanalysts have repeatedly confirmed our expectation. Each neurotic symptom, whatever its nature, is caused by other mental processes, despite the fact that the patient himself often considers the symptom to be foreign to his whole being, and quite unconnected with the rest of his mental life. The connections are there, nonetheless, and are demonstrable despite the patient's unawareness of their presence.

At this point we can no longer avoid recognizing that we are talking not only about the first of our fundamental hypotheses, the principle of psychic determinism, but also about the second, that is the existence and significance of mental processes of which the individual himself is unaware or unconscious.

In fact, the relation between these two hypotheses is so intimate that one can hardly discuss the one without bringing in the other also. It is precisely the fact that so much of what goes on in our minds is unconscious, that is, unknown to ourselves, that accounts for the *apparent* discontinuities in our mental lives. When a thought, a feeling, an accidental forgetting, a dream, or a pathological symptom seems to be unrelated to what went on before in the mind, it is because its causal connection is with some *unconscious* mental process rather than with a conscious one. If the unconscious cause or causes can be discovered, then all apparent discontinuities disappear and the causal chain or sequence becomes clear.

A simple example of this would be the following. A person may find himself humming a tune without having any idea of how it came to his mind. This apparent discontinuity in our subject's mental life is resolved, in our particular example, by the testimony of a bystander, however, who tells us that the tune in question was *heard* by our subject a few moments before it entered his conscious thoughts, apparently from nowhere. It was a sensory impression, in this case an auditory one, which caused our subject to hum the tune. Since the subject was unaware of hearing the tune, his subjective experience was of a discontinuity in his thoughts, and it required the bystander's testimony to remove the appearance of discontinuity, and to make clear the causal chain.

The example just given was chosen for its simplicity. In fact, it is rare for an unconscious mental process—in this case an auditory perception—to be discovered so simply and easily. The natural question to ask is whether there is any more general method for discovering mental processes of which the subject himself is unaware. Can they be observed directly, for example? If not, how did Freud discover the frequency and importance of such processes in our mental lives?

The fact is that we have as yet no method which permits us to observe unconscious mental processes directly. All of our methods for studying such phenomena are indirect. They permit us to infer the existence of these phenomena, and often to determine their nature and their significance in the mental life of the individual who is the object of our study. The most useful and reliable method we have at present for studying unconscious mental processes is the technique which Freud evolved over a period of several years. This technique he called psychoanalysis for the very reason that he was able, with its help, to discern and detect psychic processes that would otherwise have remained hidden and unsuspected. It was during the same years in which he was developing the technique of psychoanalysis that Freud became aware, with the help of his new technique, of the importance of unconscious mental processes in the mental life of every individual, whether mentally sick or healthy. It may be of interest to trace briefly the steps that led up to the development of Freud's technique.

As Freud himself has told us in his autobiographical sketch (1925), he began his medical career as a neuroanatomist, and a very competent one. Faced, however, with the necessity of earning a living, he entered medical practice as a neurologist and had then to treat patients whom we should today call either neurotic or psychotic. This is still true at the present time of every specialist in the field of neurology, except for those with full-time academic or hospital positions who see no private patients at all. The practice of a neurologist, now, as then, consists of psychiatric patients. At the time when Freud began his practice, there was no rationally, i.e., etiologically oriented form of psychiatric treatment. Indeed, there were few in the entire field of medicine. Bacteriology, if no longer in its infancy, was certainly in early adolescence, aseptic surgery had only just been developed, and the great advances in physiology and pathology had hardly begun to make possible substantial improvements in the treatment of patients. It is obvious to us today that the more thorough a physician's medical training, the better his therapeutic results—clinical medicine has become to a certain extent a science. It is hard to realize that hardly more than a century ago, this was not at all the case; that the well-trained and scholarly physician was hardly superior to the most ignorant quack in his ability to treat illnesses, even though he might be able to diagnose them much better. It is strange to us, for example, to read of Tolstoy's contempt for physicians, and we are inclined to attribute it to the author's idiosyncrasy, like the conviction of an eminent novelist of a later day, Aldous Huxley, that corrective lenses are no longer necessary for myopia. But the fact is that even the well-trained physician of Tolstoy's earlier days really could not cure sick people and, by the criterion of results, seemed a perfectly suitable target for his critics' scorn. It was only during the latter half of the nineteenth century that medicine as taught in the universities showed itself to be clearly superior in its *results* to naturopathy, Christian Science, homeopathy, or superstitious folklore.

As a well-trained scientist would be expected to do, Freud

utilized the most scientific methods of treatment that were at his disposal. For example, for hysterical symptoms he employed the electrical treatments recommended by the great neurologist, Erb, much of whose work in the field of clinical electrophysiology is valid to this day. Unfortunately, however, Erb's recommendations for the treatment of hysteria were not so well founded, and, as Freud tells us, he had eventually to conclude that the Erb treatment of hysteria was worthless, and that the results claimed for it are simply untrue. In 1885 Freud had gone to Paris, where he studied for several months in Charcot's clinic. He became familiar with hypnosis as a method for the production of hysterical symptoms and for their treatment, as well as with the syndrome of hysteria, both major and minor, which Charcot had outlined. Like other up-to-date neurologists of his time, Freud tried to banish his patients' symptoms by hypnotic suggestion, with varying degrees of success. It was at about this time that his friend Breuer told him of an experience with a hysterical patient which was of crucial importance in the development of psychoanalysis.

Breuer himself was a practicing physician of considerable talent and with an excellent physiological training. Among other things, he collaborated in the discovery of a respiratory reflex known as the Hering-Breuer reflex, and he introduced the use of morphine in acute pulmonary edema. What Breuer told Freud was that several years earlier he had treated a hysterical woman by hypnosis and had found that her symptoms disappeared when she had been able in her hypnotic state to recall the experience and the accompanying emotion which had led to the symptom in question—her symptoms could be talked away under hypnosis. Freud eagerly applied this method to the treatment of hysterical patients of his own with good results. The results of this work were published in collaboration with Breuer (1895) in articles, and finally in a monograph.

As Freud went on, however, he found that hypnosis was not uniformly easy to induce, that the good results were apt to be transitory, and that some at least of his female patients became sexually attached to him in the course of the hypnotic treatment—something which was most unwelcome to him. At this point the memory of an experiment of the French hypnotist Bernheim came to his rescue. Bernheim had demonstrated to a group, of which Freud was a member, that a subject's amnesia for his hypnotic experiences could be lifted *without* rehypnotizing the patient, by urging him to remember what he insisted he could not. If the urging was persistent and forceful enough, the patient *did* remember what he had forgotten without having been rehypnotized. Freud argued on this basis that he should be able to lift a *hysterical* amnesia without hypnosis too, and set about doing so. From this beginning he evolved the psychoanalytic technique, the essence of which is that the patient undertakes to report to the analyst without exception whatever thoughts come into his mind and to refrain from exercising over them either conscious direction or censorship.

It has happened frequently in the history of science that an innovation in technique has opened up a whole new world of data, and made it possible to understand, that is, to construct valid hypotheses about what was previously incorrectly or incompletely understood. Galileo's invention of the telescope was such a technical advance that made possible immense progress in the field of astronomy, and Pasteur's use of microscopy in the study of infectious disease was equally revolutionary in its effect in that field of science. The development and application of the psychoanalytic technique made it possible for Freud, the genius who developed and applied it, to make discoveries which have revolutionized both the theory and practice of psychiatry, in particular of psychotherapy, as well as to make contributions of the most fundamental sort to the science of human psychology in general.

The reason for the great value of having the patient relinquish conscious control of his thoughts is this: what the patient thinks and says under those circumstances is determined by *unconscious* thoughts and motives. Thus Freud, by listening to the patient's "free" associations—which were after all free only from *conscious* control—was able to get a picture, by inference, of what was going on unconsciously in his patient's mind. He was therefore in the unique position of being able to study his patients' unconscious mental processes, and what he discovered, in the course of years of patient and careful observation, was that not only hysterical symptoms but also many other normal and pathological aspects of behavior and thinking were the result of what was going on unconsciously in the mind of the individual who exhibited them.

In the course of studying unconscious mental phenomena, Freud soon found that they could be divided into two groups. The first group comprised thoughts, memories, etc., which could readily be made conscious by an effort of attention. Such psychic elements have ready access to consciousness, and Freud called them "preconscious." Any thought which happens to be conscious at a given moment, for example, is preconscious both before and after that particular moment. The more interesting group of unconscious phenomena, however, comprised those psychic elements which could only be made conscious by the expenditure of considerable effort. In other words, they were barred from consciousness by a considerable force, which had to be overcome before they could become conscious. This is what we find, for example, in a case of hysterical amnesia.

It was for this second group of phenomena that Freud reserved the term "unconscious" in the stricter sense. He was able to demonstrate that their being unconscious in this sense in no way prevented them from exerting the most significant influence on mental functioning. In addition, he was able to show that unconscious processes might be quite comparable to conscious ones in precision and complexity.

As we said earlier, we have as yet no way of observing unconscious mental activities directly. We can only observe their effects as expressed in the subject's thoughts and feelings which he reports to us, and in his actions, which may be either reported or observed. Such data are derivatives of unconscious mental activities, and from them we can draw inferences concerning the activities themselves.

The data are particularly full and clear when one uses the analytic technique which Freud devised. However, there are other sources of data which furnish evidence for our fundamental proposition that unconscious mental processes have the capacity to produce effects on our thoughts and actions, and it may be of interest to make a brief survey of their nature.

Evidence of this sort which is of the nature of an experiment is provided by the well-known facts of posthypnotic suggestion. A subject is hypnotized, and while in the trance is told something which he is to do after he has been roused from the trance. For example, he is told, "When the clock strikes two, you will get up from your chair and open the window." Before being awakened, the subject is also told that he will have no memory of what happened during the trance and he is then told to wake up. Shortly after he has awakened, the clock strikes two, and he goes over and opens the window. If he is then asked why he does so, he will either say, "I don't know. I just felt like it," or, more usually, he will give some rationalization, such as that he felt warm. The point is that he is *not conscious* at the time he carries out the action which the hypnotist ordered him to perform why he did so, nor can he become conscious of his real motive by any simple act of memory or introspection. Such an experiment shows clearly that a truly unconscious mental process (obedience to a command in this case) can have a dynamic or motive effect on thought and behavior.

Other evidences of this fact may be derived from clinical, or even general observation. Take for example certain phenomena of dreams. It is true, of course, that for any adequate study of dreams and dreaming in general, it is essential to use the technique of investigation that Freud devised, that is, the psychoanalytic technique. Indeed, Freud's study of dreams by this technique is one of his major achievements, and his book, *The Interpretation of Dreams*, ranks as one of the truly great and revolutionary scientific books of all time. However, we need not go into the study of dream interpretation in detail for our present purpose. As we said earlier, we shall reserve a full discussion of dream psychology for Chapter VII. At this point we need make only the following observations on the subject.

It is well known from many sources, for example the journals and logs of early Arctic expeditions, that starving men regularly, or at least very often, dream of food and of eating. I think that we can easily recognize that it is hunger which gives rise to such dreams, and of course the men are quite consciously aware of their hunger when they are awake. But *during their sleep*, when they are dreaming of gorging themselves at banquets, they are *not conscious* of hunger, but only of a dream of satiation, so that we can say that at the time the dream was dreamed, something was going on *unconsciously* in the dreamers' minds that gave rise to the dream images which were consciously experienced.

Other dreams of convenience, such as those in which the dreamer dreams that he is drinking, only to wake to the realization that he is thirsty, or dreams that he is urinating or defecating, and wakes with the urge to relieve himself, similarly demonstrate that during sleep the unconscious activity of the mind can produce a conscious result—in these cases that an unconscious bodily sensation and the wishes connected with it give rise to a conscious dream of the desired satisfaction or relief. Such a demonstration is important in itself, and can be made without any special technique of observation. However, by means of the psychoanalytic technique, Freud was able to demonstrate that behind *every* dream there are active unconscious thoughts and desires, and thus to establish as a *general rule* that when dreams occur they are caused by mental activity which is unconscious to the dreamer, and which would remain so without the use of the psychoanalytic technique.

Until Freud's investigations in the last decade of the nineteenth century, dreams had been largely neglected as an object of serious scientific study and one may add, rightly so, since before him there was no adequate technique for studying them, with the result that whatever serious studies had been made of them had shed but little light upon them. It was his discovery of the psychoanalytic method that enabled Freud to discover more about dreams than it had been possible for any of his predecessors to learn.

There is another group of phenomena to which Freud has called attention, which also demonstrate how unconscious mental activities can affect our conscious behavior. Like dreams, these are normal features of mental life; like dreams also, they had been previously neglected because they could not be fruitfully studied until the psychoanalytic method had been evolved. As we have done with dreams, we shall discuss these phenomena briefly at this point, reserving a fuller discussion of them for Chapter VI. They occur in waking life rather than in sleep, and are what we call in general slips: slips of the tongue, of the pen, of memory, and similar, related actions for which we have no very exact, generic name in English. In German they are called *Fehlleistungen*, literally, erroneous actions. As in the case of dreams, some slips are clear and simple enough for us to be able to guess with a high degree of accuracy and conviction what their unconscious meaning is. It is notoriously easy to forget something that is unpleasant or annoying, like paying a bill, for example. The amorous swain, on the other hand, does not forget an appointment with his sweetheart, or if he does, he is likely to find that she holds him to account for this unconscious sign of neglect of her just as though it had been a consciously intended one. It is not hard to guess that a young man has some hesitation about embarking on marriage if he tells us that while driving to his wedding he stopped for a traffic light, and only when it had changed did he realize that he had stopped for a green light instead of a red one. Another rather transparent example which might be called a symptomatic action rather than a slip of any sort, was furnished by a patient whose appointment had been canceled one day for his analyst's convenience. The patient found himself somewhat at loose ends during the time which was usually occupied by coming for his treatment, and decided to try out a pair of antique dueling pistols which he had recently bought. So at the time when he would ordinarily have been lying on the analyst's couch, he was shooting a dueling pistol at a target! Even without the patient's associations one would feel fairly safe in assuming that he was angry at his analyst for having failed to see him that day. We should add that, as in the case of dreams, Freud was able by applying the psychoanalytic technique to show that unconscious mental activity plays a role in the production of all slips, not just ones in which the significance of such activity is readily apparent, as is true for the examples we have offered above.

Another, easily demonstrable bit of evidence for the proposition that an individual's unconscious mental processes are of significance in his mental life is the following. The motives for a person's behavior may often be obvious to an observer, though unknown to himself. Examples of this are familiar to us from clinical and personal experience. It may be very obvious from her behavior, for instance, that a mother is dominating and demanding toward her child at the same time that she believes herself to be the most self-sacrificing of mothers, who wants only to do what is best for her child with no thought of her own wishes. I think that most of us would be ready to assume that this woman had an unconscious desire to dominate and control her child, despite not only her unawareness, but even her vigorous denial of any such desire. Another, somewhat amusing example is the pacifist who is ready to quarrel violently with anyone who contradicts his view on the undesirability of violence. It is obvious that his conscious pacifism is accompanied by an unconscious desire to fight, which in this case is the very thing that his conscious attitude condemns.

So far we have used examples from normal mental life as evidence for the existence of unconscious mental processes. In fact, however, the importance of unconscious mental activity was first and foremost demonstrated by Freud in the case of the symptoms of mentally ill patients. As a result of Freud's discoveries the idea that such symptoms have a meaning that is unknown to the patient is by now so generally accepted and understood that it hardly requires illustration. If a patient has a hysterical blindness, we naturally assume that there is something that he unconsciously does not wish to see, or that his conscience forbids him to look at. It is true that it is by no means always easy to guess the unconscious meaning of a symptom correctly and that the unconscious determinants for even a single symptom may be very many and quite complex, so that even if one can guess correctly about its meaning, the guess is only a part, and sometimes a small part, of the whole truth. This is immaterial for our present purpose, however, which is simply to indicate by illustration various sources of evidence for our fundamental proposition concerning unconscious mental processes.

Even though now, in retrospect, we can see, as in our illustrations, that we can establish even without the aid of the psychoanalytic technique the power of unconscious mental activity to influence conscious thoughts and behavior both in healthy and in mentally ill persons, as well as in the experimental situation of hypnosis, we must nevertheless remember that it was the use of that technique that did *originally* make the discovery possible and that was essential to the fuller study of unconscious mental phenomena.

This study convinced Freud that in fact the majority of mental functioning goes on without consciousness and that consciousness is an unusual rather than a usual quality or attribute of mental functioning. This is in sharp contrast to the view that prevailed before Freud's time that consciousness and mental functioning were synonymous. We believe today that the two are by no means so and that consciousness, though an important characteristic of the operations of the mind, is by no means a necessary one. We believe that it need not and often does not attach even to mental operations which are decisive in determining the behavior of the individual, or to those which are most complex and most precise in their nature. Such operations—even complex and decisive ones—may be quite unconscious.

SUGGESTED READING

FREUD, S., Introductory Lectures on Psycho-Analysis. *Standard Edition** Vols. 15 and 16, 1963. Also in: *Complete Introductory Lectures on Psychoanalysis.* New York: Norton, 1966.

* The Standard Edition of the Complete Psychological Works of Sigmund Freud. Volumes I-XXIII. London: Hogarth Press.
When American editions are available, they are also given.

CHAPTER II

THE DRIVES

The two hypotheses which we have just discussed are fundamental to any exposition of psychoanalytic theory. They form a groundwork, so to speak, on which all of the remainder rests; or, if one prefers a different metaphor, they are guides which direct and determine our approach in formulating all of our subsequent hypotheses concerning the various parts or elements of the psychic apparatus, and their manner of functioning.

Let us continue our attempt to present the schema of the mind which psychoanalytic theory has to offer us by a discussion of the instinctual forces which are believed to energize it and to impel it to activity.

The psychological theories which Freud developed were always physiologically oriented as far as it was possible for them to be so. Indeed, as we know from some of his correspondence which has been recently published, he made a most ambitious attempt to formulate a neurological psychology in the early 1890's (Freud, 1954). He was forced to abandon the attempt because the facts did not permit a satisfactory correlation between the two disciplines, but Freud certainly shared the belief which is currently held by most psychiatrists and perhaps by most nonmedical psychologists as well, that some day mental phenomena will be describable in terms of brain functioning. As yet it does not seem possible to accomplish this satisfactorily, though some interesting attempts are being made in this direction. When such attempts will be successful, no one can say. In the meantime the formal or theoretical links between psychoanalysis and other branches of biology are few. The two chief ones concern the psychic functions which are related to sense perception, and the instinctual forces called "drives," which form the subject matter of this chapter.

First a word about nomenclature. What are here called drives, are often referred to alternatively in the psychoanalytic literature as instincts. This is a more familiar word than "drive" in the present context, to be sure, but in this case the less familiar word seems preferable, for the reason that the aspect of human psychic functioning which it is intended to describe is distinctly different from what are called instincts in the lower animals, although, to be sure, they are closely related to them. The distinction to be made is this. An instinct is an innate capacity or necessity to react to a particular set of stimuli in a stereotyped or constant way—a way that is usually thought of as comprising behavior which is considerably more complex than what we speak of as a simple reflex, like the knee jerk, for instance. However, like a simple reflex, an instinct in an animal with a central nervous system presumably is composed of a stimulus, some kind of central excitation, and a motor response which follows a predetermined course. What we call a drive in man, on the other hand, does not include the motor response but only the state of central excitation in response to stimulation. The motor activity which follows this state of excitation is mediated by a highly differentiated part of the mind which is known as the "ego" in psychoanalytic terminology, and which permits the possibility that the response to the state of excitation that constitutes drive or instinctual tension will be modified by experience and reflection, instead of being predetermined, as is the case with the instincts of lower animals (Hartmann, 1948).

This difference between the instinctual life of man and

similar manifestations in the lower animals must not be carried too far. In the adult human, for example, there is obviously an intimate connection between the sexual drive and that innate pattern of response which we call orgasm. We may add that in the case of any instinctual urge or drive in man, the motor response is predetermined by genic factors in a broad, general way. It still holds true, however, that the degree to which the response is so determined is much less in man than it appears to be in other animals and that the degree to which environmental or experiential factors can change the response is much greater in man. Therefore we prefer to take account of these differences by speaking of "drives" rather than "instincts" in man.

A drive, then, is a genically determined, psychic constituent which, when operative, produces a state of psychic excitation or, as we often say, of tension. This excitation or tension impels the individual to activity, which is also genically determined in a general way, but which can be considerably altered by individual experience. This activity should lead to something which we can call either a cessation of excitation or tension, or gratification. The former would be the more objective, the latter, the more subjective terminology. Thus we see that there is a sequence which is characteristic of the operation of the drive. This sequence we may call either tension, motor activity, and cessation of tension, or need, motor activity, and gratification, as we prefer. The former terminology deliberately neglects the elements of subjective experience, while the latter explicitly refers to it.

The attribute which drives possess of impelling the individual to activity impressed Freud as being analogous to the concept of physical energy, which it will be recalled is defined as the capacity to do work. Consequently Freud assumed that there is a psychic energy which is a part of the drives, or which somehow derives from them. This psychic energy is not to be conceived of as the same as physical energy in any way. It is merely analogous to it in the respects we have already mentioned. The concept of psychic energy, like the concept of physical energy, is a hypothesis which is intended to serve the purpose of simplifying and facilitating our understanding of the facts of mental life which we can observe.

Freud continued the analogy between his psychological hypotheses and those of physics by speaking of the quantum of psychic energy with which a particular object or person was invested. For this concept Freud used the German word *Besetzung*, which has been translated into English by the word "cathexis." The accurate definition of "cathexis" is the amount of psychic energy which is directed toward or attached to the mental representative of a person or thing. That is to say, cathexis refers to a purely mental phenomenon. It is a psychological, not a physical concept. Psychic energy cannot flow out through space and cathect or attach itself to the external object directly. What are cathected of course are the various memories, thoughts, and fantasies of the object which comprise what we call its mental or psychic representatives. The greater the cathexis, the more "important" the object is, psychologically speaking, and vice versa.

We may illustrate our definition of cathexis by the example of a small child whose mother is the source of many important, instinctual gratifications, as we should naturally expect to be the case. We express this fact in our new terminology by saying that the child's mother is an important object of its drives, and that this object is highly cathected with psychic energy. By this we mean that the child's thoughts, images and fantasies which concern its mother, that is her mental representative in the child's mind, are highly cathected.

Before leaving this topic, the following remarks are in order, by way of further emphasis of what has already been said. The concept of psychic energy is one which has given rise to much debate among psychoanalysts, and to not a little confusion as well. Much of the difficulty seems to arise from the word "energy." In physics there are various kinds of energy: kinetic energy, potential energy, radiant energy, to name a few. Psychic energy therefore *sounds* like one of the several forms of physical energy, viz., kinetic energy, potential energy, radiant energy, and psychic energy. It is *not*. Psychic energy is a term for a psychological concept, not for a physical one. It can be defined only in psychological terms. It cannot, as yet, be defined in physical terms at all. It is true that psychology is somehow an aspect of the activity of the central nervous system. It is a branch of animal biology, and thus, eventually, of physics and chemistry. At present, however, we know little of the connections between the two, as we said earlier. We don't know, for example, what activity of the brain, what physical processes, correspond to a wish, a longing, a need for gratification of a particular sort. Until we do, we cannot begin to connect physical energy with its psychic analogue. We must resign ourselves to the limitations imposed by our present state of knowledge, and avoid making a meaningless equation between the psychic and the physical. To apply to psychic energy the laws of thermodynamics, to discuss the entropy of mental processes, as some authors have attempted to do, is meaningless. It is, in the literal sense of the word, nonsense.

Let us now consider the question of the classification and nature of the drives. Freud's hypotheses about their classification changed and developed over the course of some three decades, that is from about 1890 to 1920 (Bibring, 1941), and there have been some significant additions to his ideas by others in the past ten years. In his first formulation he proposed to divide the drives into the sexual and the self-preservative ones. He soon abandoned the idea of a self-preservative *drive*, since he considered it to be an unsatisfactory hypothesis, and for many years all instinctual manifestations were considered to be part of, or derived from, the sexual drive. The study of various psychic phenomena, however, and in particular those of sadism and masochism, eventually led Freud to revise his theories once more, and in *Beyond the Pleasure Principle* (Freud, 1920) he formulated the theory of drives which is generally accepted by analysts today, although as we shall see, not all analysts accept it entirely in the form in which Freud presented it originally.

In this latest formulation, Freud proposed to account for the instinctual aspects of our mental lives by assuming the existence of two drives, the sexual and the aggressive. As their names suggest, this dualism is related in a very rough way to what we mean when we speak of sex and aggression, but in fact a concise definition of the two drives is not possible. We can come somewhat closer to what we mean, if we say that the one drive gives rise to the erotic component of mental activities, while the other gives rise to the purely destructive component.

Such cautious, meticulous phrasing is necessary because Freud's theory assumes, and this is a most important thing to remember about the dual theory of drives, that in all of the instinctual manifestations which we can *observe*, whether normal or pathological, *both* the sexual and the aggressive drives participate. To use Freud's terminology, the two drives are regularly "fused" though not necessarily in equal amounts.

Thus even the most callous act of intentional cruelty, that seems on the surface to satisfy nothing but some aspect of the aggressive drive, still has some unconscious sexual meaning to its author and provides him with a degree of unconscious sexual gratification. In the same way there is no act of love, however tender, which does not simultaneously provide an unconscious means of discharge to the aggressive drive.

In other words, the drives which we postulate are not observable as such in human behavior in pure or unmixed form. They are abstractions from the data of experience. They are hypotheses—operational concepts, to use a term which is fashionable nowadays—which we believe enable us to understand and explain our data in as simple and systematic a way as possible. So we must never expect or look for a clinical example in which the aggressive drive appears isolated from the sexual one, or vice versa. The aggressive drive is no more *synonymous* with what we ordinarily speak of as aggression than is the sexual drive with a desire for sexual intercourse.

In our present theory, then, we distinguish two drives. One of these we call the sexual or erotic one and the other, the aggressive or destructive one. In keeping with this distinction we also assume that there are two kinds of psychic energy, that which is associated with the sexual drive, and that which is associated with the aggressive one. The former has a special name, "libido." The latter has no such name, though at one time it was suggested that it be called "destrudo," by analogy from "destroy." It is ordinarily referred to simply as aggressive energy, though sometimes it is called "aggression." The latter usage is unfortunate, since, as we have just said, the meaning of aggressive energy and of the aggressive drive is *not* the same as the behavior which we refer to ordinarily as aggression, and to use the same word for both can only lead to unnecessary confusion by tending to blur the important distinction that should be made between them.

It is also important to realize that the division of drives into sexual and aggressive in our present theory is based on psychological evidence. In his original formulation Freud attempted to relate the psychological theory of the drives to more fundamental, biological concepts, and proposed that the drives be called life and death drives respectively. These drives would correspond approximately to the processes of anabolism and catabolism, and would have much more than psychological significance. They would be instinctual characteristics of all living matter—instincts of protoplasm itself, as it were.

However correct or incorrect these biological speculations of Freud may be, it is certain that they have led to a great deal of misunderstanding. It cannot be emphasized too strongly that the division of drives that we use is based on clinical grounds and will stand or fall on those grounds alone. Whether Freud was right or wrong in his ideas about life and death drives has nothing to do with the case. In fact there are some analysts who accept the concept of a death drive and some (perhaps the majority at present) who do not; but those who do not, as well as those who do, are in general persuaded of the value *on the clinical level* of considering instinctual manifestations to be composed of admixtures of sexual and aggressive drives.

Freud first defined a drive as a stimulus of the mind which came from the body (Freud, 1905b). Such at that time he was concerned only with the sexual drives, such a definition appeared to fit the facts very well. Not only are sexual excitement and gratification obviously related to stimulation of and physical changes in various parts of the body, but also the hormones liberated by various endocrine glands have a profound effect on the entire sexual life and behavior. However, in the case of the aggressive drive the evidence for a somatic basis is not at all clear. At first the suggestion was made that the skeletal musculature bore very much the same relationship to this drive as did the sexually excitable parts of the body to the sexual drive. Since we know at present of no evidence, whether physiological, chemical, or psychological to support this hypothesis, it has been largely abandoned. It appears to be tacitly assumed that the somatic substrate for the aggressive drive is furnished by the form and function of the nervous system. Perhaps some analysts would prefer not to go even that far, and to leave the question of the somatic basis of the aggressive drive to one side as unanswerable for now.

Rather than go further with such theoretical questions as these, it will probably be more rewarding to turn to aspects of the drives which are closely related to observable facts. There are many ways in which one might do this, but perhaps as good a way as any is to discuss an aspect of the drives which has proved to be particularly significant for both theory and practice, that is, their genetic development.

For simplicity's sake let us start with the sexual or erotic drive, since we are more familiar with its development and vicissitudes than we are with those of its sometime partner and sometime rival, the aggressive drive. Psychoanalytic theory postulates that those instinctual forces are already at work in the infant, influencing behavior and clamoring for gratification, which later produce the sexual desires of the adult, with all of their pain and bliss. Indeed the word "postulates" is an inadequate one in this connection. It would be better to say that this proposition is considered to have been amply proved.

The proofs which are available come from at least three sources. The first of these is the direct observation of children. It is truly remarkable how obvious are the evidences of sexual desires and behavior in small children, if one will observe them and talk with them with an unbiased and objective mind. Unfortunately, "there's the rub," because it is precisely on account of each person's own need to forget and deny the sexual wishes and conflicts of his own early childhood that before Freud's investigations almost no one was able to recognize the obvious presence of sexual wishes in the children whom he observed. The other sources of evidence on this point come from the analyses of children and of adults. In the former one can see directly, and in the latter infer reconstructively, the great significance of infantile sexual desires as well as their nature.

One more point should be made clear. The similarity between the sexual wishes of the child of from three to five years and those of the adult is so striking, when the facts are known, that one has no hesitation in calling those of the child by the same name as those of the adult. But how are we to identify the derivatives or manifestations of the sexual drive at a still earlier age? Following Freud (1905b), we may rely on the following observations. (1) In the course of normal development there are certain features of pleasurable behavior in earlier childhood which later become subordinated to genital excitement and gratification and which contribute to it. This is true of kissing, looking, fondling, exhibiting, and the like. (2) In certain cases of abnormal sexual development (sexual perversions) one or several infantile interests or actions become the chief source or sources of adult sexual gratification. These are commonly anal as well as oral or visual. (3) Evidence from the therapeutic application of the psychoanalytic method to neurotic patients indicates that such "perverse" wishes are active in the minds of these patients also. However, instead of being conscious and exciting, as they are to sexually perverse individuals, they are unconscious and a source of anxiety and guilt.

We are now in a position to describe in a schematic way what is known of the typical sequence of the manifestations of the sexual drive from infancy on, a sequence which Freud first outlined in the edition of his *Three Essays on Sexuality* which appeared in 1915.

The reader must understand that the stages to be described are not as distinct from one another as our schematic presentation would imply. In reality one stage merges with the next and the two overlap, so that the transition from one to the other is a very gradual one. One must also understand that the times given for the duration of each stage are to be taken as very approximate and average ones.

For the first year and a half of life, approximately, the mouth, lips and tongue are the chief sexual organs of the infant. By this we mean that its desires as well as its gratifications are primarily oral ones. The evidence for this is to a large extent reconstructive, that is, it is based on the analyses of older children and of adults, but it is also possible to observe quite directly the importance to children of this age, and even older, of sucking, mouthing and biting as sources of pleasure.

In the next year and a half, the other end of the alimentary canal, that is the anus, comes to be the most important site of sexual tensions and gratifications. Pleasurable and unpleasurable sensations are associated both with the retention of feces and with their expulsion, and these bodily processes, as well as feces themselves and fecal odors, are the objects of the child's most intense interest.

Toward the close of the third year of life the leading sexual role begins to be assumed by the genitals, and it is normally maintained by them thereafter. This phase of sexual development is referred to as the phallic one for two reasons. In the first place the penis is the principal object of interest to the child of either sex. In the second, we believe that the little girl's organ of sexual excitement and pleasure during this period is her clitoris, which is embryologically the female analogue of the penis. To be sure, this may continue to be true throughout later life, although usually the vagina replaces the clitoris in this respect.

These then are the three stages of psychosexual development in the child—oral, anal, and phallic—the last of which merges into the stage of adult sexual organization at puberty. This adult stage is known as the genital one, and if proper usage is observed, the phrase "genital phase" will be reserved for it. We may interpolate that the distinction between the phallic and the genital phases is one of substance and not just of name, since the capacity for orgasm is usually only acquired at puberty. However, proper usage is not always observed in this respect in the psychoanalytic literature, and the word "genital" is frequently used instead of the correct "phallic." In particular, the oral and anal phases are usually called *pregenital* rather than *prephallic*.

In addition to the three main modalities of sexuality in the child which give their names to the principal phases we have been discussing, there are other manifestations of the sexual drive which deserve mention. One of these is the desire to look, which is usually most marked in the phallic phase, and its counterpart, the wish to exhibit. The child wishes to see the genitals of others as well as to show its own. Of course its curiosity and exhibitionism include other parts of the body and other bodily functions as well.

Another component of sexuality which is regularly present in the child is that which is connected with the urethra and urination. It is called urethral erotism. Cutaneous sensations also contribute their share, and so do hearing and smelling, so that there is room for considerable individual variation from one child to another on this score alone. Whether the variations that do occur in the relative importance of the different sexual modalities are due to constitutional differences between one child and another, or whether they are due to the influence on the child of the environment, with its frustrations and seductions, is a question to which there is, as yet, no certain answer. Analysts tend to assume, with Freud, that in some cases constitutional factors are the more important, in others, environmental ones, while in most instances each set of factors contributes its share to the final result (Freud, 1905b).

We have described the sequence of phases which normally occurs in childhood in the manifestations of the sexual drive. It seems reasonable to assume that this sequence results in changes in the degree of interest and importance which attaches in the child's psychic life to the various objects and modes of gratification of the sexual drive. For example the nipple or breast is of far greater psychic importance during the oral than during the anal or the phallic phase, and the same is true of sucking, the mode of gratification which is characteristic for the earliest oral phase. We have also seen that these changes come about gradually rather than abruptly, and that the old objects and modes of gratification are only gradually given up even after the new ones have been established for some time in the leading role.

If we describe these facts in terms of our newly defined concepts, we say that the libidinal cathexis of an object of an earlier phase diminishes as the next phase is reached and we add that, though diminished, the cathexis persists for some time after the later phase has become established and the objects appropriate to it have become the principal objects of libidinal cathexis.

The theory of psychic energy affords us an explanation of what happens in these changes which is both simple and consonant with the facts as we know them. We assume that the libido which cathected the object or mode of gratification of the earlier phase gradually becomes detached from them and instead cathects an object or mode of gratification of the next phase. Thus libido which first cathected the breast, or, to be more precise, the psychic representative of the breast, later cathects feces, and still later, the penis. According to our theories there is a flow of libido from object to object and from one to another mode of gratification during the course of psychosexual development, a flow which proceeds along a course which is probably determined in broadest outline by constitutional factors which are common to all, but which can vary considerably from person to person.

We have good reason to believe, however, that no really strong libidinal cathexis is ever completely abandoned. Most of the libido may flow on to other objects, but some at least normally remains bound to the original one. This phenomenon, that is, the persistence of the libidinal cathexis of an object of infancy or childhood into later life, we speak of as a "fixation" of the libido. For example, a boy may remain fixated to his mother and thus be unable in adult life to transfer his affections to another woman as he should normally be able to do. In addition, the word "fixation" may refer to a mode of gratification. Thus we speak of persons who are fixated to oral or anal modes of gratification.

The use of the word "fixation" is often assumed to indicate or to imply psychopathology. This is because the persistence of early cathexes was first recognized and described by Freud and those who followed him in neurotic patients. It is likely, as we have said above, that it is a general characteristic of psychic development. Perhaps when excessive in degree it is more likely to result in a pathological outcome; perhaps other factors, as yet unknown, determine whether a fixation will be associated with mental illness or not.

A fixation, whether to an object or to a mode of gratification, is usually unconscious, either wholly or in part. It might be supposed on first thought that a strong fixation, that is the persistence of a strong cathexis, would be conscious, while a weak one would be unconscious. Actually, our best evidence is that there is no relation between the strength of the persistent cathexis and its accessibility to consciousness. For example, despite the very great strength of their cathexes, the sexual interests of our childhood are regularly forgotten in large part as we grow out of early childhood, as we have remarked earlier in this chapter. In fact, the word "forgotten" is too weak and pallid a one to be properly descriptive of what happens. It is more accurate to say that the memories of these interests are energetically barred from becoming conscious. The same thing may be true of other, somewhat later fixations also.

In addition to what we have described as the forward flow of libido in the course of psychosexual development, an ebb may also occur. For this ebb we have a particular name, "regression." When we use the word specifically in connection with a drive, as we are doing here, we speak of instinctual regression. This term designates the return to an earlier mode or object of gratification.

Instinctual regression is closely related to fixation, since in fact when regression occurs, it is usually to an object or mode of gratification to which the individual was already fixated. If a new pleasure proves unsatisfactory and is given up, the individual tends to revert to one that is tried and true, as one would expect.

An example of such a regression would be the response of a small child to the birth of a sibling, with whom he had to share his mother's love and attention. Although he had given up thumb-sucking several months before his sibling's arrival, he reverted to it after the sibling was born. In this case, the earlier object of libidinal gratification to which the child regressed was its thumb, while the earlier mode of gratification was sucking.

As in our example, regression often appears under unfavorable circumstances. However, this is by no means always the case. Children, or for that matter, adults may indulge in regressive behavior for pleasure, as in the case of anal games or jokes. Regression is not to be equated with psychopathology. It is a normal phenomenon in mental life under some circumstances, an unfavorable or a pathological phenomenon under others (Kris, 1952; A. Freud, 1965).

A characteristic of infantile sexuality that is of special importance should be mentioned at this point. It concerns the relationship of the child to the objects (principally persons) of his sexual longings. To take a very simple case, if the infant cannot always have its mother's breast, it soon learns to pacify itself by sucking its own fingers or toes. This ca-

pacity to gratify its own sexual needs by itself is referred to
as autoerotism. It gives the child a certain independence
from the environment as far as obtaining gratification goes
and also leaves the way open for what may be a fateful turning away from the world of outer reality altogether to an
excessive, or even an exclusive interest in the self, such as
one finds in serious pathological conditions like schizophrenia.

If we turn now to a consideration of the aggressive drive,
we must confess that much less has been written about its
vicissitudes than about those of the sexual drive. This is
largely due to the fact that it was not until 1920 that Freud
considered the aggressive drive to be an independent, instinctual component of mental life which was comparable to
the sexual component that had been long since recognized
and made the object of special study.

The manifestations of the aggressive drive show the same
capacity for fixation and regression and the same transition
from oral to anal to phallic that we have described for the
manifestations of the sexual drive. That is to say, aggressive
impulses in the very young infant are apt to be discharged by
oral activity such as biting. Somewhat later soiling, or retention of feces become important outlets for the aggressive
drive, while to the slightly older child the penis and its
activity are used, or at least conceived of (used in fantasy)
as a weapon and a means of destruction respectively.

However, it is clear that the relationship between the
aggressive drive and the various parts of the body which we
have just mentioned is not nearly as close as is the relationship in the case of the sexual drive. The child of five or six
years, for example, does not actually use his penis as a
weapon to any great extent; ordinarily he uses his hands, his
teeth, his feet, and words. What is true, however, is that the
weapons he uses in his games and fantasies, such as spears,
arrows, guns, etc., can be shown by analysis to represent his

penis in his unconscious thought. It appears, therefore, that in his fantasies he is unconsciously destroying his enemies with his powerful and dangerous penis. Despite this, we must conclude that the sexual drive is much more intimately related to its erogenous body zones than is the aggressive drive either to the same or to any similar part of the body. Perhaps this distinction does not hold true for the earliest, oral phase. There is little that an infant of a few months does use except its mouth, and we may well assume that oral activities are the chief outlet for its aggressive drive (biting) as well as for its sexual one (sucking, mouthing).

It is interesting that the question of the relation of the aggressive drive to pleasure is likewise still doubtful. We have no hesitation about the connection between the sexual drive and pleasure. Gratification of the sexual drive means not just any indifferent discharge of tension, but a pleasurable one. The fact that the pleasure can be interfered with or even replaced by guilt, shame, or disgust in certain instances, does not alter our view concerning the original relationship between sexuality and pleasure. But does gratification of the aggressive drive (or to put it in other words: discharge of aggressive tension) also bring pleasure? Freud thought not (Freud, 1920). Other, subsequent writers supported the view that it does (Hartmann et al. 1949), and the majority of psychoanalysts appear to have accepted this view.

Incidentally, a word of warning may be helpful concerning the frequent misuse of the words "libido" or "libidinal" in the psychoanalytic literature. They must often be understood to refer not only to the energy of the sexual drive, but also to that of the aggressive one. It is understandable that this should be so for the literature before the time when the concept of the aggressive drive was formulated. At that time "libidinal" was synonymous with "instinctual." But the effect of the original usage is so strong that even now one must often understand that "libido" is being used to include aggressive as well as sexual energy. }

SUGGESTED READING

FREUD, S., Three Essays on the Theory of Sexuality. *Standard Edition*, Vol. 7, pp. 125–243, 1953. Also, New York: Basic Books, 1962.
FREUD, S., New Introductory Lectures on Psycho-Analysis. *Standard Edition*, Vol. 22. Chapter 4, Lecture XXXII, 1964. Also in: *Complete Introductory Lectures on Psychoanalysis*. New York: Norton, 1966.

CHAPTER III

THE PSYCHIC APPARATUS

Let us ask ourselves now, "What is the picture of the mind that we have obtained thus far from our discussion of psychoanalytic theory?"

In framing the answer to our question we see that in the first place we began with two fundamental and well-established hypotheses concerning mental functioning which were essentially of a descriptive character. One of these was the law of psychic causality, and the other was the proposition that psychic activity is principally unconscious.

We understand that these two hypotheses are to be our guide-posts as it were in our further discussion of psychoanalytic theory. As we have just said, they are primarily descriptive in nature. However, in our next topic, the drives, we immediately found ourselves dealing with concepts that were basically dynamic ones. We discussed psychic energy, that impelled the organism to activity until gratification was achieved; the genetically determined pattern of change from one phase of instinctual organization to another as the infant matured; the individual variations that might occur within the broad limits of this pattern; the flow of libido and aggressive energy from object to object during the course of development; the establishment of fixation points; and the phenomenon of the return of psychic energy to those fixation points which we call instinctual regression.

In fact, it is characteristic of psychoanalytic theory that it gives us just such a moving, dynamic picture of the mind rather than a static and lifeless one. It tries to demonstrate and explain the growth and functioning of the mind to us, as well as the operations of its various parts and their mutual interactions and conflicts. Even the division of the mind which it makes into various parts is made on a dynamic and functional basis, as we shall see in the present chapter and the two succeeding ones, which deal with what Freud called the elements of the psychic apparatus.

The first published attempt which Freud made to construct a model of the psychic apparatus was that which appeared in the last chapter of *The Interpretation of Dreams* (Freud, 1900). He pictured it as similar to a compound optical instrument, like a telescope or microscope, which is made up of many optical elements arranged consecutively. The psychic apparatus was to be thought of as made up of many psychic components arranged consecutively and stretching, if one may use the word, from the perceptual system at one end to the motor system at the other, with the various memory and association systems in between.

Even in this very early schema of the mind, therefore, one sees that the divisions were functional ones. One "part" of the apparatus reacted to sensory stimuli, a closely related part, when activated, produced the phenomenon of consciousness, others stored up memory traces and reproduced them, and so on. From one system to the next there flowed some sort of psychic excitation which energized each in turn, just as a nerve impulse passes from one element of a reflex arc to another.

In addition, Freud proposed to distinguish three psychic systems, which, in his early diagrams, he intercalated among the memory and association systems. However, even in his first discussion of these three systems, they emerged as fundamentally important and strikingly novel. He elaborated his ideas concerning them in a later monograph (Freud, 1915c) which may be summarized as follows.

The contents and operations of the mind may be divided on the basis of whether they are conscious or not. Three systems are to be distinguished, the system Ucs. (from "unconscious"), Pcs. (from "preconscious"), and Cs. (from "conscious"). The abbreviations were used as names, in order to avoid confusion with the ordinary meanings of the words from which the abbreviations were derived.

At first glance it seems that this second theory of Freud's about a psychic apparatus is as far removed as possible from being a dynamic and functional one. He appears to be making a division between the parts of the mind on a purely static and qualitative basis: "Is it conscious or not?" In this case, however, first appearances are deceptive, and this second theory is fundamentally a functional one also, as the rest of the discussion will show.

Freud pointed out that the mere attribute of consciousness is an inadequate basis for differentiating among psychic contents and processes. The reason for this is that there are two classes of contents and processes which are not conscious and which can be distinguished from one another by dynamic, functional criteria. The first of these groups does not differ in any essential way from whatever happens to be conscious at the moment. Its elements can be made conscious simply by an effort of attention. Conversely, what is conscious at the moment becomes no longer so when attention is withdrawn from it. The second group of mental processes and contents which are not conscious, however, are different from the first in that they cannot become conscious by any mere effort of attention. They are barred from access to consciousness for the time being by some force within the mind itself.

A simple example of this second group would be a command given under hypnosis, as described in Chapter I, which the subject was to obey after "waking" from the hypnotic trance, but of which he was commanded to have no conscious memory. In this case all that had transpired during the hypnotic trance was barred from consciousness by the hypnotist's command to forget. Or, to be more exact, the memory of the events of the trance was barred from consciousness by the part of the subject's mind which was obedient to the command to forget them.

It was on this *functional* basis that Freud differentiated between the two systems which he called Ucs. and Pcs. respectively. Those psychic contents and processes which were actively barred from consciousness he called the system Ucs. Those which could become conscious by an effort of attention he called Pcs. The system Cs. of course designated what was conscious in the mind.

Because of their functional closeness, the systems Cs. and Pcs. were grouped together as the systems Cs.-Pcs. in contrast to the system Ucs. The close relationship of Cs. and Pcs. is easy to understand. A thought that belongs to the system Cs. at this moment, is a part of the system Pcs. a few moments later, when attention has been withdrawn from it, and it is no longer conscious. Conversely, at each moment thoughts, wishes, etc., which have till then belonged to the system Pcs., become conscious and are consequently part of the system Cs.

Since conscious processes had been known and studied by psychologists long before Freud, it was natural that the principal new contributions and discoveries which he had to make concerned the system Ucs. Indeed, for many years of its development psychoanalysis was rightly called a "depth psychology," that is, a psychology of the Ucs. It was a psychology that was chiefly concerned with the contents and processes of the mind which are barred from consciousness by some psychic force. During this period of its development psychoanalysis was very well served by the theories we have just summarized concerning the psychic apparatus.

As Freud's understanding of the system Ucs. grew, however, he realized that its contents were not as uniform as he had expected them to be. It turned out that there were other criteria than that of being actively barred from consciousness which could be applied to the contents and processes of the mind and since the application of these new criteria seemed to him to result in more homogeneous and useful groupings of mental contents and processes than the old had done, Freud proposed a new hypothesis concerning mental systems (Freud, 1923). This theory is usually referred to as the structural hypothesis, to distinguish it from the earlier one, which is often called the topographic theory or hypothesis (Arlow & Brenner, 1964).

The structural hypothesis, despite its name, resembles its predecessors in that it attempts to group together mental processes and contents which are *functionally* related and to distinguish among the various groups on the basis of *functional* differences. Each of the mental "structures" which Freud proposed in his new theory is in fact a group of mental contents and processes which are functionally related to one another. Freud distinguished three such functionally related groups or "structures" and called them the id, the ego, and the superego respectively.

As a way of giving ourselves a first, rough orientation in this final of Freud's theories, we may say that the id comprises the psychic representatives of the drives, the ego consists of those functions which have to do with the individual's relation to his environment, and the superego comprises the moral precepts of our minds as well as our ideal aspirations.

The drives, of course, we assume to be present from birth, but the same is certainly not true of interest in or control of the environment on the one hand, nor of any moral sense or aspirations on the other. It is obvious therefore that neither of the latter, that is neither the ego nor the superego develops till sometime after birth.

Freud expressed this fact by assuming that the id comprised the entire psychic apparatus at birth, and that the ego and the superego were originally parts of the id which differentiated sufficiently in the course of growth to warrant their being considered as separate functional entities.[1]

This differentiation takes place first with respect to the ego functions. It is common knowledge that the infant shows an interest in his environment and is able to exercise some degree of control over it long before he develops any moral sense. In fact, Freud's studies led him to the proposition that the differentiation of the superego does not really get under way till the age of five or six years and is probably not *firmly* established till several years later, perhaps not until ten or eleven years of age. On the other hand, the differentiation of the ego begins within the first six or eight months of life, and is well established by the age of two or three years, though very much growth and change normally occur after that age too.[2]

Because of these differences in time of development, it will be convenient for us to discuss the differentiation of the ego and of the superego separately. The nature of the time differences suggests that we start with the ego.

There is one point which the reader should bear in mind during the following discussion of the differentiation and development of the ego. That is that the many aspects of this development must be discussed and presented seriatim in a book, whereas in real life they are all happening at the same time and each is influencing and being influenced by the

---

[1] It has been suggested subsequently that there are advantages in assuming that the psychic structure of the newborn is an undifferentiated one, from which the id, the ego, and the superego all develop, rather than to assume that the id is the precursor and in a sense the parent of the other two (Hartmann, et al., 1946).

[2] Certain analysts, notably Melanie Klein and her associates, have advanced the hypothesis that the superego begins to function as an independent, psychic system well before the end of the first year of life. However, this view is not accepted by the majority of psychoanalysts at present.

other. In order to achieve a fairly adequate picture of ego development, one must be familiar with *all* of its aspects. There is no way of presenting just one aspect at a time and neglecting the others which is fully satisfactory. They *should* all be discussed simultaneously, or, since that is impossible, the reader must think about all the other aspects when he is reading about any particular one. Unless the reader has prior acquaintance with the material of the following discussion, this means that he will have to read it at least twice and probably several times. It will be only on re-reading that he will understand more clearly the intimate interrelationships of the various aspects of ego differentiation and development.

We have already said that the group of psychic functions which we call the ego are those which are similar in that each has to do, either principally or to an important degree, with the individual's relation to his environment. In the case of an adult, of course, such a broad formulation includes a very wide range of phenomena: desire for gratification, habit, social pressures, intellectual curiosity, aesthetic or artistic interest, and many others, some of which differ grossly from the rest, while others differ only by the subtlest of nuances.

In childhood, however, and particularly in early infancy there is no such profusion of reasons for interest in the environment, nor is their nature so varied and so subtle. The little child's attitude is very simple and eminently practical: "Give me what I want!" or, "Do what I want!" In other words, the only subjective importance which the environment has for the child originally is as a possible source of gratification or discharge for the wishes, urges, and psychic tensions which arise from the drives and which constitute the id. If we wish to make our statement quite complete, we must add the negative as well, that is, the environment is also important as a possible source of pain or discomfort, sensations which the child tries to avoid.

To repeat, the infant's original interest in its environment is as a possible source of gratification. The parts of the psyche which have to do with exploiting the environment gradually develop into what we call the ego. Consequently, the ego is that part of the psyche which is concerned with the environment for the purpose of achieving a maximum of gratification or discharge for the id. As we noted in Chapter II, the ego is the *executant* for the drives.

Such a cordial cooperation between ego and id is not what we are accustomed to see in our ordinary clinical work. On the contrary, there we daily deal with severe conflicts between ego and id. They are the very stuff of neurosis, and our necessarily continuous preoccupation with such conflicts in our work as clinicians makes it easy for us to forget that conflict is not the only relation between ego and id. Certainly it is not the primary one, which is rather one of cooperation, as we have said.

We do not know at what stage of psychic development conflicts do begin to arise between the ego and the id and to assume serious significance for psychic functioning, but it seems likely that this can happen only after a substantial degree of differentiation and organization of the ego has taken place. At any rate we shall postpone a discussion of such conflicts till somewhat later in our exposition of the development of the ego and the id.

Now what are the activities of the ego vis-à-vis its environment in the earliest months of life? To us as adults they may seem to be almost insignificant, yet a moment's reflection will confirm their importance and we may be sure that despite their *apparent* insignificance they are more important milestones in the life of each of us than any subsequent achievements will ever be.

One obvious group of ego functions is the acquisition of control over the skeletal musculature, which we commonly refer to as motor control. Equally important are the various modalities of sensory perception, which give essential information about the environment. The acquisition of what we might call a library of memories is also necessary as a part of one's equipment if he hopes to influence his environment effectively. It is obvious that the better one knows what has happened in the past, and the more "pasts" one has experienced, the better one will be able to exploit the present. Incidentally, it seems probable that the earliest memories are those of instinctual gratification.

In addition to these functions, there must be some psychic process in the young infant which corresponds to what we call an affect in later life. What such primitive affects, or predecessors of affects, might be is an interesting question that still lacks an answer that is wholly satisfactory. Finally, at some time or other in early infancy must come the most distinctly human ego activity of all: the first hesitation between impulse and action, the first delay in discharge, which will subsequently develop into the immensely complex phenomenon which we call thought (Rapaport, 1951).

All of these ego functions—motor control, perception, memory, affects, thinking—begin, as we can see, in a primitive and preliminary way and develop only gradually as the infant grows. Such a gradual development is characteristic of ego functions in general, and the factors which are responsible for the progressive development of the ego's functions are divisible into two groups. The first of these is physical growth, which in this case means primarily the genically determined growth of the central nervous system. The second is experience, or, if one prefers, experiential factors. For the sake of convenience we may refer to the first factor as maturation (Hartmann and Kris, 1945).

We can readily understand the importance of maturation.

An infant cannot achieve effective motor control of its extremities, for example, until after the corticospinal (pyramidal) tracts have been myelinated. Similarly the capacity for binocular vision necessarily depends on the existence of adequate neural mechanisms for conjugate eye movements and for the fusion of macular images. Such maturational factors clearly exert a profound effect on the speed and sequence of the development of the functions of the ego and the more we can learn about them from the developmental psychologist and others, the better. However, the particular direction of Freud's interest was toward the influence of experiential factors on ego development, although he was well aware of the fundamental importance of genic factors, and of the complexity of the interaction between constitution and environment which is so characteristic of psychic development.

One of the aspects of experience which Freud (1911) considered to be of fundamental importance in the earliest stages of ego formation was, strangely enough, the infant's relation with his own body. He pointed out that our own bodies occupy a very special place in our psychic lives as long as we are alive and that they begin to occupy that special place very early in infancy. He suggested that there is more than one reason for this. For example, a part of the body is different from any other object in the infant's environment in that it gives rise to two sensations rather than one when the infant touches or mouths it. It is not only *felt*, it *feels*, which is not true of any other object.

In addition, and probably even more important, the parts of its own body afford the infant an easy and ever available means of id gratification. For instance, the infant, as the result of maturation, and to some extent of experience as well, usually becomes able to put its thumb or fingers in its mouth at the age of three to six weeks (Hoffer, 1950) and thereby to gratify its desire to suck whenever it wishes to do so. We believe that to an infant so young there is nothing that compares in psychic importance with the oral gratification which accompanies sucking. We can imagine that a correspondingly great importance must attach to the various ego functions (motor control, memory, kinesthesia) which make the gratification of thumb-sucking possible, and to the objects of the drive itself, the thumb and fingers. Moreover, we must remember that the sucking (oral) organs are also of great psychic importance for the same reason, namely that they are intimately related to the all-important experience of pleasure which is produced by sucking. So both parts of the body, both the sucked and the sucking are, or come to be, of great psychic importance, and their psychic representatives come to occupy an important place among those mental contents which belong under the heading of the ego.

We should add that parts of the body can acquire great psychic importance by virtue of their being frequently the source of painful or *un*pleasurable sensations and by virtue of the additional fact that these painful sensations often cannot be escaped from. If a baby is hungry, for instance, it stays hungry until it is fed. It cannot "pull away" from the feeling of hunger as it can pull its hand away from a painful stimulus and thereby stop it.

At any rate the cumulative effect of these factors and perhaps of others more obscure to us is that the infant's own body, first in its various parts and eventually also *in toto*, occupies a particularly important place within the ego. The psychic representations of the body, that is the memories and ideas connected with it, with their cathexes of drive energy, are probably the most important part of the developing ego in its earliest stage. Freud (1923) expressed this fact by saying that the ego is first of all a body ego.

Still another process which is dependent on experience and which is of very great significance in the development of the ego is what is called *identification* with the objects, usually persons, of the environment. By "identification" we mean the act or process of becoming like something or someone in one or several aspects of thought or behavior. Freud pointed out that the tendency to become like an object in one's environment is a very important part of one's relationship to objects in general and that it appears to be of particular significance in very early life.

As early as the middle of the first year of life one can see evidence of this tendency in the infant's behavior. He learns to smile, for instance, by imitating the adult who is smiling at him, to talk by imitating what is said to him, and there is a host of imitative games which adults regularly play with growing babies at about this time which depend on the same tendency to imitate. One need only mention "peek-a-boo" and "clap-hands" to be reminded how large a part such games play at this period in childhood.

Another example of the importance of identification can be drawn from the infant's acquisition of language, which occurs somewhat later. Simple observation will show us that the child's acquisition of motor speech depends in considerable measure on the psychological tendency to imitate an object in the environment or, in other words, to identify with it. It is perfectly true that a child cannot learn to speak until his central nervous system has matured sufficiently and that the acquisition of language as a whole is far from being simply a process of imitation. Nevertheless, it is true that children ordinarily speak in imitation, at least at first. That is to say they repeat sounds that adults say for them and learn to say them in imitation of an adult, very often as part of a game. Moreover, it is most instructive to observe that *every* child talks with the same "accent" as do the adults and older children of his environment. Intonation, pitch, pronunciation, and idioms are all copied exactly, if the child's hearing is normal. So exactly, indeed, that it makes one wonder whether what we ordinarily call "tone deafness," that is the inability to detect relative differences in pitch, can really be congenital. However that may be, we can have no doubt that identification plays a very great role in the acquisition of this particular ego function that we have called motor speech.

The same thing is true of physical mannerisms, of athletic or intellectual interests and hobbies, of a tendency toward unbridled expression of the instinctual drives like temper tantrums, or of an opposite tendency toward a checking of such expression, and of many other aspects of ego functioning. Some of these aspects are gross and obvious, some are more subtle and less readily apparent, but when taken all together it is clear that they represent a very important part of the effect of experience on ego formation.

Of course the tendency to identify with a highly cathected person or thing in the environment is not limited to early childhood by any means. For example, the adolescent who dresses or talks like an idol of the entertainment world or like an athletic hero has to that extent identified with him. Such identifications in adolescence may be transient ones, of only passing significance, but they are by no means always so. Educators understand very well, for instance, that it is important that a teacher of adolescents not only teach well, but that he must also be a "good example" to his students, which is another way of saying that his students are apt to become like him, that is to identify with him. To be sure we might not always agree with our friends the educators as to what constitutes a desirable example, but we should all agree that pupils tend to identify with their teachers.

Indeed, this tendency persists throughout life, but in later life at least it is apt to be largely unconscious in its manifestations. In other words, the adult very often does not know that in some aspects of thought or behavior or both he is becoming like, that is, imitating, another person, or that he has already become like him. In earlier life the desire to be like the other person is more likely to be accessible to consciousness, though it is by no means always so. Thus, for example, a small boy makes no secret of wanting to be like his father, or later like Superman or Roy Rogers, while in later life he may grow a moustache which is precisely like his new boss's without being conscious of a desire to identify with him. His desire to do so is unconscious, even though it is expressed by his decision to grow a moustache.

What we have discussed so far is a tendency toward identifying with persons or things in one's environment which are highly cathected with libido. It should have been self-evident from our discussion that this tendency is a perfectly normal one, although it seems to be a more prominent and relatively more important one during early mental life than later on.

It is interesting to note that there is also a tendency to identify with those objects which are highly cathected with aggressive energy. This seems to be particularly true if the object or person in question is powerful, a type of identification which has been called "identification with the aggressor" (A. Freud, 1936). In such cases, of course, the individual has the satisfaction of himself participating, at least in fantasy, in the power and glory he attributes to his opponent. The same sort of satisfaction incidentally is afforded to the individual, whether he be child or adult, who identifies with an admired object cathected principally with libido. See for instance our earlier examples of identifications with parents, teachers, popular idols, and employers.

However, the best evidence we have is in favor of the view that identification is only *secondarily* connected with fantasies of replacing an admired object in order to profit therefrom by taking over the admired person's rights and properties. There is no doubt that this is a very powerful motive in many cases in which it plays a role, but it seems that the tendency to identify with an object is simply a consequence of its libidinal cathexis, since it can be observed at a time in infancy long before any such motive as envy or any fantasy such as one of replacing an envied person could very well be conceived to be operative. Whether identification can also be the direct consequence of a high cathexis with aggressive energy is a question that has yet to be answered.

Freud (1916a) emphasized another factor which plays an important part in the process of identification. This factor he called object loss, a term which can mean any one of several things. It can refer to the actual death of an object, to a fantasy that an object has died, to long-continued or permanent separation from an object, or to a fantasy of such separation. He discovered that under any of these circumstances there is a tendency to identify with the lost object. Subsequent clinical experience has repeatedly confirmed the correctness and significance of this discovery. Cases in point will vary all the way from the son who becomes a replica of his father after the latter's death and carries on his father's business just as his father used to do, as though he were the old man himself, which indeed he very nearly is, to the patient cited by Freud (1916a) who accused *herself* of crimes which in fact her dead father had committed. The first of these two examples we should call normal, of course, while the second was a patient who suffered from a severe mental illness.

As our examples suggest, the loss of a highly cathected person by death or separation may well have a crucial effect on one's ego development. In such cases there remains a lasting need to imitate or to become the image of what has been lost. The cases of this sort which have been most often studied in psychoanalytic practice are ones of depression, a clinical condition in whose psychopathology unconscious identification with a lost object regularly plays an important role.

Thus we see that identification plays its part in ego development on more than one score. It is first of all an inherent part of one's relationship to a highly cathected object, particularly early in life. In addition we have noted the tendency to identify with an admired though hated object, which Anna Freud called "identification with the aggressor." Finally there is the last-mentioned factor that the loss of a highly cathected object leads to a greater or less degree of identification with the lost object. However, regardless of the way in which identification takes place, the *result* is always that the ego has become enriched thereby, whether for better or for worse.

We wish to discuss now another topic which is also intimately related to the subject of the differentiation of the ego and the id from one another. This is the topic of the modes of functioning of the psychic apparatus which we call the *primary* and the *secondary processes* (Freud, 1911).

The primary process was so named because Freud considered it to be the original or primary way in which the psychic apparatus functioned. We believe that the id functions in conformity with the primary process throughout life and that the ego does so during the first years of life, when its organization is immature and it is still very much like the id, whence it so recently sprang, in its functioning. The secondary process, on the other hand, develops gradually and progressively during the first years of life and is characteristic of the operations of the relatively mature ego.

Each of the terms "primary process" and "secondary process" is used in the psychoanalytic literature to refer to two related but distinct phenomena. The words "primary process," for example, may refer either to a certain type of thinking which is characteristic for the child whose ego is still immature, or to the way in which we believe drive energy, whether libidinal or aggressive, is shifted about and discharged in the id or in the immature ego. In an analogous way, "secondary process" may refer to a type of thinking which is characteristic for the mature ego or it may refer to the processes of binding and mobilization of psychic energy which are believed to occur in the mature ego. The two types of thinking have the greater clinical importance and are fairly accessible to study. The two ways of dealing with and discharging psychic energy occupy a more important place in our theory, but are less accessible to study, as is true for all our hypotheses concerning psychic energy.

Let us first discuss what phenomena in the management of psychic energy are meant when we speak of primary or of secondary process.

As for the primary process, its basic characteristics can be described rather simply in terms of our previous theoretical formulations concerning drive energy. We have simply to say that the drive cathexes which are associated with the primary process are highly mobile ones. We believe that this cathectic mobility accounts for two striking characteristics of the primary process: (1) the tendency to immediate gratification (discharge of cathexis) which is characteristic for the id and the immature ego, and (2) the ease with which the cathexis can be shifted from its original object or method of discharge in the event that these are blocked or inaccessible and can instead be discharged by a similar, or even by a rather different route.

The first characteristic, the tendency to immediate gratification or discharge of cathexis, is clearly the dominant one in infancy and childhood, while the ego functions are still immature. In addition it is very much more common in later life than our vanity would like to admit and the investigation of unconscious mental processes by the method of psychoanalysis, in particular of those processes which we call the id, has shown that the tendency to immediate discharge of cathexis is characteristic of the id throughout our lives.

As for the second characteristic, the ease with which one method of discharge of cathexis can substitute for another may perhaps best be illustrated with some simple examples. We are offered one such example by the infant who sucks his thumb when he is unable to get the breast or the bottle. The cathexis of drive energy associated with the impulse or desire to suck is primarily, i.e., first, directed toward the psychic representatives of the breast or bottle. The cathexis is a mobile one, however, and if discharge cannot be effected by sucking either breast or bottle because they are inaccessible, the cathexis shifts to the infant's thumb which *is* accessible, the infant sucks its thumb instead, and discharge of cathexis is effected.

Another instance would be that of the child who plays with mud pies. Play with feces is no longer an accessible form of discharge of cathexis because it has been forbidden, so the child, because of the mobility of the cathexis attached to the psychic representatives of its feces, can obtain the same gratification by shifting the cathexis to mud and achieving discharge of cathexis by playing with mud instead. In the same way we are familiar with the child who beats or teases his little brother when he is angry with his mother, or the man who shouts at his children at night because he didn't dare to express his anger at his employer during the day.

When we turn to a consideration of the secondary process, we find that a very different state of affairs exists. Here the emphasis is on the ability or capacity to *delay* the discharge of cathectic energy. We might say that the point seems to be, to be able to delay discharge until the environmental circumstances are most favorable. To be sure, this is an anthropomorphic formulation, but after all, we are talking about the ego, which is *anthropos* itself (Hartmann, 1953b). In any case the capacity to delay discharge is an essential feature of the secondary process.

Another of its essential features is that the cathexes are much more firmly attached to a particular object or method of discharge of cathexis than was the case with the primary process. Here again, as in the case of the first characteristic, that is the capacity to delay gratification, the differences between primary and secondary processes are quantitative rather than qualitative.

By the same token the transition from the one to the other is gradual, both historically, in tracing the growth and development of a particular individual, as well as descriptively, in attempting to draw the line between primary and secondary processes in studying the mental functioning of a particular person. It is not usually hard to say that certain thinking or behavior bears such and such traces of the primary or secondary process, but no man can say, "Here ends the primary process and there begins the secondary." The change from primary to secondary process is a gradual one which is a part of the differentiation and growth of those mental processes which form what we call the ego.

As we said earlier, the terms primary and secondary process also designate two different types or modes of thinking. Again we believe that primary process thinking appears earlier in life than does secondary process thinking and that the latter develops gradually as one part or aspect of ego development.

If we try now to define and describe these two modes of thinking, we shall find that the secondary one is easier to describe than the primary one, because it is the more familiar to us. It is ordinary, conscious thinking as we know it from introspection, that is, primarily verbal and following the usual laws of syntax and logic. It is the mode of thinking that we ordinarily attribute to the relatively mature ego and since it is familiar to us all, it needs no special, further description.

Primary process thinking, on the other hand, is the mode of thinking which is characteristic of those years of childhood when the ego is still immature. It is different in important respects from our familiar ways of conscious thinking, which we call the secondary process; so different, indeed, that the reader may doubt whether primary process thinking has any place in the normal as opposed to the pathological functioning of the mind. It is important to emphasize, therefore, that primary process thinking is *normally* the dominant mode of thought for the immature ego, and that it normally persists in some degree into adult life as well, as we shall soon see.

To proceed now with our description of primary process thinking, we may start with one of its characteristics which often produces a strong impression of strangeness and incomprehensibility. This is the absence of any negatives, conditionals, or other qualifying conjunctions. If something is stated, one can tell only by the context whether it is meant to be understood in the positive or in the negative, or perhaps even in the conditional or the optative sense. Opposites may appear in place of one another and mutually contradictory ideas may coexist peacefully. It really seems that we shall have a difficult time to show that this kind of thinking is not wholly pathological, but before we discuss this point further, let us complete our description of the primary process as a mode of thought.

In primary process thinking representation by allusion or analogy is frequent and a part of an object, memory or idea may be used to stand for the whole, or vice versa. Moreover, several different thoughts may be represented by a single thought or image. In fact verbal representation is not used nearly as exclusively in primary as in secondary process thinking. Visual or other sense impressions may appear instead of a word, or for that matter instead of a paragraph or a whole chapter of words. As a final characteristic we may add that a sense of time, or a concern with time does not exist in primary process thinking. There is no such thing as "before" or "after," as "now" or "then," as "first," "next," or "last." Past, present and future are all one in the primary process.

Now it is true that primary process thinking is apparent in many cases of severe mental illness and may be so conspicuous a part of mental life as to contribute prominently to the symptoms which these patients manifest. This is the case in the various deliria associated with toxic or organic disease of the brain as well as in severe diseases of undetermined etiology such as schizophrenia and manic-depressive psychosis. However, primary process thinking is not in itself pathological. The abnormality in such cases is the relative absence or disappearance of secondary process thinking, rather than the presence of primary process thinking. It is the *dominance* or *exclusive operation* of the primary process that constitutes an abnormality when it occurs in adult life. Despite the initial impression of strangeness which primary process thinking makes upon us, the following considerations may help to make it more understandable to us. They may even persuade us that it is in fact more familiar to us than we had imagined.

The lack of a sense of time, for instance, we can understandably relate to what we know of the intellectual development of little children. It is several years before a child develops a sense of time, before there is anything comprehensible to him but the "here and now," so that this characteristic of primary process thinking is but a familiar trait of early childhood.

The same is true for the tendency to represent ideas in a nonverbal way. This is, after all, the way the preverbal child must think.

As for the confusing and illogical, syntactical features which we have described, the use of qualifying conjunctions and even the use of the negative particle are much more common in written than in spoken speech, where so much of the sense is conveyed by context, gestures, facial expression, and the tone of the speaker's voice. Moreover, the more colloquial and informal the manner of speaking, the simpler the syntax, and the more ambiguous are the words themselves likely to be if they should be removed from context. For instance, the words "He's a great one," can mean very different things if the speaker intends them to be serious, funny, or sarcastically critical. In fact, if the last of these possibilities is true, that is, if the speaker is being sarcastic, the word "great" will mean precisely the opposite of the definition which the dictionary gives for it. Such representation by the opposite, which at first sight is one of the most bewildering of the characteristics of primary process thinking, thus turns out to be common enough in everyday usage. So common, indeed, that we are hardly aware of its frequency unless we pay special attention to it.

Similarly, representation of a part by the whole, or vice versa, or representation by analogy or allusion, are ways of thinking that are seriously pursued in poetry and are found just as frequently in other less serious mental productions such as jokes and slang. Even the representation of ideas in a nonverbal way creeps into our conscious lives quite often. We speak of pictures "that tell a whole story, better than words could do"; and though the artistically sophisticated among us may not have a very high critical regard for serious paintings which try to tell a story, we will all recognize the frequency of such attempts in humorous cartoons, caricatures, and advertising illustrations, for instance.

These examples all go to show that the characteristics of primary process thinking are not as alien to the conscious thinking of adult life as we assumed at first. They obviously persist throughout life and continue to play a rather considerable role, though a subordinate one. In addition, as we shall see in later chapters, the ego normally preserves a capacity for reverting temporarily to immature patterns which are characteristic of childhood. This is particularly evident in the games, jokes and play of adults, whether spiced with alcohol or not. It also occurs during sleep in dreaming as well as in the daydreams of waking life. In all such cases there is apparent a temporary increase in the importance of primary process thinking as compared with secondary process thinking, the type which is normally the dominant one in adult life, as we have said.

Although we have now covered the essentials of primary and secondary process thinking, there are a few more points to be added which will facilitate the reader's approach to the psychoanalytic literature concerning these subjects.

In the first place, there are a couple of terms in accepted use in the psychoanalytic literature to designate some of the features of primary process thinking which it would be well to define. The first of these terms is "displacement," the second is "condensation."

When used in its technical, psychoanalytic sense "displacement" refers to the representation of a part by the whole, or vice versa, or, in general, the substitution of one idea or image by another which is associatively connected with it. Freud assumed that such substitutions were due to or depended on a shift in the cathexis, that is, in the charge of psychic energy, from the one to the other thought or idea. Hence his choice of the word "displacement": what is displaced is the cathexis. Incidentally this term illustrates the close relation between primary process thinking and the characteristic ways of regulating drive energy which are also called primary process. In this case the ready tendency to displacement which is characteristic of primary process thinking is related to the mobility of cathexes which we have described as characteristic of the primary process proper.

The term "condensation" is used to indicate the representation of several ideas or images by a single word or image, or even a part of one. As in the case of displacement, the choice of the term "condensation" refers to the energy displacements on which the process is supposed to depend. Freud assumed that when many mental representations are represented by one, the cathexes of the many are concentrated (condensed) on the one.

There is one other characteristic of primary process thinking which is usually considered as though it were a separate and special one, although it would seem to be rather an example of one of the characteristics we have already discussed, that is displacement. This characteristic is what we call symbolic representation in the analytic sense of the word "symbolic."

Fairly early in his study of dreams and neurotic symptoms Freud (1900) found that some elements in dreams or symptoms have a meaning which is relatively constant from patient to patient, which is different from their ordinarily accepted meaning, and, strangest of all, which is unknown to the patient himself! For instance, a pair of sisters in a dream often stands for some thoughts about breasts, a journey or absence stands for death, money stands for feces, and so on. It is as though there is a secret language that people use unconsciously, without being able to understand it consciously, and the vocabulary of this language, so to speak, Freud called symbols. In other words, in the primary process, money may be used as a symbol, that is, as a full equivalent for feces, travel may be used for death, etc. This is truly a remarkable state of affairs, and it is not surprising that this discovery excited great interest and equally great opposition. To be sure, it is possible that both the interest and the opposition were as much due to the fact that many of the objects and ideas which are represented symbolically are forbidden ones, that is, sexual or "dirty."

The list of what may be represented by a symbol is not very long. It comprises the body and its parts, particularly the sexual organs, buttocks, anus, urinary and alimentary tracts, and the breasts; members of the immediate family, as mother, father, sister and brother; certain bodily functions and experiences, such as sexual intercourse, urination, defecation, eating, weeping, rage, and sexual excitement; birth; death; and a few others. The reader will notice that these are things which are of great interest to the small child, in other words that they are things important to an individual at a time when his ego is still immature and the primary process plays a major role in his thinking.

This completes our discussion of the primary and secondary processes. We wish to turn now to another aspect of the theory of drive energy as it has to do with the differentiation of the ego from the id and its subsequent development.

The aspect to which we refer is called the *neutralization of drive energy* (Freud, 1923; Hartmann et al., 1949). As a result of neutralization, drive energy which would otherwise press imperiously to discharge as soon as possible, like all id cathexes, becomes available to the ego and at the ego's disposal for carrying out its various tasks and wishes according to the secondary process. We thus relate unneutralized drive energy to the primary process and neutralized drive energy to the secondary process, although we are not certain of the precise relationship between neutralization and the establishment and operation of the secondary process.

What we do know are, first, that neutralization is progressive rather than a sudden transition, and second, that the energy which it makes available to the ego functions is essential to the ego. Without it the ego cannot function adequately, if at all (Hartmann, 1953a).

When we say that neutralization is progressive we mean that it is a transformation that occurs little by little over an extended period of time. Like the other changes which are associated with ego development it is a change that takes place gradually and that parallels the ego's growth, to which, as we have said, it contributes such an important share.

If we try now to define neutralized energy, the simplest, comprehensive definition we can offer is that it is energy which has been appreciably altered from its original, sexual or aggressive character. We should interpolate that this concept of the denaturation of drive energy was first introduced by Freud at a time when the only instinctual drive which was recognized was the sexual one (Freud, 1905b). As a result, in discussing the process which we are now considering, he referred to it as desexualization. In more recent years the word "desaggressivization" has been introduced as a companion term (Hartmann et al., 1949) but for the sake of simplicity and euphony it seems preferable to speak simply of neutralization, whether of sexual or of aggressive energy.

The term neutralization implies that an activity of the individual which originally afforded drive satisfaction through discharge of cathexis ceases to do so and comes to be in the service of the ego, apparently nearly or quite independent of the need for gratification or discharge of cathexis in anything which even approaches its original instinctual form. Perhaps the following example will serve to make things more understandable.

The child's earliest attempts to talk afford a discharge for various drives cathexes, as do the other activities of the immature ego in general. Just what drive energies of the little child are discharged in talking may be difficult or impossible to know fully and accurately, but we shall certainly agree on several of them: expression of emotion, identification with an adult or older sibling, and playing a game with and winning the attention of an adult, let us say. We shall also agree, however, that in time the use of language comes to be largely *independent* of such gratification and is available for the communication of thought even in the absence of such direct gratifications as those which first accompanied it: what was originally drive energy has been neutralized and is at the service of the ego.

We wish to emphasize that the relationship between such an activity as talking and drive satisfaction is normal at an early stage of life. Without the contribution made by the energy of the drives the acquisition of language would be seriously impeded, if indeed it could take place at all. One can see clinical examples of this fact in the mutism of withdrawn, psychotic children, who have no gratifying relationship with adults and whose speech only returns or first develops when in the course of treatment they begin to have such relationships again, or for the first time. On the other hand, if the drive energy involved does not become sufficiently neutralized, or if, in later life, the neutralization is undone, and talking, or the neutral energy available for it, is re-instinctualized, then neurotic conflicts may interfere with what had been hitherto an ego function which is available to the individual regardless of inner conflict. Examples of the consequence of such instinctualization are afforded by childhood stuttering (inadequate neutralization) and hysterical aphonia (re-instinctualization). We may add in passing that re-instinctualization (deneutralization) is one aspect of the phenomenon of regression, to which we have already referred in Chapter II and which we shall discuss again in Chapter IV.

The concept that neutralized energy is at the disposal of the ego for the execution of many of its functions accords with the fact that these operations of the ego are autonomous in the sense that they are ordinarily undisturbed by the flux of the drives, at least after early childhood, or by the intrapsychic conflicts which are stirred up by the drives (Hartmann et al., 1946). However, their autonomy is a relative, not an absolute one, and as we have said above, in some pathological situations the energy at their disposal may be re-instinctualized and the functions themselves become affected by, or even at the mercy of the wishes arising from the drives, or by the conflicts over those wishes.

SUGGESTED READING

FREUD, S., The Ego and the Id. *Standard Edition*, Vol. 19, pp. 3–66, 1961. Also New York: Norton, 1961.

FREUD, S., New Introductory Lectures on Psycho-Analysis. *Standard Edition*, Vol. 22. Chapter 3, Lecture XXXI, 1964. Also in: *Complete Introductory Lectures on Psychoanalysis*. New York: Norton, 1966.

RAPAPORT, D., ed., *Organization and Pathology of Thought*. New York: Columbia University Press, 1951.

CHAPTER IV

THE PSYCHIC APPARATUS (continued)

In Chapter III we discussed various topics in connection with the differentiation of the ego from the id, its gradual growth, and its functioning. We spoke of the basic psychic functions which are grouped together under the heading, "the ego," such as motor control, sensory perception, memory, affects, and thinking, and drew attention to the fact that the factors which influence ego development fall into two broad categories which we called maturational and environmental or experiential. We discussed the latter category at some length and pointed out the exceptional importance for ego development of one of the objects of the infant's environment, namely his own body. In addition we discussed the very great influence which other persons of the child's environment have on the growth and development of his ego via the process of identification. We turned then to what we call the mode of functioning of the various parts of the psychic apparatus and discussed the primary and secondary processes and primary and secondary process thinking. Finally we discussed the role played in ego formation and functioning by the neutralization of psychic energy deriving from the drives.

In this chapter we shall organize our discussion around two principal topics which in turn are closely related to one another. The first of these concerns the ability of the ego to acquire knowledge of its environment and mastery over it.

The second deals with the complex and extremely important ways in which the ego achieves a degree of control and mastery over the id, that is over the wishes and impulses arising from the drives. The one topic has to do with the ego struggling with the outer world in its role of intermediary between id and environment, the other with the ego in the same role struggling with the id itself, or as one might say, with the inner world.

Let us begin with the first of these topics, that is with the ego's mastery of the environment. It is clear that at least three ego functions which we have previously discussed are of fundamental importance in this connection. The first of these functions comprises the sensory perceptions which inform the ego about the surroundings in the first place. The second includes the ability to remember, to compare, and to think according to the secondary process, which permits a much higher level of knowledge about the environment than the elementary sensory impressions alone could ever provide. The third consists of the motor controls and skills which permit the individual to undertake to alter his physical environment by active means. As one would expect, these functions are interrelated rather than separated from one another. For example, motor skills may be essential in gaining sensory impressions, as is the case with the acquisition of stereoscopic vision or the use of the hands in palpation. However, in addition to these various and interrelated ego functions we also distinguish a particular one that plays a most significant role in the ego's relation to the environment and which we call *reality testing* (Freud, 1911, 1923).

By reality testing we mean the ability of the ego to distinguish between the stimuli or perceptions which arise from the outer world, on the one hand, and those which arise from the wishes and impulses of the id, on the other. If the ego is able to perform this task successfully, we say that the individual in question has a good or adequate sense of reality. If his ego cannot perform the task, we say that his sense of reality is poor or defective.

How does a sense of reality develop? We believe that it develops gradually, like other ego functions, as the infant grows and matures over a considerable period of time. We assume that during the first several weeks of its life the infant is unable to distinguish at all between the stimuli from its own body and instinctual drives and those from its environment. It develops the capacity to do so progressively, partly in consequence of the maturation of its nervous system and sensory organs and partly in consequence of experiential factors.

Freud (1911) drew attention to the fact that frustration was one of the latter. In fact he considered that it was of great importance in the development of reality testing during the early months of life. He pointed out, for example, that the infant experiences many times that certain stimuli, e.g., those from the breast and milk, which are important sources of gratification, are sometimes absent. As the infant discovers, this may be true even though the particular stimuli are highly cathected, that is, in this example, even though the infant is hungry.

Such experiences of frustration, which are inevitably repeated over and over in a variety of ways during infancy, Freud considered to be a most significant factor in the development of a sense of reality. Through them the infant learns that some things in the world come and go, that they can be absent as well as present, that they are "not here," however much he may wish them to be so. This is one of the starting points for recognizing that such things (mother's breast, for example) are not "self" but "outside self."

Conversely there are some stimuli which the infant cannot *make* go away. No matter how much he may wish them "not here," here they stay. These stimuli arise from within the body and are in their turn starting points for recognizing that such things (a stomach-ache, for instance) are not "outside self" but "self."

The capacity to tell whether something is "self" or "not self" is obviously a part of the general function of reality testing, a part to which we refer as the establishment of firm ego boundaries. Actually, it would probably be more accurate to speak of self-boundaries than of ego boundaries, but the latter phrase has become solidly established in the literature by now.

Under the influence of such experiences as we have just outlined, the ego of the growing child gradually develops a capacity to test reality. We know that in childhood this capacity is but partial and varies in effectiveness from time to time. For example, we well know the tendency of the child to experience a game or fantasy as real, at least as long as it lasts. In addition, however, we must recognize that even in normal adult life our view of reality is constantly influenced by our own wishes, fears, hopes, and memories. There are few if any of us who ever see the world clear and see it steady. For the vast majority of us our view of the world about us is more or less influenced by our inner mental lives.

To take a simple example, think how different a foreign people seem to us to be when our respective countries are enjoying peaceful relations from what they seem to be when our countries are at war. They become transformed from pleasant, even admirable people to despicable and vicious ones. What has really caused the change in our estimate of their characters? I think we should have to agree that the decisive factors producing the change have been psychic processes occurring within ourselves. No doubt, these psychic processes are quite complex ones, but one can readily guess that at least one important one is an arousal of hatred for the enemy, a desire to hurt or destroy him, and the resultant guilt, that is fear of punishment and fear of retaliation. It is in consequence of such turbulent feelings within us that our erstwhile admirable neighbors become despicable and vicious in our eyes.

The incompleteness or the unreliability of the capacity of our egos for reality testing is thus reflected in the prevalence of prejudices such as we have just discussed. It is also apparent from the widespread and tenacious belief in superstitions and magical practices, whether religious or not, as well as in religious beliefs in general. Nevertheless the adult normally attains a considerable degree of success in his ability to test reality, at least in usual or everyday situations, an ability which is lost or considerably impaired only by a severe mental illness. Patients who are sick with such an illness have much more serious disturbances in their ability to test reality than one is accustomed to see in normal or neurotic people. As an example, one may merely cite the mentally ill patient who believes his delusions or hallucinations to be real, for instance, when in fact they have their origins primarily in the fears and wishes within himself.

Indeed, disturbance in reality testing is such a regular feature of various, severe, mental illnesses that it has become a diagnostic criterion of them. The serious consequences of such a disturbance serve to emphasize to us the importance of the capacity of reality testing to the ego in its normal role as executant for the id. An intact reality sense enables the ego to act efficiently upon the environment in the interests of the id. It is thus a valuable asset to the ego when the latter is allied with the id and attempting to exploit the environment with regard to opportunities for gratification.

Let us now look at the other aspect of the ego's role as an intermediary between the id and the environment which we proposed to consider in this chapter. In this new aspect we find the ego delaying, controlling, or otherwise opposing discharge of id energies rather than furthering or facilitating their discharge.

As we understand the relationship between ego and id, the

capacity of the ego to control the discharge of id energies is in the first place something which is necessary or valuable for the efficient exploitation of the environment, as we mentioned above. If one can wait a little bit, he can often avoid some unpleasant consequence of gratification or increase the pleasure to be gained. As a simple example, a year-and-a-half-old child who wants to urinate may be able to avoid the unpleasure of a scolding if his ego can delay the onset of urination till he gets to the toilet, and at the same time he can gain an extra pleasure of praise and affection. In addition, we have seen that some delay of discharge of drive energy is an essential part of the development of the secondary process and of secondary process thinking, which is certainly a valuable asset to the ego in exploiting the environment.

We can understand, therefore, that the very process of ego development results in a certain degree of delay in the discharge of id energies and a certain measure of control of the id by the ego. Anna Freud (1954a) expressed this aspect of the relationship between the id and the ego by comparing it to the relationship between the individual and the civil service in a modern state. She pointed out that in a complex society the citizen must delegate many tasks to civil servants if he wants them done efficiently and to his own best interests. The creation of a civil service is therefore to the individual citizen's advantage and brings him many benefits which he is happy to enjoy, but at the same time he discovers that there are certain disadvantages also. The civil service is often too slow in satisfying a particular need of the individual and seems to have its own ideas of what is best for him, ideas that do not always coincide with what he wants at the moment. In a similar way the ego may impose delay on the id drives, may argue the claims of the environment against them, and even appropriates for its own use some of the energy of the drives by means of neutralization.

We might expect from what we have learned so far about the relationship between ego and id that the relationship between the ego and the environment would never be strong enough to force the ego into serious or long-continued opposition to the instinctual demands of the id. After all, we have said repeatedly that the relationship of the ego to reality was primarily in the service of the id and we should expect therefore that in the event of a really major conflict between the id wishes and the realities of the environment, the ego would be substantially allied with the id.

What we find to be the case, however, is rather different from our expectation. We learn that the ego may in fact array itself against the id under certain circumstances and may even directly oppose the discharge of its drive energies. This opposition of ego to id is not clearly evident until after there has been a certain degree of development and organization of the ego functions, of course, but its beginnings are no later than the latter part of the first year of life. A simple example of such opposition would be the ego's rejection of a wish to kill a sibling. As we know, very small children often act upon such a wish by attacking the sibling, but with the passage of time and under the pressure of environmental disapproval the ego eventually opposes and rejects this id wish, to such an extent in fact that at last it seems to cease to exist. At least as far as external behavior is concerned, the ego has prevailed and the wish to kill has been given up.

Thus we see that although the ego is primarily the executant of the id and continues to be so in many respects throughout life, it begins to exercise an increasing degree of control over the id rather early in life and gradually comes to be in opposition to some id strivings and even in open conflict with them. From being the obedient and helpful servant of the id in every respect, the ego becomes in some part the opponent and even the master of the id.

But this revision of our conception of the role of the ego

must raise some questions in our minds which deserve to be answered. How are we to account for the fact that the ego, a part of the id which began as the servant of the drives, becomes to some extent their master? Also what particular means does the ego use for keeping the id impulses in check when it succeeds in doing so?

The answer to the first question lies partly in the nature of the infant's relation to its environment and partly in certain psychological characteristics of the human mind. Some of these characteristics are new and some are already familiar to us from our previous discussion. What they have in common is that they are all related to ego functioning.

First for the environment. We know that the infant's environment is of very special, biological significance to it, or rather that parts of its environment are. Without these parts, which are at first its mother and later both parents, it could not survive. It is not surprising to us, therefore, that the human infant's unusually great and uniquely prolonged physical dependence on its parents is paralleled by its psychological dependence on them. For the infant, as we have seen, is dependent for most of its sources of pleasure upon its parents and we realize that it is in consequence of these several factors that the infant's mother, for example, can become such an important object of the infant's environment that in case of a conflict between a demand of the mother and a direct id wish of the infant, the ego sides with the former against the latter. For example if the mother forbids the expression of a destructive impulse, such as tearing the pages out of books, the ego will often take the mother's side against the id.

This part of our answer is easy to understand and requires no very technical or involved discussion. In passing on to the rest of our answer to the first of the questions which we asked above, we shall have to discuss more than one factor and at some length.

First of all we may re-emphasize that ego formation and ego functioning use energy which comes either wholly or in large part from the id. Unless we are to assume that the id is an infinite reservoir of psychic energy, we must conclude that the mere fact of the existence of the ego and its functioning implies a reduction in the amount of drive energy in the id. Some of it has been used up to make and run the ego. Indeed, in looking about us at our fellow men we sometimes have the impression that there is no id left in some particularly passionless members of the species and that *all* of their psychic energy has gone into ego formation, even though we know that such an extreme is an impossible one. The important point, however, is that the development of the ego results inevitably in some degree of weakening of the id. From this point of view one may say that the ego grows like a parasite at the expense of the id, and this may well contribute in some measure to the fact that the ego eventually is strong enough to become in part the master of the id rather than remaining forever and completely its servant, although, as we have said earlier, it seems unlikely that it can fully explain this outcome.

At this point we may profitably mention several processes which are of importance in ego formation and functioning and which contribute significantly to the process of diminishing the psychic energy of the id and of increasing that of the ego.

One such process which we have seen to be a principal part of ego development and which must operate in the manner just described is the neutralization of drive energy. This process of denaturation, which we described at some length in Chapter III, clearly results in a reduction of the libidinal and aggressive energies of the id and an increase in the energy which is available to the ego.

Another of the factors which we know to be important in ego development and which plays a significant role in diverting psychic energy from the id to the ego is the process of identification. Identification was also discussed in Chapter III, and the reader will remember that it consists essentially in the individual becoming like an object (person or thing) of the outside world which was psychologically important to the individual, that is, which was highly cathected with drive energy.

The "becoming like," as we have seen, produces a change in the ego, and one of the consequences of this change is that either all or part of the cathexes which were previously attached to an external object become attached instead to the copy of that object in the ego. The fact that some of the id energies are now attached to a part of the ego contributes to the enrichment of the energies at the disposal of the ego at the expense of the id and to the strengthening of the ego vis-à-vis the id.

There is still another way that deserves our attention by which id demands are weakened and thereby rendered more liable to control by the ego and that is the process of fantasied gratification. It is a remarkable, though a commonplace fact that a fantasy, whether a daydream or a dream during sleep, in which one or several id wishes are represented as fulfilled, results actually in a partial gratification of the id impulses which are concerned and in a partial discharge of their energy. Thus for example a sleeper who is thirsty may dream of quenching his thirst and may feel sufficiently satisfied by the dream so that he goes on sleeping even though the water tap is only in the next room.

It is obvious even on brief reflection that the part played in our mental lives by fantasy is a very great one indeed, and we do not propose even to outline the general importance of the function of fantasy at this point. We wish only to point out that one effect of fantasy may be that an id impulse is so nearly satisfied that it is relatively easy for the ego to check or control it thereafter, and that fantasy therefore can play a role in making it possible for the ego to master a part of the id. We may add what should be obvious, namely that such fantasies occur frequently in normal mental life.

We come now to the final one of the psychological characteristics which we wish to discuss as playing a part in enabling the ego to become to some extent the master of the id. This characteristic is probably the decisive one in the entire situation and is the one which is really responsible for the ability of the ego to oppose and master the impulses of the id to a certain degree and at certain times. It is the human tendency to develop anxiety under certain circumstances, a tendency which will not only require a rather lengthy and technical discussion to elucidate it, but also a considerable introduction, since the current, psychoanalytic theory of anxiety cannot be understood without first presenting what Freud (1911) called the pleasure principle. This hypothesis we have not yet discussed and we propose to do so now.

Expressed in simplest terms, the pleasure principle states that the mind tends to operate in such a way as to achieve pleasure and to avoid its opposite. The German word which Freud used to express the opposite of pleasure is *Unlust*, which has often been translated as "pain," so that the pleasure principle is sometimes alternatively called the pleasure-pain principle. However, "pain," unlike *Unlust*, also denotes the physical sensation of pain, as well as the opposite of pleasure, and in order to avoid ambiguity on that score it has been suggested by more recent translators that the somewhat clumsy, but unambiguous word "unpleasure" be used instead of "pain."

Freud added to the concept of the pleasure principle the ideas that in earliest life the tendency toward achieving pleasure is imperious and immediate and that the individual only gradually acquires the ability to postpone the achievement of pleasure as he grows older.

Now this concept of the pleasure principle sounds very

much like the concept of the primary process which we discussed in Chapter III. According to the pleasure principle there is a tendency to the achievement of pleasure and avoidance of unpleasure, a tendency which in earliest life brooks no delay. According to the primary process, cathexes of drive energy must be discharged as soon as possible, and we further assume that this process is dominant in mental functioning at the start of life. In addition, in connection with the pleasure principle Freud asserted that with age there is a gradual increase in the individual's capacity to postpone the attainment of pleasure and the avoidance of unpleasure, while in connection with the primary process he formulated the idea that the development of the secondary process and its increase in relative importance permit the individual to postpone the discharge of cathexes as he grows older.

In most of its essentials, therefore, Freud's early concept of the pleasure principle corresponds to his later one of the primary process. The only real difference, as distinct from terminological ones, is that the pleasure principle is formulated in *subjective* terms while the primary process is formulated in *objective* ones. That is to say, the words "pleasure" or "unpleasure" refer to subjective phenomena, in this case to affects, while the phrases "discharge of cathexis" or "discharge of drive energy" refer to the objective phenomena of energy distribution and discharge, in this case within the id. It should be noted, by the way, that according to our theories an affect or emotion is an ego phenomenon, however much it may depend for its genesis on processes within the id.

Freud was naturally well aware of the great similarity between the formulation of the pleasure principle and the formulation of that aspect of id functioning which he had named the primary process. In fact he tried to unify the two concepts and it is really because he felt that his attempt to do so was unsuccessful that we must discuss the two hypotheses separately at this point.

The attempt to unify the two concepts was made on the basis of a very simple assumption, the assumption in fact that an increase in the amount of undischarged, mobile cathexes within the mental apparatus corresponds or gives rise to a feeling of unpleasure, while the discharge of such cathexes, with a corresponding lessening of their remaining amount, leads to a feeling of pleasure. In simpler and somewhat less precise terms we may say that Freud (1911) originally assumed that an increase in psychic tension caused unpleasure while a decrease in such tension caused pleasure. If this assumption were correct, the pleasure principle and the primary process would come to be merely different wordings of the same hypothesis.

The argument would run about as follows: The pleasure principle says that in the very young child there is a tendency to achieve pleasure through gratification which may not be postponed. The primary process says that in the very young child there is a tendency to discharge of cathexis, that is, of drive energy which may not be postponed. But, according to Freud's original assumption the pleasure of gratification is one with or perhaps one aspect of the discharge of cathexis. If the assumption were true, therefore, the two formulations would say the same thing in different words and the pleasure principle and the primary process would be merely two alternative formulations of the same hypothesis.

Unfortunately for our natural longing for simplicity in our theories Freud (1924c) concluded that although pleasure accompanied a discharge of mobile psychic energy in the vast majority of cases, while unpleasure was the consequence of the accumulation of such energy, still there were important cases in which this did not seem to be so. In fact he asserted that there were even cases where the reverse was true. As an example he pointed out that at least up to a certain point an increase in sexual tension is experienced as pleasurable.

Freud's final decision, therefore, was that the relationships between the phenomena of the accumulation and discharge of mobile drive energy, on the one hand, and the affects of pleasure and unpleasure, on the other, were neither simple nor determinable. He offered one guess, namely that the rate and rhythm of increment or discharge of cathexis might be a determining factor and left the matter about at that. There have been subsequent attempts to develop a satisfactory hypothesis about the relationship between pleasure and the accumulation and discharge of drive energy, but none of them is widely enough accepted at present to justify its inclusion here (Jacobson, 1953).

The consequence of these facts is that we cannot yet satisfactorily formulate the pleasure principle in terms of later concepts which deal principally with psychic energy. We must therefore hold to the earlier version of it which is formulated in terms of the subjective experiences of pleasure and unpleasure: the mind, or the individual in his mental life, seeks to attain pleasure and to avoid unpleasure.

The reader will recall that our reason for introducing a discussion of the pleasure principle at this point was to pave the way for the subject of anxiety and it is to this latter topic that we shall now turn our attention. The importance of the pleasure principle in the psychoanalytic theory of anxiety will become apparent in the course of our discussion.

Freud's original theory of anxiety was that it resulted from a damming up and inadequate discharge of libido. Whether the abnormal accumulation of libido within the psyche was the result of external obstacles to its proper discharge (Freud, 1895) or whether it was due to inner obstacles such as unconscious conflicts or inhibitions concerning sexual gratification was relatively unimportant from the point of view of the theory of anxiety. In either case the result was an accumulation of undischarged libido which might be transformed into anxiety. The theory did not explain how the transformation took place nor what factors determined the precise time when it took place. It is also important to note that according to this theory the term "anxiety" denoted a pathological type of fear which was, to be sure, related phenomenologically to the normal fear of an external danger, but which had a distinctly different origin. Fear of external danger was, presumably, a learned reaction, that is, a reaction based upon experience, while anxiety was transformed libido, that is, a pathological manifestation of drive energy.

This was the status of the psychoanalytic theory of anxiety until 1926. In that year there was published a monograph by Freud called *The Problem of Anxiety* in its American translation and *Inhibition, Symptoms, and Anxiety* in the British one. In this monograph Freud pointed out that anxiety is the central problem of neurosis, and he proposed a new theory concerning anxiety which was based on the structural hypothesis and which we shall presently summarize.

Before we do so it is worth while to note in passing the close relationship between the subject matter of *Inhibition, Symptoms, and Anxiety*, that is Freud's second theory of anxiety, and that of two earlier works to which we have frequently referred during the course of Chapters II and III, *Beyond the Pleasure Principle* and *The Ego and the Id*. These two monographs contain the fundamental concepts which differentiate modern psychoanalytic theory from what went before. These concepts are the dual theory of the drives and the structural hypothesis. They permit a more consistent and more convenient way of viewing mental phenomena than was possible before, as well as of understanding their complicated interrelationships. The new theories also paved the way for important advances in the clinical application of psychoanalysis. An outstanding example of this has been the development of ego analysis and of the entire field of psychoanalytic ego psychology which has taken place since they were formulated.

Freud himself wrote several papers in which he showed how the new theories could be fruitfully applied to clinical problems (Freud, 1924b, 1924c, 1924d, 1926). *Inhibition, Symptoms, and Anxiety* is by far the most important single instance of such a fruitful application. In it Freud advanced a clinically applicable theory of anxiety which was based on the insights afforded by the structural hypothesis.

In attempting to understand the new theory we must realize first of all that Freud considered anxiety to have a biological, inherited basis. In other words, he believed that the human organism is congenitally endowed with the capacity for reacting with the psychological and physical manifestations which we call anxiety. Indeed, he pointed out that in man as in lower animals this capacity has a definite survival value for the individual, at least in his "natural" state. If a human being, without the protection of his parents, could not be frightened by anything, he would soon be destroyed.

What Freud tried to explain in his theory of anxiety, therefore, was neither the nature nor the basic origin of anxiety, but rather its place and its importance in the mental life of man. As we shall see, the formulations that he proposed in *Inhibition, Symptoms, and Anxiety* in part included his earlier formulations and in part went far beyond them.

In addition one major part of his earlier theory was completely abandoned: he gave up entirely the idea that undischarged libido was *transformed* into anxiety. He took this step on clinical grounds and demonstrated the validity of his new position by a rather detailed discussion of two cases of childhood phobia.

In his new theory Freud proposed to relate the appearance of anxiety to what he called "traumatic situations" and "danger situations." The first of these he defined as a situation in which the psyche is overwhelmed by an influx of stimuli which is too great for it either to master or to discharge. He believed that when this occurs anxiety develops automatically.

Since it is part of the function of the ego both to master incoming stimuli and to discharge them effectively, it would be expected that traumatic situations would occur more often in the early months and years of life when the ego is still relatively weak and undeveloped. Indeed Freud considered that the prototype of the traumatic situation is the experience of birth as the emerging infant is affected by it. At that time the infant is subjected to an overwhelming influx of external and visceral sensory stimuli and responds with what Freud considered to be the manifestations of anxiety.

Freud's chief interest in birth as a traumatic situation accompanied by anxiety was apparently that it could be viewed as a prototype of later, psychologically more significant traumatic situations and as such fitted in with his new ideas rather neatly. Otto Rank (1924) attempted to apply this idea of Freud's clinically in a much bolder way than Freud had himself intended and proposed the notion that all neuroses are traceable to the birth trauma and can be cured by reconstructing what that trauma must have been and making the patient conscious of it. Rank's theories created a considerable stir among psychoanalysts at the time they were first proposed, but they have been pretty well discarded by now.

Freud paid considerable attention in his monograph to the traumatic situations which occur in early infancy after birth. As an example of such situations he chose the following. A young infant is dependent on its mother, not only for the satisfaction of most of its bodily needs, but also for the instinctual gratifications, which, at least in the early months of life, infants experience chiefly in connection with bodily satisfaction. Thus, for example, when an infant is nursed, not only is its hunger sated. It also experiences simultaneously the instinctual pleasure which is associated with oral stimulation, as well as the pleasure of being held, warmed, and fondled. Before a certain age an infant cannot achieve these pleasures, that is, these instinctual gratifications, by itself. It needs its mother to be able to do so. If, when its mother is absent, the infant experiences an instinctual need which can be gratified only through its mother, then a situation develops which is traumatic for the child in the sense in which Freud used this word. The infant's ego is not sufficiently developed to be able to postpone gratification by holding the drive wishes in abeyance and instead the infant's psyche is overwhelmed by an influx of stimuli. Since it can neither master nor adequately discharge these stimuli, anxiety develops.

It is worth noting that in our example, and of course in all the other cases which our example is intended to typify, the flood of stimuli giving rise to this primitive, automatic type of anxiety is of *internal* origin. Specifically it arises from the operation of the drives or more precisely of the id. For this reason anxiety of the automatic type which we have been discussing has been referred to at times as "id anxiety." This name is rarely used today, however, since it permitted the misconception that the id was the *site* of this kind of anxiety. Actually, Freud's idea, contained in the structural hypothesis, was that the ego is the site of all emotions. The experiencing of any emotion is a function of the ego, according to Freud, and of course this must be true of anxiety also. What facilitated the misconception that the id was the site of automatically induced anxiety was that the ego hardly exists as a differentiated, much less an integrated structure at such an early age as the one to which our example of the preceding paragraph refers. Tiny infants, as we have said before, have only the rudiments of an ego and even the little bit that has begun to differentiate from the rest of the id is still hardly distinguishable from it. Nevertheless, whatever ego *can* be differentiated in such young children is the site of the anxiety which develops.

Freud also believed that the tendency or capacity of the mental apparatus to react to an exclusive influx of stimuli in the way described above, that is, by developing anxiety, persists throughout life. In other words, a traumatic situation, in Freud's special sense of this word, may develop at any age. To be sure, such situations will develop much more often in very early life for the reason which we gave above, namely that the ego is as yet undeveloped, since the better developed the ego, the better able it is to master or discharge incoming stimuli whether of internal or of external origin. The reader will remember that it is only when such stimuli can *not* be adequately mastered or discharged that the situation becomes a traumatic one and anxiety develops.

If Freud was correct in his assumption that birth is a prototype of later traumatic situations, then the birth experience is an example of a traumatic situation in infancy which is caused by stimuli that are principally of external origin. In other cases the offending stimuli originate primarily from the drives, that is their origin is an internal one, as was true for example of the infant whose mother was not there to supply the gratification for which its id was clamoring and which only she could give.

As far as we know, traumatic situations arising as a consequence of the demands of the id are the most common and the most important in early life. Freud also believed that such situations arise in later life in those cases which he classified as "actual" anxiety neuroses (see Chapter VIII) and that the anxiety from which those patients suffer is in fact due to the overwhelming influx of stimuli arising from sexual drive energy which has not been adequately discharged because of external hindrances.

However, this particular assumption of Freud's has relatively little practical significance, since the diagnosis of actual neurosis is rarely if ever made at present. Another application of the same basic idea has assumed more clinical importance, however, namely the assumption that the so-called traumatic neuroses of adult life, as, for example, battle neuroses and what used to be called shell-shock, are the result of an overwhelming influx of *external* stimuli which has then automatically given rise to anxiety. Freud himself raised this possibility and many authors have subsequently appeared to assume that it was true, or at least that Freud believed it to be true. Actually Freud (1926) expressed the opinion that a traumatic neurosis probably could not arise in such a simple way, without what he called the "participation of the deeper layers of the personality."

Freud's concept of traumatic situations and of the automatic development of anxiety in traumatic situations constitutes what we might call the first part of his new theory of anxiety. It is the part which is closest to his earlier theory, although it differs substantially from the earlier one with regard to the mode of production of anxiety. The reader will remember that according to Freud's earlier view anxiety arose from the transformation of libido, while according to his later view it developed as the result of an overwhelming influx of stimuli which might or might not arise from the drives.

We may now summarize the first part of Freud's new theory as follows:

(1) Anxiety develops automatically whenever the psyche is overwhelmed by an influx of stimuli too great to be mastered or discharged.

(2) These stimuli may be either of external or of internal origin, but most frequently they arise from the id, that is, from the drives.

(3) When anxiety develops automatically according to this pattern, the situation is called a traumatic one.

(4) The prototype of such traumatic situations is birth.

(5) Automatic anxiety is characteristic of infancy, because of the weakness and immaturity of the ego at that time of life, and is also found in adult life in cases of so-called actual anxiety neurosis.

The second part of the new theory is that, in the course of growth, the young child learns to anticipate the advent of a traumatic situation and to react to it with anxiety before it becomes traumatic. This type of anxiety Freud called signal anxiety. It is produced by a situation of *danger* or the anticipation of danger, its production is a function of the ego, and it serves to mobilize the forces at the command of the ego to meet or to avoid the impending traumatic situation.

To illustrate the meaning of the words "danger situation" Freud returned to the example of the infant left alone by its mother. The reader will recall that if, while still alone, the infant should be assailed by some need for whose gratification the mother's presence was necessary, the situation would become traumatic and anxiety would develop automatically. Freud argued that after it has reached a certain stage of development the infant's ego will recognize that a relationship exists between its mother's departure and the development of the highly unpleasurable state of automatically induced anxiety that sometimes appears after she has gone. In other words, the ego will know that if mother is present, anxiety will not develop, while it may do so if she is gone. As a result the ego comes to consider separation from the mother as a "danger situation," the danger being the appearance of an imperious demand for gratification from the id while mother is away, with the consequent development of a traumatic situation.

What does the infant do in such a danger situation? Part of what it does is familiar to anyone who has had experience with children. By various expressions of distress the child attempts to keep mother from leaving or to summon her if she has already left. However, Freud was more interested in what goes on intrapsychically in the infant than in the various ego activities which are intended to alter the external environment, important as these may be. He suggested that in a danger situation the ego reacts with anxiety which it actively produces itself and which he proposed to call signal anxiety, since it is produced by the ego as a signal of danger.

But one moment before we proceed. How can the ego actively produce anxiety, whether as a signal or for any other purpose? The answer to this question depends upon our recalling that the ego is after all a group of related functions. We believe that in a danger situation certain of these functions, e.g., sensory perception, memory, and some type of thought process, are concerned with recognizing the danger, while other parts of the ego, or other ego functions react to the danger with what is perceived as anxiety. Indeed we can even guess from our clinical experience that the perception of danger probably gives rise to a fantasy of the traumatic situation and that this fantasy is what causes signal anxiety. Whether or not this guess is correct, we can say that some ego functions are responsible for recognizing the danger and others for reacting to it with anxiety.

Let us continue now with Freud's exposition of what happens when the ego recognizes a danger situation and reacts to it by producing signal anxiety. It is at this point that the pleasure principle enters the picture. Signal anxiety is unpleasant and the more intense the anxiety, the more unpleasant it is. We assume of course that in some degree the intensity of the anxiety is proportional to the ego's estimate of the severity or of the immediacy of the danger or of both. So we expect that in the case of any considerable danger situation the anxiety and the unpleasure will also be considerable. The unpleasure then automatically sets into action what Freud called the "all-powerful" pleasure principle. It is the operation of the pleasure principle which then gives the ego the necessary strength to check the emergence or continued action of whatever id impulses might be giving rise to the danger situation. In the example of the infant left by its mother these impulses might be expressed by the desire to be nursed and fondled by her, for instance.

Freud outlined a series of *typical* danger situations which may be expected to occur in sequence in the child's life. The first of these, chronologically, is separation from a person who is important to the child as a source of gratification. This is often referred to in the psychoanalytic literature as "loss of the object," or as "loss of the loved object," although at the age when this is *first* perceived as a danger the child is still much too young for us to attribute to it such a complex emotion as love. The next typical danger situation for the child is the loss of love of a person of its environment on whom it must depend for gratification. In other words, even though the person is present, the child may fear the loss of its love. This is referred to as the "loss of the object's love." The next, typical danger situation is different for the two sexes. In the case of the little boy the danger is the loss of his penis, which is referred to as castration in the psychoanalytic literature. In the case of the little girl the danger is some analogous genital injury. The last danger situation is that of guilt, or disapproval and punishment by the superego.

The first of these dangers we assume to be characteristic of the earliest stage of ego development, perhaps up to the age of one and a half years, when there is added to it the second, while the third does not occupy the center of the stage until the age of two and a half to three years. The last of the typical danger situations appears only after the age of five or six years, when the superego has been formed. All of these dangers persist at least to some degree throughout life *unconsciously*—in neurotic patients, to an excessive degree— and the relative importance of each danger varies from person to person. It is obviously of the greatest practical importance in clinical work with a patient to know which danger is the chief one that the patient unconsciously fears.

Freud asserted that anxiety is the central problem of mental illness, and his assertion is accepted by most of us today. We may incidentally remind ourselves that this was not always so. Before the publication of *Inhibition, Symptoms, and Anxiety* the main emphasis in psychoanalytic thinking about the neuroses, both theoretically and clinically, was on the vicissitudes of the libido, in particular on libidinal fixations. At that time, as we have said earlier, anxiety was thought to be libido which had been transformed as a consequence of its inadequate discharge. It was natural therefore that the libido should be the principal focus of attention in discussions of theory and that the clinician's principal concern should be to undo fixations and in general to insure adequate discharge of libido. This is not intended to imply that it is any less important now than formerly to remove fixations. It is only that we now tend to look at these problems, both clinically and theoretically, from the point of view of both the ego and the id, rather than from the side of the id alone.

With all the emphasis in the current psychoanalytic literature on the importance of anxiety in mental illness it is easy to lose sight of the fact that the role of anxiety in enabling the ego to check or inhibit instinctual wishes or impulses which seem to it to be dangerous is an essential one in normal development. This function of anxiety is by no means pathological in itself. On the contrary, it is a necessary part of mental life and growth. Without it, for example, any sort of education, in the broadest sense of the word, would be impossible. The individual would be at the mercy of each impulse as it arose in his id and would have to attempt to gratify each one in turn or simultaneously, unless the attempt to do so resulted in a traumatic situation in which the individual was overwhelmed with anxiety.

Another point about signal anxiety is this: it is, or should be, very much less in intensity than the anxiety which accompanies a traumatic situation. In other words, this signal which the ego learns to give in the course of its development is less intensely unpleasurable than the anxiety which might develop if the signal were not given and a traumatic situation developed. Signal anxiety is an attenuated anxiety.

Let us now recapitulate this second part of the new theory of anxiety:

(1) In the course of development the ego acquires the capacity to produce anxiety when a danger situation arises (threat of a traumatic situation) and later, in anticipation of danger.

(2) Through the operation of the pleasure principle this signal anxiety enables the ego to check or inhibit id impulses in a situation of danger.

(3) There is a characteristic set or sequence of danger situations in early and later childhood which persist as such to a greater or less degree throughout life *unconsciously*.

(4) Signal anxiety is an attenuated form of anxiety, it plays a great role in normal development, and it is the form of anxiety which is characteristic of the psychoneuroses.

We have now completed our answer to the first of the two questions which we raised on page 69. This was the question of accounting for the fact that, although the ego begins as a part of the id which is the servant of the rest, it eventually becomes to some extent the master of the id as time goes on. We wish now to apply ourselves to answering the second question which we raised on page 69, namely, just how the ego manages to keep the id impulses in check when it succeeds in doing so.

We understand from our discussion of anxiety that when the ego opposes the emergence of an id impulse it does so because it judges that the emergence of that impulse will create a danger situation. The ego then produces anxiety as a signal of danger, wins the help of the pleasure principle in this way, and is able to offer successful opposition to the emergence of the dangerous impulses. In psychoanalytical terminology we speak of such opposition as the *defense* or as the defensive operation of the ego. Our question may then be framed as follows, "What are the defenses which the ego has to offer against the id?"

The answer to this question is a very simple, although a very general one. The ego can use anything which lies to its hand that will serve the purpose. Any ego attitude, any perception, a change in attention, furtherance of another id impulse which is safer than the dangerous one and will compete with it, a vigorous attempt to neutralize the energy of the dangerous drive, the formation of identifications, or the promotion of fantasy can be used alone or in any combination in a defensive way. In a word the ego can and does use all of the processes of normal ego formation and ego function for defensive purposes at one time or another.

In addition to these defensive operations of the ego, however, in which the ego makes use of processes which are already familiar to us from previous discussion, there are certain processes of the ego which have to do primarily with the ego's defenses against the id. To these Anna Freud (1936) gave the name of "defense mechanisms" and our chief concern in our further discussion of the ego's defenses will be with them.

Any list which we might give of the defense mechanisms would be necessarily incomplete and open to criticism, since there are still differences of opinion among analysts about what should and what should not be called a defense mechanism as opposed to the other means which are available to the ego for the mastering of the impulses of the id. What we shall do therefore is to try to define and discuss those defense mechanisms which are generally recognized as such and which are generally admitted to be of considerable importance in mental functioning.

The mechanism which was earliest recognized and which

has been most extensively discussed in the psychoanalytic literature is the one which we call *repression* (Freud, 1915b). Repression consists in an activity of the ego which bars from consciousness the unwanted id impulse or any of its derivatives, whether memories, emotions, desires, or wish-fulfilling fantasies. All are as though they did not exist as far as the individual's *conscious* life is concerned. A repressed memory is a forgotten one from the subjective point of view of the individual in whom repression has taken place. Indeed, we may remark parenthetically that we don't know for sure whether there is any type of forgetting other than repression.

The act of repression sets up within the mind a permanent, or at least a long-lasting opposition between ego and id at the locus of the repression. We believe that on the one hand the repressed material continues to be charged with a certain cathexis of drive energy which constantly presses for satisfaction, while on the other side the ego maintains the repression by means of a constant expenditure of a portion of the psychic energy at its disposal. This energy is called a countercathexis, since it has the function of opposing the cathexis of drive energy with which the repressed material is charged.

The equilibrium between cathexis and countercathexis is never a statically fixed one. It is the result of a balance between opposing forces and it may shift at any time. As long as the countercathexis expended by the ego remains stronger than the cathexis of the repressed material, the latter remains repressed. If the countercathexis becomes weak, however, the repressed material will tend to emerge into consciousness and action. That is, the repression will begin to fail, as we say, and the same will be the case if the intensity of the drive cathexis is increased without there being a corresponding increase in countercathexis.

Perhaps it is worth while to illustrate these possibilities.

The countercathexis put forth by the ego can be diminished in several ways. It seems to happen for example in many toxic and febrile conditions, of which a very familiar one is alcohol intoxication. A person may exhibit in his overt behavior or speech libidinal and aggressive tendencies while drunk that he himself knows nothing of when he is sober, and the same may be true of other toxic states. A comparable reduction in countercathexis seems to occur frequently during sleep, as we shall see in Chapter VII, with the result that repressed wishes and memories may appear consciously in a dream in a way that would be quite impossible in the dreamer's waking state.

Contrariwise, we have good reason to believe that at puberty, for example, there is an increase in the energy available to the id, so that at that time of life repressions which have been fairly solid for several years may break down either partly or completely. In addition, we assume that lack of gratification tends to increase the strength of the id impulses. Just as the starving man will eat food that would ordinarily disgust him, so the individual who has been severely deprived sexually, for example, will be more liable to have his repressions fail than if he had not been so long or so severely deprived. Another factor which probably weakens repressions by increasing the strength of the id impulses is that of seduction or temptation.

We must also point out that if a repression is weakened and is about to fail, or even if it does fail to some degree, this does not mean that the struggle is necessarily ended between the ego and the id about those particular impulses and that the impulses will thereafter have fairly direct and free access to consciousness as well as the ego's help in achieving gratification. This outcome is of course a possible one. In the transition from childhood to adulthood, for example, it is necessary, in our society at least, for many sexual repressions to be abrogated wholly or in part if the adult sexual adjustment is to be a normal one. However, another outcome is also frequent. As soon as the id impulse starts to break through to consciousness and to satisfaction, the ego reacts to the breakthrough as a new danger and once more produces the signal of anxiety, in this way mobilizing fresh strength for a renewed defense against the unwanted and dangerous impulse. If the ego's attempt is successful, an adequate defense is reestablished, whether it be by repression or in some other way, which in turn requires a further expenditure of countercathectic energy by the ego for its maintenance.

With reference to the possibility of shifts in the equilibrium between the ego and the id which exists in repression, we should add that it is possible (Freud, 1924a; 1933, p. 127) that there may be such a thing as the *completely* successful repression of a wish, let us say, which results in the actual *disappearance* of the wish and the abolition of its energic cathexis, or at least in the complete diversion of its cathexis to other mental contents. In practice we know of no example of such an ideally complete repression. In fact, in our clinical work we deal chiefly with cases in which repression has been conspicuously *un*successful, with the result that psychoneurotic symptoms have developed (see Chapter VIII). At any rate the only cases of which we have positive knowledge are those in which the repressed material continues to be cathected with drive energy which must consequently be opposed by a countercathexis.

There are two more points which should be made clear about the mechanism of repression. The first of these is that the entire process goes on unconsciously. It is not only the repressed material that is unconscious. The activities of the ego which constitute repression are quite as unconscious. One is no more aware of "repressing" something than one is of forgetting something. The only thing one can be aware of is the end result. However, there is a conscious activity which is somewhat analogous to repression. This activity is

usually referred to as *suppression* in the psychoanalytic literature. It is the familiar decision to forget about something
and to think no more about it. It is more than likely that
there are intermediates between suppression and repression
and it may even be that there is no truly sharp line of demar-
cation between the two. However, when we use the word
"repression," we mean that the barring from consciousness
and the erection of a durable countercathexis have taken
place unconsciously.

The second of our final points is that when something is
repressed it is not enough to say that it is forcibly barred
from entering consciousness. It is equally important to realize that the repressed has become functionally separated
from the ego as a whole and has become instead a part of the
id.

Such a statement requires some explanation. Until now in
our discussion of repression we have spoken of an opposition
or conflict between the ego on the one hand and an impulse
of the id on the other. It would certainly make no great sense
to say that repression makes an id impulse a part of the id.
What we must realize in this connection is that the memories, fantasies, and emotions which are intimately associated
with the id impulse in question comprise many elements
which were parts of the ego *before* repression took place.
After all, before the repression the ego functions were at the
service of this particular id impulse as they were at the service of other ones, so that id impulse and ego operations
formed a harmonious whole rather than two conflicting
parts. When repression took place it was the *whole* that was
repressed, with the result that something was really sub-
tracted from the organization of the ego and added to the id.
It is easy to understand, if one bears this fact in mind, that an
undue degree of repression is harmful to the integrity of the
ego. We can realize now that each repression actually diminishes the extent of the ego and therefore renders it less effec-

tive than it has been. We may add, as an additional method by which repression reduces the effectiveness or "strength" of the ego, that each repression requires of the ego a further expenditure of its limited store of energy in order to maintain the necessary countercathexis.

The second defense mechanism which we shall discuss is one which is called *reaction formation*. This is a mechanism whereby one of a pair of ambivalent attitudes, e.g., hate, is rendered unconscious and kept unconscious by an overemphasis of the other, which in this example would be love. Thus hate *appears* to be replaced by love, cruelty by gentleness, stubbornness by compliance, pleasure in dirt by neatness and cleanliness, and so on, yet the missing attitude persists unconsciously.

Incidentally, although we are most used to thinking of reaction formations like those mentioned above, which operate in the direction of the individual giving up some form of socially unacceptable behavior in favor of behavior which is more acceptable to his parents or teachers, it is also perfectly possible for the reverse to happen, that is for hate to appear as a reaction formation against love, stubbornness for compliance, and so on down the list. What is decisive in determining the precise nature of the reaction formation in each particular case is the answer to the question, "What is it that the ego fears as a danger and to which it therefore reacts with the signal of anxiety?" If the ego for some reason fears the impulse to hate, or, more precisely, if it fears the impulses associated with hating, then the operation of the defense mechanism of reaction formation will check those impulses and keep them in check by emphasizing and strengthening the attitude of love. If it is love that is feared, then the reverse will take place.

For example, a person may develop an attitude of great tenderness and affection toward people or animals in order to check and to keep unconscious very cruel or even sadistic impulses toward them. Conversely it may develop in the course of psychiatric or analytic treatment that the patient's conscious anger with his therapist is primarily motivated by the unconscious need of his ego to defend itself against the emergence of feelings and fantasies of love for the therapist. One consequence of our knowledge of the operation of this defense mechanism is that whenever we observe an attitude of this sort which is unrealistic or excessive, we wonder whether it may not be so overemphasized as a defense against its opposite. Thus we should expect that a devoted pacifist or anti-vivisectionist, for instance, has unconscious fantasies of cruelty and hatred which appear to his ego to be particularly dangerous.

We believe that reaction formation takes place unconsciously, as we said previously is the case with repression, and as is the case indeed with most if not all of the ego's defense mechanisms. However, here again there is some advantage in recognizing the analogues to reaction formation that do exist in our conscious mental lives. What happens unconsciously in reaction formation is at least similar to what goes on consciously in the mind of the sycophant, the hypocrite, or even, under certain circumstances, of the good host. Each of these says to himself, "I will pretend that I like this person, although my true or deeper feelings toward him are different, or even directly opposite." What we must beware of is mistaking the similarity for identity. When such a process occurs consciously it signifies a merely temporary adjustment. True reaction formation, on the other hand, permanently alters both the ego and the id of the individual in whom it occurs in much the same way as repression does.

Before we pass on to the next of the defense mechanisms, we wish to make a final observation which will serve to illustrate the complexity and the interrelationship of the activities of the ego in general, as well as the difficulties that lie in the path of any attempt to simplify the discussion of the defense mechanisms of the ego by being too schematic.

Let us consider the case of a child of two years of age whose mother gives birth to a sibling. We know that one inevitable result of such an experience on the part of the two-year-old is that he wants to get rid of the baby who in his eyes is depriving him of the love and attentions which he wants to get from his mother. Such a hostile wish against the baby is expressed by the child in either word or deed to a recognizable degree and may even result in some serious danger to the baby. However, the child soon discovers that his hostility toward his sibling is most unwelcome to his mother, and the usual outcome is that he defends himself against the emergence of these hostile impulses because of fear of loss of his mother's love. It may be that the defense which his ego employs is that of repression. In that case we believe that his hostile impulses and their derivatives are excluded from the ego, become joined to the id, and are barred from consciousness by a permanent countercathexis.

In addition to the disappearance from the child's consciousness of hostile impulses toward its sibling, it is not uncommon to observe some degree of love for the sibling, which may vary considerably in intensity, but which we can confidently ascribe to the defensive activities of the ego also, in particular, to a reaction formation. It seems that the ego has employed two mechanisms to defend itself against the hostile id impulses which frighten it. It has used not only repression but reaction formation as well.

In fact our clinical experience tells us that defense mechanisms are rarely employed singly, or even in pairs. On the contrary, many are used together, though in any given case one or two are usually the most important or primary mechanisms.

Even this does not exhaust the complications inherent in

our simple example, however. We can understand very well that in repressing his hostility the child reacted as though his mother had said to him, "I won't love you if you hate baby." His response was, "I don't hate baby, therefore I needn't be afraid you won't love me." The phrase, "I don't hate baby," is a verbalization of what repression accomplished. To avoid the possibility of misunderstanding we may remark parenthetically that we do not mean to imply that such a conversation actually took place between mother and child, but only that the effect was as if there had been such a conversation. Even though the words themselves were never uttered, the thoughts expressed by the words correspond to things that did really happen. But the words which we have used so far have to do only with the repression and, as we have seen, reaction formation was also a part of the child's defense. By his reaction formation the child said in effect, "I don't hate baby, I love him." Where did the "I love him" come from? To be sure, we feel empathically that it has an inner defensive value, that it is much harder to admit feelings of hate toward one whom we profess to love than toward one whom we regard indifferently. To be sure also, many mothers say not only, "You mustn't hate baby," but also say very explicitly, "You must love baby," so that for their children to "love baby" is logically a reassurance against the fear of losing mother's love. But analytic experience teaches us in addition that when a two-year-old "loves baby" he does so in a very special and meaningful way. He acts as though he himself were the mother and imitates her in his actions and attitude toward baby. In other words, he unconsciously identifies with mother.

We are therefore led to the unexpected conclusion that the process of identification may be a part of reaction formation or perhaps a necessary prelude to it and we wonder whether defense mechanisms may not be of two types, those which are elementary or not further reducible and those which are reducible to what we might call the elementary mechanisms. This is a question which still awaits a definitive answer. In her classic work on *The Ego and the Mechanisms of Defense*, Anna Freud (1936) referred to a suggestion by some authors that repression is the basic mechanism of defense and that all other mechanisms either reinforce a repression or are called into operation after the failure of repression. Anna Freud herself proposed by implication the value of studying and presumably classifying the defense mechanisms on a genetic or developmental basis, that is, by beginning with the most primitive defensive mechanisms, or even, perhaps, with precursors of defense mechanisms proper and working up step by step to the final, relatively highly developed, defense mechanisms. It is interesting that this suggestion, which seems to be such a stimulating one, has not so far been followed up, at least as far as one can judge from the literature.

However, to return for the present to the suggestion that repression is *the* defense mechanism and that all others are at best auxiliary to repression, we must confess our inability to make a final decision in the matter. The difficulty arises from our inability to characterize or describe repression except in terms of its result. The result of repression is that something is "forgotten," that is, barred from access to consciousness. It is true of every other defense mechanism as well that something is barred from consciousness. Whether it is also true of these other defense mechanisms that the details of the process of barring from consciousness and the details of the end result as well are sufficiently similar to the corresponding details of the mechanism which we are agreed to call by the special name of repression, we cannot say with assurance as yet.

Let us continue with our catalogue of the defense mechanisms. The word *isolation* has been used in the psychoanalytic literature to designate two defense mechanisms which are not at all similar, although they are both characteristic of patients with a particular type of neurotic symptom which we ordinarily call obsessional. The most common meaning of the word is a mechanism which Freud originally called isolation of affect, but which might better be called repression of affect or repression of emotion. In such cases a fantasy connected with a wish or a crucial memory from the past may have ready access to consciousness, but the emotion, usually a painful one, which should be connected with it does not become conscious. Moreover, such patients usually manage to keep from feeling too much emotion of any sort. To be sure this process of repression of emotion begins as a barring from consciousness of painful or frightening emotions, that is, it operates clearly in the interests of the pleasure principle and in many cases it goes no farther than this. However, in some unfortunate individuals it goes so far that in the end the individual has hardly any awareness of emotions of any kind and seems like a caricature of that equanimity which ancient philosophers put forward as an ideal.

The other meaning of isolation is a much rarer mechanism which Freud discussed in the section of *The Problem of Anxiety* (1926) which had to do with the psychopathology of obsessions. It is an unconscious process by which a particular thought is literally isolated from the thoughts that preceded it and those that follow by a brief period of mental blankness. By thus depriving the isolated thought of any associational connections in the mind, the ego endeavors to minimize the possibility of its re-entry into consciousness. The thought is treated as "untouchable."

As we have said, both types of isolation are characteristically found in association with obsessional symptoms. Another defense mechanism which is characteristically related to such symptoms is the mechanism of *undoing*. This is an action which has the purpose of disproving or undoing the harm which the individual in question unconsciously imagines may be caused by his wishes, whether these be sexual or hostile ones. For example, a small child whose hostile wishes toward a sibling or parent are a source of anxiety to him may behave in the following way. First he hits the object of his anger, then he kisses it. By the second action he *undoes* the first. It is not difficult to find analogous behavior among older children and adults as well.

Many instances of ritualistic behavior both in children and in adults contain elements which are explainable on this basis, that is they are consciously or unconsciously intended to undo the effect of some id impulse which the ego considers to be dangerous. Sometimes the meaning of the ritual is obvious, as in the example quoted above. It may even be nearly if not quite conscious to the patient himself. More usually the meaning of the undoing mechanism is not easy to discover because it has been distorted and disguised before it has been allowed to become conscious. One thing we can say is that the whole idea of undoing is a magical one and presumably has its origin in those early years of childhood when magical ideas dominate so much of mental life.

Another important defense mechanism is that of *denial*. Anna Freud (1936) used this word to refer to the denial of an unpleasant or unwanted piece of external reality either by means of a wish-fulfilling fantasy or by behavior. For instance, a little boy who was afraid of his father might say that he was himself the strongest man in the world and had just won the world's heavyweight championship and might go around the house wearing a belt indicative of the championship. In this example what the little boy denies are his own small size and his weakness relative to his father. These facts of reality are rejected and replaced by a fantasy and behavior which gratify the boy's wishes for physical superiority over his father.

The term "denial" seems also to have been used by other authors to refer to a similar attitude toward the data of inner experience, that is, toward inner reality. In the above example, for instance, the statement might be made that the little boy denied his own fear. Such use of the word "denial" seems undesirable, since using it in this sense makes it very similar to the concept of suppression which we defined somewhat earlier, or perhaps makes it essentially a step on the road to repression. The original meaning of "denial" refers rather to the blocking of certain sense impressions from the outside world. If they are not actually denied access to consciousness, they at least have as little attention paid to them as possible and the painful consequences of their presence are partly nullified.

Another confusion that sometimes arises in connection with the use of the word "denial" in discussions of the problems of defense is due to the fact that it is the very nature of defense that *something* is denied, just as it is most often the nature of defense that something is barred from consciousness. The id says "Yes," and the ego says "No," in every defensive operation. To infer from this, however, as some authors seem to have done, that the specific mechanism which Anna Freud described as denial by fantasy is involved in the operation of every defense mechanism hardly seems justified.

We might add that the defense mechanism of denial is either closely related to certain aspects of play and daydreams or that it plays a significant role in these two activities throughout life. The whole concept of recreational activities as means of escape from the cares and frustrations of our daily lives obviously comes close to the operation of denial as a defense mechanism.

The next mechanism we wish to discuss is that which is called *projection*. This is a defense mechanism which results in the individual attributing a wish or impulse of his own to some other person, or for that matter, to some nonpersonal object of the outside world. A grossly pathological example of this would be a mentally ill patient who projected his violent impulses and as a result incorrectly believed himself in danger of physical harm from the F.B.I., the Communists, or the man next door, as the case might be. Such a patient would ordinarily be classified clinically as suffering from a paranoid psychosis.

It is important to note, however, that although projection plays such an important role in paranoid psychoses, it operates in the minds of people who are not mentally sick also. Analytic experience has shown that many people attribute to others wishes and impulses of their own which are unacceptable to them and which they unconsciously try to get rid of, as it were, by the mechanism of projection. It is *as though*, such persons said unconsciously, "It's not *I* who have such a bad or dangerous wish, it's *he*." The analysis of these individuals has shown us that the crimes and vices which we attribute to our enemies in times of war, the prejudices which we bear against strangers, against foreigners, or against those whose skins differ in color from our own, and many of our superstitious and religious beliefs are often wholly or in part the result of an unconscious projection of wishes and impulses of our own.

We can understand from these examples that if projection is used as a defense mechanism to a very great extent in adult life, the user's perception of external reality will be seriously distorted, or, to put it in other words, his ego's capacity for reality testing will be considerably impaired. Only an ego which will readily abandon its capacity to test reality correctly will permit itself the extensive use of this defense. Incidentally, these remarks apply equally to the use of denial as a defense mechanism in adult life.

Projection, therefore, is a defense mechanism which normally plays its greatest role in early life. The very small child quite naturally attributes to others, whether persons, animals, or even inanimate objects, the feelings and reactions which he himself experiences, even when he is not engaged in a defensive struggle against his own feelings or wishes, and the tendency to repudiate unwanted impulses or behavior by attributing them to others is clearly apparent in the early years of life. It often happens that a child, when scolded for or accused of some misdeed, says that it was not he but some other child, often an imaginary one, who really did it. As adults we are inclined to view such an excuse as a conscious deception on the part of the child, but child psychologists assure us that the very young child really accepts his projection as the truth and expects his parents or nurse to do so too.

A final word about the possible origin of the mechanism of projection may be in order. It has been suggested (Stärcke, 1920; van Ophuijsen, 1920; Arlow, 1949) that the model for the psychological mechanism of separating some of one's thoughts or wishes from one's own mental life and projecting them into the outer world is the physical experience of defecation, which is familiar to the child from earliest infancy. We know from psychoanalytically guided observations that the small child considers its feces to be a part of its own body and it appears that when projection is used as a defense mechanism the user unconsciously tries to rid himself of his unwanted mental contents as though they were intestinal contents.

Another defense mechanism is that which is called the turning of an instinctual impulse against oneself, or, more briefly, *turning against the self*. We may indicate what this means by an illustration from childhood behavior, since childhood is a time when this mechanism, like projection and denial, is readily observable in overt behavior. The child who feels rage, for example, against another, but dares not express it against its original object, may instead beat, strike, or injure himself. This mechanism, like projection, despite its seeming strangeness, plays more of a role in normal mental life than is ordinarily recognized. It is frequently accompanied by an unconscious identification with the object of the impulse against the emergence of which the individual is defending himself. In the example above, for instance, it is *as though* the child, in hitting himself, were saying, "I'm him, and *this* is how I'll hit him!"

The reader will recall that we have already discussed the process of identification at some length in Chapter III, where we viewed it as a most important factor in ego development. Identification is frequently used for purposes of defense, but there is at present no general agreement whether it should be classified as a defense mechanism as such, or whether it is more correct to look at it as a general tendency of the ego which is frequently utilized in a defensive way. In this connection we may repeat what we said at the beginning of our discussion of the defense mechanisms of the ego, namely that the ego can and does use as a defense *anything* available to it that will help to lessen or avoid the danger arising from the demands of an unwanted instinctual drive.

When identification is used by the ego in a defensive way it is often unconsciously modeled after the physical action of eating or swallowing. This means that the person using the mechanism of identification unconsciously imagines that he is eating or being eaten by the person with whom he becomes identified. Such a fantasy is the reverse of that associated with the mechanisms of projection, where the reader will remember that the unconscious model appears to be the act of defecation.

The terms *introjection* and *incorporation* are also found in the literature to designate the unconscious fantasy of union with another by ingestion. Some authors have attempted to distinguish among these several terms, but in general usage they are essentially synonymous with the term *identification*.

We should make mention of one more mechanism which occupies a most important position among the defensive

operations of the ego, namely *regression*. Despite its importance as a defense, however, regression, like identification, is
probably a mechanism of broader significance than the defense mechanisms proper. We may assume that the tendency
to regression is a fundamental characteristic of our instinctual lives and as such we have already mentioned it in Chapter II. The importance of instinctual regression as a defense
is that in the face of severe conflicts over wishes of the
phallic phase of instinctual development, for example, these
wishes may be partly or wholly given up and the individual
may return or regress to the aims and desires of the earlier
anal and oral phases, thus avoiding the anxiety which would
be caused by a persistence of the phallic wishes. In some
cases such an instinctual regression, which incidentally is
more often a partial than a complete one, suffices to settle the
conflict between ego and id in favor of the former and there
results a relatively stable, intrapsychic equilibrium on the
basis that prephallic drive wishes have been more or less
completely substituted for the phallic ones. In other cases
the regression fails to achieve its defensive purpose and instead of a relatively stable equilibrium there results a renewed conflict, this time on a prephallic level. Such cases, in
which a considerable degree of instinctual regression has
taken place without achieving a resolution of the intrapsychic conflict in favor of the ego, are usually to be found
clinically among the more severe cases of mental illness.

A regression of this sort in the instinctual life appears to be
accompanied in many cases by some degree of regression in
ego functioning or development as well. When such a regression of ego functioning is a prominent feature of an individual's mental life that persists into adulthood, it is nearly
always to be reckoned as pathological.

This completes the list of the defense mechanisms which
we shall discuss: repression, reaction formation, isolation of
affect, isolation proper, undoing, denial, projection, turning

against the self, identification or introjection, and regression. They are all operative to a greater or less degree in normal psychic development and functioning as well as in various psychopathological states.

Allied to them, yet distinct from them, is the mental mechanism which Freud (1905b) called *sublimation*. As originally conceived, sublimation was the normal counterpart of the defense mechanisms, the latter being thought of as primarily associated with psychic dysfunction at that time. Today we should say rather that the term sublimation expresses a certain aspect of normal ego functioning. We have said repeatedly in Chapter III and in the present chapter that the ego normally functions in such a way as to achieve the maximum degree of drive satisfaction consistent with the limitations imposed by the environment. To illustrate the concept of sublimation let us take as an example the infantile wish to play with feces, which is, of course, a drive derivative. In our culture this wish is usually strongly opposed by the small child's parents or parent substitutes. It often happens then that the child gives up playing with its feces and turns instead to making mud pies. Later, modeling in clay or plastilene may be substituted for playing with mud and in exceptional cases the individual may become an amateur or even a professional sculptor in adult life. Psychoanalytic investigation indicates that each of these substitute activities affords a degree of gratification of the original, infantile impulse to play with feces. However, in each instance the originally desired activity has been modified in the direction of social acceptability and approval. Moreover, the original impulse as such has become unconscious in the mind of the individual engaged in modeling or sculpturing in clay or plastilene. Finally, in most such substitute activities the secondary process plays a greater role than it did in the original, infantile wish or activity. To be sure, this last is less obvious in such an example as we have chosen than it would be in the case of a person who became a specialist in intestinal parasites rather than a sculptor.

What we call a sublimation is such a substitute activity, which at the same time conforms with the demands of the environment and gives a measure of unconscious gratification to an infantile drive derivative which has been repudiated in its original form. In our examples, playing with mud pies, modeling, sculpting, and the study of intestinal parasites are all sublimations of the wish to play with feces. We might equally well say that they are all manifestations, at different age levels, of the normal functioning of the ego, acting to harmonize and satisfy the demands of the id and of the environment as fully and as efficiently as possible.

SUGGESTED READING

FREUD, s., Inhibitions, Symptoms and Anxiety. *Standard Edition*, Vol. 20, pp. 77–174, 1959. Also published as *The Problem of Anxiety*, New York: Norton, 1964.

FREUD, A., *The Ego and the Mechanisms of Defense. The Writings of Anna Freud*, Vol. IV. New York: International Universities Press, 1966.

CHAPTER V

THE PSYCHIC APPARATUS (*concluded*)

In this final chapter on the so-called structural hypothesis of the psychic apparatus we shall discuss some aspects of the individual's relationship to the persons of his environment and also the topic of the development of the superego. As usual we shall try to begin with the state of affairs in very early life and to follow our topic forward during the course of the child's development and into later life.

Freud was the first to give us a clear picture of the very great importance to our psychic life and development of our relationship to other people. The earliest of these of course is the child's relationship to its parents, a relationship which is in most cases at first principally restricted to its mother or mother substitute. A little later come its relationship to its siblings, or other close playmates, and to its father.

Freud pointed out that the persons to whom the child is attached in its early years have a place in its mental life which is unique as far as influence is concerned. This is true whether the child's attachment to these persons is by bonds of love, of hate, or of both, the last being by far the most usual. The importance of such early attachments must be due in part to the fact that these early relationships influence the course of the child's development, something that later relationships cannot do to the same extent by virtue of the very fact that they are later. In part also it is due to the fact that in its early years the child is relatively helpless for a very long period of time. The consequence of this protracted helplessness is that the child is dependent on its environment for protection, for satisfaction, and for life itself for a much longer period than is any other mammal. In other words, biological factors per se play a great role in determining the significance as well as the character of our interpersonal relationships, since they result in what we might call the prolonged postpartum fetalization that is characteristic of our development as human beings.

In psychoanalytic literature the term "object" is used to designate persons or things of the external environment which are psychologically significant to one's psychic life, whether such "things" be animate or lifeless. Likewise the phrase "object relations" refers to the individual's attitude and behavior toward such objects. For convenience we shall use these terms in the following discussion.

In the earliest stages of life we assume, as we have said in Chapter III, that the infant is unaware of objects as such and that he learns only gradually to distinguish self from object during the course of the first several months of his development. We have also stated that among the most important objects of infancy are the various parts of the child's own body, e.g., his fingers, toes and mouth. All of these are extremely important as sources of gratification and hence, we assume, they are highly cathected with libido. To be more precise we should say that the psychic representatives of these parts of the infant's body are highly cathected, since we no longer believe, as some analysts formerly did, that libido is like a hormone which can be transported to a part of the body and fixed there. This state of self-directed libido Freud (1914) called *narcissism*, after the Greek legend of the youth, Narcissus, who fell in love with himself.

The present place of the concept of narcissism in psychoanalytic theory is uncertain to some degree. This is because the concept was developed by Freud before the dual theory of instincts had been formulated. As a result only the sexual drive found a place in the concept of narcissism, and the latter has never been explicitly brought into line with either the dual theory of instincts or with the structural hypothesis. Should we consider, for example, that self-directed energy arising from the aggressive drive is also a part of narcissism? Again, what part of the psychic apparatus is cathected by drive energy which is narcissistic in its nature? Is it the ego proper, or is it special parts of the ego, or even, perhaps, other parts of the psychic apparatus which are as yet undefined? These are questions to which definitive answers have yet to be given.

However, in spite of the fact that the concept of narcissism has not been brought up to date, so to speak, it remains a useful and necessary working hypothesis in psychoanalytic theory. In general the term is used to indicate at least three somewhat different, though related things when it is applied to an adult. These are: (1) a hypercathexis of the self, (2) a hypocathexis of the objects of the environment, and (3) a pathologically immature relationship to these objects. When the term is applied to a child, of course, it generally indicates what we consider to be a normal stage or characteristic of early development. It might be worth adding that Freud believed that the major portion of libido remains narcissistic, that is, self-directed, throughout life. This is usually referred to as "normal" or "healthy" narcissism. He also believed that those libidinal forces which cathect the psychic representatives of the objects of the outer world bear the same relationship to the main body of narcissistic libido as do the pseudopodia of an amoeba to its body. That is to say, object libido derives from narcissistic libido and may return to it if the object is later relinquished for any reason.

Let us return now to the topic of the development of object relations. The child's attitude toward the first objects of which it is aware is naturally an exclusively self-centered one. The child is at first concerned only with the gratifications which the object affords, that is, with what we might call the need-satisfying aspect of the object. Presumably the object is at first only cathected when the infant begins to experience some need which can be gratified by or through the object and is otherwise psychically nonexistent for the infant. We assume that only gradually does there develop a continuing relation with an object, by which we mean a persistent object cathexis, even in the absence of an immediate need which the object is to satisfy. We may express this same idea in more subjective terms by saying that it is only gradually that the infant develops an interest in objects of its environment which persists even when it is not seeking pleasure or gratification from those objects. At first, for example, mother is of interest to the infant only when it is hungry or needs her for some other reason, but later in infancy or early childhood mother is psychologically important on a continuing basis and no longer only episodically.

We are not well acquainted with the exact ways in which a continuing object relation does develop, or the stages through which it passes, particularly the very early stages. One fact that is worth mentioning is that the earliest objects are what we call part objects. This means, for example, that it is a long time before the mother exists as a single object for the child. Before that, her breast, or the bottle, her hand, her face, etc., are each separate objects in the child's mental life and it may well be that even different aspects of what is physically the same object may also be distinct objects to the child, rather than united or related ones. For instance, the mother's smiling face may be at first a different object to the child from her scowling or angry one, her loving voice a different object from her scolding one, etc., and it may be that it is only after some time that these two faces or two voices are perceived by the child as a single object.

We believe that a continuing object relation probably develops in the latter part of the first year of life. One of the important characteristics of such early object relations is a high degree of what we call *ambivalence*. That is to say, feelings of love may alternate with equally intense feelings of hate, depending on the circumstances. We may doubt indeed whether the destructive fantasies or wishes toward the object which may be presumed to be present in the latter part of the first year of life should be considered as hostile in intent. To be sure, they would result in the destruction of the object if they were carried out, but a tiny infant's wish or fantasy of swallowing the breast or the mother is as well a primitive forebear of love as of hate. However, there is no doubt that by the second year of life the child is beginning to have feelings of rage as well as of pleasure toward the same object.

This early ambivalence persists normally to some extent throughout life, but ordinarily its degree is much less even in later childhood than it is in the second through the fifth years and it is still less in adolescence and adult life. To be sure, the diminution in ambivalence is often more apparent than real. The *conscious* feelings for the object often reflect one half of the ambivalence, while the other half is kept unconscious, though nonetheless powerful in its effect on the individual's mental life. Such persistent ambivalence is often associated with severe neurotic conflicts and symptoms, as one might expect.

Another characteristic of early object relationships is the phenomenon of identification with the object. This is something which we have already discussed in Chapter III. There we pointed out the great importance of the part played by identification in the complex processes of ego development. Although there are many motives for identification, we stated that any object relation carries with it a tendency to identify with, that is, to become like the object and that the more primitive the stage of ego development, the more pronounced is the tendency to identification.

We can understand, therefore, that object relations in early life in particular play a most important part in ego development, since a part of the ego is in a way a precipitate of these relations. In addition it has been emphasized in recent years that inadequate or unsatisfactory relationships with the objects, that is with the external environment of very early life may prevent the proper development of those functions of the ego which we discussed in Chapter IV: reality testing and mastery of the drives (Spitz, 1945; Beres and Obers, 1950). In this way the stage may be set in very early life for serious psychological difficulties either in later childhood or in adult life (Hartmann, 1953a).

As we said in Chapter III, a tendency to identify with highly cathected objects persists *unconsciously* in all of us throughout life, although it does not normally occupy the predominant position in the object relationships of later life which it characteristically assumes in early childhood. This unconscious persistence of the tendency to identify with the object is but one example of a general attribute of many early modes or characteristics of mental functioning, which, though outgrown as far as conscious mental life is concerned, yet live on without our even being aware of their continued existence and operation.

However, if identification continues to play a dominant role in object relations in adult life, we consider it to be evidence of a maldevelopment of the ego which is severe enough to be considered to be pathological. The first striking examples of such maldevelopment were reported by Helene Deutsch (1934, 1942), who called them "as if" personalities. These were people whose personalities changed with their object relations in a chameleon-like fashion. If such a person was in love with an intellectual, his personality and interests conformed to the intellectual type. If he then gave up this relation and became attached to a gangster instead, he conformed as wholeheartedly to that attitude and way of life.

As would be expected from our previous discussion, Helene Deutsch found that the early object relationships of these patients, e.g., their relationships to their parents, had been grossly abnormal. Similar cases of arrested or improper ego development have since been reported by others, e.g., Anna Freud (1954b).

The early stages of object relations which we have thus far attempted to characterize are usually referred to as pregenital object relations, or sometimes more specifically as anal or oral object relations. Incidentally, the customary use of the word "pregenital" in this connection is inaccurate. The proper term would be "prephallic." At any rate, in the psychoanalytic literature, the object relations of the child are usually named according to the erogenous zone which happens to be playing the leading role in the libidinal life of the child at the time.

Such a designation has primarily a historical significance. Freud studied the stages of libidinal development before he studied the other aspects of the mental life of these early periods which he was also the first to clarify, so that it was only natural that the names of the stages of libidinal development were later used to characterize all the phenomena of that period of the child's life. When it comes to object relations, however, the use of libidinal terminology has more than just a historical value. It serves to remind us that after all it is the drives and perhaps primarily the sexual drive, that seek after objects in the first place, since it is only through objects that discharge or gratification can be achieved. The importance of object relations is *primarily* determined by the existence of our instinctual demands, and the relationship between drive and object is of fundamental importance throughout life. We stress this fact because it is one which is sometimes lost sight of in the face of the more recently discovered connections between object relations and ego development.

When the child is from two and a half to three and a half years old, it enters into what ordinarily become the most intense and fateful object relations of its entire life. From the point of view of the drives, as the reader will remember from our discussion in Chapter II, the child's psychic life changes at this age from the anal to the phallic level. This means that the leading, or most intense wishes and impulses which the child experiences toward the objects of his instinctual life will henceforth be phallic ones. Not that the child quickly or totally gives up the anal and oral wishes which dominated his instinctual life at still earlier ages. On the contrary, as we said in Chapter II, these prephallic wishes persist well into the phallic stage itself. However, during this stage they play a subordinate rather than a dominant role.

The phallic stage is different from the previous ones from the point of view of the ego as well as from that of the drives. In the case of the ego, however, the differences are due to the progressive development of the ego functions which characterizes all the years of childhood and most particularly the early ones, while the changes in the instinctual life, that is in the id, from oral to anal to phallic are due, we believe, primarily to inherited, biological tendencies.

The ego of the three- or four-year-old is more experienced, more developed, more integrated, and consequently different in many ways from the ego of the one- or two-year-old child. These differences are apparent in that aspect of ego functioning with which we are principally concerned at the moment, namely in those characteristics of the child's object relationships which are related to the ego. By this age the child no longer has part object relationships if it has developed normally. Thus, for example, the several parts of mother's body, her varying moods, and her contrasting roles of the "good" mother who gratifies the child's wishes and the "bad" one who frustrates them are all recognized by the child of this age as comprising a single object called mother. Moreover, the child's object relationships have by now acquired a considerable degree of permanence or stability. The cathexes which are directed toward an object persist in spite of the temporary absence of need for the object, something which is not true in very early stages of ego development. They even persist despite fairly prolonged absence of the object itself. In addition, by the time the phallic phase is well under way at least, the child is able to distinguish pretty clearly between self and object and to conceive of objects as individuals like himself with similar feelings and thoughts. To be sure, this latter process goes so far as to be somewhat unrealistic, both because animals and toys are thought to be just like humans and because the child's own thoughts and impulses are apt to be projected onto other persons in an incorrect way, as we have seen in Chapter IV. However, the principal point which we wish to make here is that the child's ego development has reached such a level by the time of the phallic stage that object relationships are possible which are comparable to those of later childhood and of adult life, even though they may not be identical with them in every respect. The nature of the four- or five-year-old's self-awareness and of his perception of objects are such as to make possible the existence of feelings of love or hate for a particular object as well as of feelings of jealousy, fear, and rage toward a rival which contain all of the essential characteristics of such feelings in later life.

The most important object relations of the phallic phase are those which are grouped together as the *oedipus complex*. Indeed the period of life from about two and a half to six years is called the oedipal phase or the oedipal period as often as it is called the phallic stage or phase. The object relations which comprise the oedipus complex are of the greatest importance both to normal and to pathological mental development. Freud considered the events of this phase of life to be crucial, in fact (Freud, 1924a), and although we now know that still earlier events may be crucial to some individuals, so that the events of the oedipal period are of less importance in their lives than those of the preoedipal or prephallic period, it still seems probable that the events of the oedipal period are of crucial significance for most persons and of very great significance for nearly all.

Our knowledge about the oedipus complex developed in this way. Freud discovered rather early that there were regularly present in the unconscious mental lives of his neurotic patients fantasies of incest with the parent of the opposite sex, combined with jealousy and murderous rage against the parent of the same sex. Because of the analogy between such fantasies and the Greek legend of Oedipus, who unknowingly killed his father and married his mother, Freud called this constellation the oedipus complex (Freud, 1900). In the course of the first ten or fifteen years of this century, it became apparent that the oedipus complex was not just characteristic of the unconscious mental life of neurotics, but was on the contrary present in normal persons as well. The existence of such wishes in childhood and the conflicts to which they give rise are in fact an experience which is common to all of mankind. It is true, as many anthropologists have made clear, that in cultures different from our own there are consequent differences in the mental life and conflicts of childhood, but the best evidence which is available at present speaks for the existence of incestuous and parenticidal impulses and of conflicts about them in every culture we know of (Róheim, 1950).

In addition to the realization that the oedipus complex is universal, our understanding of the oedipal wishes themselves was increased during the first two decades of this century to include what were at first called the inverse or negative oedipal wishes, that is, fantasies of incest with the parent of the same sex and murderous wishes toward the parent of the opposite sex. In its turn, this constellation of fantasies and emotions was thought at first to be exceptional, but was in time recognized to be general instead.

This then, in briefest summary, is the full statement of what we call the oedipus complex. It is a twofold attitude toward both parents: on the one hand a wish to eliminate the jealously hated father and take his place in a sensual relationship with the mother, and on the other hand a wish to eliminate the jealously hated mother and take her place with the father.

Let us see whether we can give more real meaning to this extremely condensed formulation by attempting to trace the typical development of the oedipus complex in a schematic way. But before we start, a word of warning. The most important single fact to bear in mind about the oedipus complex is the strength and force of the feelings which are involved. It is a real love affair. For many people it is the most intense affair of their entire lives, but it is in any case as intense as any which the individual will ever experience. The description that follows cannot begin to convey what the reader must keep in mind as he reads it: the intensity of the tempest of passions of love and hate, of yearning and jealousy, of fury and fear that rages within the child. *This* is what we are talking about when we try to describe the oedipus complex.

At the start of the oedipal period the little child, whether boy or girl, ordinarily has its strongest object relation with its mother. By this we mean that the psychic representatives of the mother are more strongly cathected than any others except for those of the child's own self, principally its body. As we shall see later, this is an important exception. The first clear step into the oedipal phase, then, is the same for either sex, as far as we know, and consists of an expansion or extension of the already existing relationship with the mother to include the gratification of the child's awakening genital urges. At the same time there develops a desire for her exclusive love and admiration, which is presumably connected with a wish to be grown up and to "be daddy" or "do what daddy does" with mother. What it is that "daddy does" the child at this age naturally cannot understand clearly. From its own physical reactions, however, regardless of any chances it may have had for observation of its parents, it must connect these wishes with exciting sensations in its genitals and, in the case of the boy, with the sensation and phenomenon of erection. As Freud discovered very early in his work with neurotic patients, the child may develop any one or several of various fantasies about the sexual activities of its parents which it wishes to repeat with mother. For example, it may conclude that they go to the toilet together, or that they look at each other's genitals, or take them in each other's mouths, or handle them in bed together. These conjectures or fantasies of the child, as one can see, are in general related to the child's pleasurable experiences with adults with which it was already familiar by the beginning of the oedipal phase and to its own autoerotic activities. There can be no doubt, in addition, that as the months and years go by, the child's sexual fantasies grow with its experience and knowledge. We should also add that the desire to give mother babies, as father did, is one of the very important oedipal wishes and that the sexual theories of this period are very much concerned with the problem of how this is done, as well as of how the babies come out when they are made.

Along with the sexual yearnings for mother and the desire to be her exclusive love object go wishes for the annihilation or disappearance of any rivals, who are generally father and siblings. Sibling rivalry admittedly has more than one source, but its principal one is surely the desire for the exclusive possession of the parent.

These jealous, murderous wishes arouse severe conflicts within the child on two grounds. The first of these is the obvious fear of retaliation, particularly from the parent, who at that age seems to the child to be truly omnipotent. The second is that they conflict with feelings of love and admiration and often enough, with feelings of longing and dependence as well for the parent or older sibling, as well as the fear of parental disapproval for wishing to destroy a younger sibling. In other words, the child fears both retaliation and loss of love as consequences of its jealous wishes.

From this point, it will be convenient for us to consider separately the evolution of the oedipus complex in the girl and in the boy. We shall start with the latter.

Experience with the analyses of many adults and children, as well as evidence from anthropology, religious and folk myths, artistic creations, and various other sources, has shown us that the retaliation which the little boy fears as the consequence of his oedipal wishes for his mother is the loss of his own penis. It is this which is meant in psychoanalytic literature by the term *castration*. The evidence as to *why* this should be the boy's fear, regardless of the individual or cultural environment of his childhood, has been presented or formulated differently by different authors, and we need not concern ourselves with a discussion of them at this point. For our purpose it is enough to know the fact that it is so.

The observation by the child that there are in fact real people who do *not* have penises, that is, girls or women, convinces him that his own castration is a genuine possibility and the fear of losing his highly prized sexual organ precipitates an intense conflict over his oedipal wishes. This conflict eventually leads to the repudiation of the oedipal wishes. In part they are abandoned and in part they are repressed, that is to say they are banished into the inaccessible recesses of the child's unconscious mind.

The situation is complicated by the fact that the little boy is also stirred to a jealous rage against his mother for her rejection of his wish for exclusive possession of her caresses and her body and this either reinforces or gives rise to a wish to get rid of her (kill her) and to be loved by his father in her place. Since this too leads to the fear of castration, once he has learned that to be a woman is to be without a penis, these wishes also must eventually be repressed.

Thus we see that both the masculine and the feminine wishes of the oedipal period arouse castration anxiety and since the little boy is really neither physically nor sexually mature, he can only resolve the conflicts stirred up by his wishes either by giving up the wishes or by holding them in check by various defense mechanisms and other defensive operations of the ego.

In the case of the little girl the situation is somewhat more complicated. Her desire to play the man with her mother does not founder on castration fear, since of course she does not have a penis to begin with. It comes to grief as a result of the realization that she *is* not so equipped, a realization which brings with it intense feelings of shame, inferiority, jealousy (penis envy), and rage against her mother for having permitted her to be born without a penis. In her rage and despair she normally turns to her father as her principal love object and hopes to take mother's place with him. When these wishes too are frustrated, as in the ordinary course of events they must be, the little girl may again return to the earlier attachment to her mother and remain committed in her psychosexual behavior throughout life to the wish to have a penis and be a man. More normally, however, the little girl, rebuffed by her father in her desire to be his sole sexual object, is forced to renounce and repress her oedipal wishes. The analogues in the little girl to the castration anxiety which is such an immensely powerful determinant in the fate of the little boy's oedipal wishes, are first, the mortification and jealousy which are referred to by the term "penis envy" and second, the fear of genital injury which is consequent upon the wish to be penetrated and impregnated by her father.

The reader will understand that this highly condensed presentation of the essentials of the oedipus complex is likewise a highly schematic one. In fact, each child's mental life during this period is unique for him or her and is profoundly influenced both by experiences during the first two years of life, which have preceded the oedipal period, and by the events of the oedipal period themselves. For example, one can imagine what immense consequences would ensue upon the illness, absence, or death of a parent or sibling, or upon the birth of a new sibling, or upon an observation of parental or other adult intercourse, or upon the sexual seduction of the child by an adult or older child if any one of these should occur during the oedipal period.

In addition to these environmental factors, we believe that it is likely that children vary in constitutional capacities or predispositions. Freud (1937) mentioned the variations in instinctual endowment that may occur, for example, in the tendency to bisexuality, that is, in the predisposition in the boy toward femininity and in the girl toward masculinity. He postulated, and most analysts agree, that some degree of bisexuality in the psychic sphere is normally present in every human being. This is indeed a corollary of the fact that the oedipus complex normally includes fantasies of sexual union with *both* parents. It is clear, however, that variations in the relative strength of the masculine and the feminine components of the sexual drive might considerably influence the relative intensity of the various oedipal wishes.

For instance, an unusually strong, constitutional tendency toward femininity in a boy would be expected to favor the development of an oedipal constellation in which the wish to take the mother's place in sexual union with the father was more intense than the wish to take the father's place with mother. The converse would be true in the case of an unusually strong, constitutional tendency toward masculinity in a girl. Whether or not this would be the actual result in any particular case would naturally depend on how much the constitutional tendency was favored or opposed by environmental factors. Moreover, what the relative importance may be of constitution and environment is something which we have no way of estimating satisfactorily at present. In fact, in our clinical work we are as a rule ignorant of constitutional factors and tend therefore to lose sight of their possible importance as compared to the environmental factors, which are usually more obvious and hence more impressive.

There is at least one other important aspect of the oedipal phase that we have not yet mentioned and that should not be passed over. That is the genital masturbation which ordinarily constitutes the child's sexual *activity* during this period of its life. Both the masturbatory activity and the fantasies which accompany it substitute in great part for the direct expression of the sexual and aggressive impulses which the child feels toward its parents. Whether this substitution of autoerotic stimulation and fantasy for real actions toward real people is in the long run more beneficial or more harmful to the child depends in part on what value standards one chooses to adopt, but in any case the question seems to be an idle one. The substitution is inevitable, because in the last analysis it is forced on the child by his biological immaturity.

With the passing of the oedipal phase, genital masturbation is usually abandoned, or greatly diminished, and does not reappear till puberty. The original oedipal fantasies are repressed, but disguised versions of them persist in consciousness as the familiar daydreams of childhood, and they continue to exert an important influence on nearly every aspect of mental life: on the forms and objects of adult sexuality; on creative, artistic, vocational, and other sublimated activity; on character formation; and on whatever neurotic symptoms the individual may develop (see Chapters VIII and IX).

This is not the only way in which the oedipus complex

influences the future life of the individual, however. It has in addition a specific consequence which is of very great importance in subsequent mental life and which we propose to discuss now. This consequence is the *formation of the super-ego*, the third of the group of mental functions which Freud postulated in his so-called structural hypothesis of the psychic apparatus.

As we said in Chapter III, the superego corresponds in a general way to what we ordinarily call conscience. It comprises the moral functions of the personality. These functions include (1) the approval or disapproval of actions and wishes on the grounds of rectitude, (2) critical self-observation, (3) self-punishment, (4) the demand for reparation or repentance of wrongdoing, and (5) self-praise or self-love as a reward for virtuous or desirable thoughts and actions. Contrary to the ordinary meaning of "conscience," however, we understand that the functions of the superego are often largely or completely unconscious. It is thus true, as Freud (1933) said, that while, on the one hand, psychoanalysis showed that human beings are less moral than they had believed themselves to be, by demonstrating the existence of unconscious wishes in each individual which he consciously repudiates and denies, it has demonstrated on the other hand that there are more and stricter moral demands and prohibitions in each one of us than we have any conscious knowledge of.

To return to the topic of the origin of the superego, it is fairly generally agreed at present that its earliest beginnings, or perhaps one had better say, its precursors, are present in the prephallic or preoedipal phase. The moral demands and prohibitions of parents, or of the nursemaids, governesses, and teachers who may act as substitutes for the parents, begin to influence the mental life of the child very early. Certainly their influence is apparent by the end of the first year. We may mention in passing that the moral demands of this very early period are rather simple ones, if we judge them by our adult standards. Among the most important of them are those that have to do with toilet training. Ferenczi referred to these precursors of the superego as "sphincter morality."

In the preoedipal phase, however, the child treats the moral demands which are made upon him as a part of his environment. If mother, or some other moral arbiter, is there in the flesh and if the child wants to please her, he will refrain from transgression. If he is alone, or if he is angry at mother, he will either displease her or do as he wishes, subject only to his fear of punishment. During the course of the oedipal phase itself matters begin to change in this respect and somewhere around the ages of five or six years morality begins to be an inner matter. It is then, we believe, that the child first begins to feel that moral standards and the demand that wrongdoing must be punished, repented, and undone, come from within himself, rather than from another person whom he must obey. In addition we believe that it is not until the age of nine or ten years that this process of internalization has become stable enough to be essentially permanent, even though it is normally still subject to addition and modification throughout adolescence and to some extent perhaps even into adult life.

What is it that happens to produce this fateful internalization? As far as we understand it, in the course of abandoning and repressing or otherwise repudiating the incestuous and murderous wishes which constitute the oedipus complex, the child's relations with the objects of these wishes are in considerable part transformed into identifications with them. Instead of loving and hating his parents, who he believes would oppose and punish such wishes, he becomes like his parents in his repudiation of his wishes. Thus the original nucleus of the prohibitions of the superego is the demand that the individual repudiate the incestuous and hostile wishes that comprised that individual's oedipus complex. Moreover, this demand persists throughout life, unconsciously of course, as the essence of the superego.

We see, therefore, that the superego has a particularly intimate relationship to the oedipus complex and that it is formed as a consequence of the identifications with the moral and prohibiting aspects of his parents, identifications which arise in the child's mind in the process of the dissolution or passing of the oedipus complex. The superego, we may say, consists originally of the internalized images of the moral aspects of the parents of the phallic or oedipal phase.

Let us now examine certain aspects of this process of identification in greater detail. As we do so, we must bear in mind that the ego's main task at the time the identifications in question take place is the defensive struggle against the oedipal strivings. We understand that it is principally castration anxiety in the boy and its analogues in the girl that constitute the fear that motivates this struggle and that the struggle itself occupies the center of the stage of the child's psychic life at this age. All else is a part of it, a consequence of it, or subordinate to it.

From the point of view of the ego the establishment of the identifications which form the superego is a very great aid to its defensive efforts against the id impulses which it is struggling to master. It means that the parental prohibitions have been permanently installed within the mind, where they can keep an ever watchful eye on the id. It is as though, by identifying with his parents in this way, the child can ensure that they are always present, so that whenever an id impulse threatens to assert itself the parents are at hand, ready to enforce their demand that it be repudiated.

We see then that the superego identifications are an advantage to the ego from the point of view of defense. Indeed, we might go farther and say that they are an essential support to the ego in this respect. However, from the point of view of the ego's independence and its freedom to enjoy instinctual gratification the superego identifications are a very great disadvantage. From the time of the formation of the superego, the ego loses a large share of its freedom of action and remains forever afterward subject to the domination of the superego. The ego has acquired not merely an ally in the superego, it has acquired a master. Thenceforward the demands of the superego are added to those of the id and of the external environment to which the ego must bow and among which it must try to mediate. The ego is able to participate in the power of the parents by identifying with them, but only at the cost of remaining to some extent permanently subject to them.

Freud (1923) made two further observations concerning the formation of these identifications that are of interest to mention here. The first of these observations is that the child experiences his parents' prohibitions in large part as verbal commands or scolding. The consequence of this is that the superego bears a close relationship to auditory memories and in particular to memories of the spoken word. Some intuitive perception of this fact is probably responsible for the common figure of speech which refers to the "voice of conscience." In states of psychological regression, such as dreams (Isakower, 1954) and certain types of severe mental illness (Freud, 1923), the functioning of the superego is perceived in the form of spoken words which the subject experiences as coming from a source outside himself, just as his parents' commands did when he was little. It must not be supposed, however, that the superego is exclusively related to auditory perceptions and memories. Memories of other sensory perceptions, such as visual and tactile ones, are related to it as well. For example, one patient, who was very much frightened by his own hostile fantasies, at the height of an attack of acute anxiety felt that his face was being slapped whenever he thought of being angry. In this case the

operation of the superego was experienced as physical punishment which was felt as coming from someone outside
himself in quite the same way as his parents had punished
him on occasion in his childhood.

The second of Freud's (1923) observations was that in
large measure the parental images which are introjected to
form the superego are those of the parents' superegos. That
is, it happens in general that parents, in bringing up their
children, tend to discipline them very much as they were
themselves treated by their parents in their own childhoods.
Their own moral demands, acquired in early life, are applied
to their children, whose superegos in consequence reflect or
resemble those of their parents. This characteristic has an
important social consequence, as Freud (1923) pointed out.
It results in a perpetuation of the moral code of a society and
is responsible in part for the conservatism and resistance to
change which social structures show.

Let us now consider some aspects of superego formation
which are rather more closely concerned with the id than
with the ego. For one thing, as Freud (1923) pointed out,
the superego identifications are in some degree the consequence of the abandonment of the incestuous object relations
of the oedipus complex. In this sense these identifications are
partly the consequence of object loss. The reader will remember that this was one of the mechanisms of identification
which we discussed in Chapter III. As we understand it,
when the instinctual cathexes are withdrawn from their original objects, their constant search for another object leads to
the formation of an identification with the original object
within the ego itself to which the cathexes are then attached.
What were object cathexes thus become narcissistic ones. In
the case in which we are now interested, of course, the identifications which are thus formed within the ego comprise that
special part of the ego which we call the superego.

From the point of view of the id, then, the superego is the

substitute for and the heir of the oedipal object relations. It is for this reason that Freud described it as having its roots deep within the id. We see, moreover, that the formation of the superego results in the transformation of a very substantial amount of object cathexes into self-directed or narcissistic ones. It is ordinarily the most openly sexual cathexes and the most directly or violently hostile ones which are thus given up, while feelings of tenderness and of less violent hostility continue to be attached to the original objects. That is, the child continues to have feelings of tenderness and of less violent hatred or rebelliousness toward his parents. In order to avoid misunderstanding we should make it clear that by no means all of the child's directly incestuous and murderous impulses toward his parents are abandoned. On the contrary, at least a portion of them, and in many, perhaps even in most persons, a considerable portion of them are simply repressed, or otherwise defended against. This portion lives on in the id, as do any other repressed wishes, still directed toward the original objects and kept from open expression in act or conscious thought and fantasy only by the constant opposition of the countercathexes which the ego has directed against them. However, these repressed oedipal wishes, with their cathexes, do not contribute to the formation of the superego (Freud, 1923). For that reason they have been omitted from our present discussion despite their obvious importance.

It is a surprising, but easily observable fact that the severity of an individual's superego does not necessarily, nor even regularly, correspond to the severity with which his parents opposed his instinctual wishes when he was a child. On the basis of our discussion so far we should expect this to be the case. Since the superego is the introjected parent, we should expect that the child with a severe parent would have a severe superego and vice versa. To some extent this is no doubt true. It is very likely that direct castration threats toward a little boy during the oedipal phase, for instance, or similar threats to a little girl of the same age tend to result in the formation of an undesirably severe superego and in consequence an undesirably severe prohibition of sexuality or aggressiveness, or both, in later life.

However, it appears that other factors than the severity of the parent play the major part in determining the severity of the superego. The principal factor appears to be the intensity of the aggressive component of the child's own oedipal wishes. In simpler, though less exact language we may say that it is the intensity of the child's own hostile impulses toward his parents during the oedipal phase that is the principal factor in determining the severity of the superego, rather than the degree of the parents' hostility or severity toward the child.

We believe that we can understand or explain this in the following way. When the oedipal objects are abandoned and replaced by superego identifications, the drive energy which formerly cathected those objects comes to be at least in part at the disposal of the newly established part of the ego which we call the superego. Thus the aggressive energy at the disposal of the superego derives from the aggressive energy of the oedipal object cathexes and the two are at least proportional, if not equal in amount. That is, the greater the amount of aggressive energy in the oedipal object cathexes, the greater the amount of such energy which is subsequently at the disposal of the superego. This aggressive energy can then be turned against oneself whenever occasion arises in order to enforce obedience to the prohibitions of the superego or to punish one for transgressing them. In other words, the severity of the superego is determined by the amount of aggressive energy at its disposal and this in turn bears a closer relationship to the aggressive cathexes of the child's oedipal impulses toward its parents than it does to the severity of the parents' prohibitions during the child's oedipal phase. The little child whose oedipal fantasies were especially violent and destructive will tend to have a stronger sense of guilt than one whose fantasies were less destructive.

Our final comment on superego formation from the point of view of the id is this. One way of formulating the conflicts of the oedipal period is to say that the id impulses associated with the objects of that period, that is, with the parents, appear to the child to expose him to the danger of bodily injury. In the case of the boy the fear is that he will lose his penis. In the case of the girl it is some analogous fear of genital injury, or an intensely unpleasant feeling of mortification because of the lack of a penis, or both. In any case there is a conflict between the demands of object cathexes on the one hand and narcissistic or self-cathexes on the other hand. It is instructive to note that the issue is decided in favor of the narcissistic cathexes. The dangerous object cathexes are repressed or abandoned, or they are mastered or repudiated in other ways, while the narcissistic cathexes are maintained essentially intact. We are thus reminded once more of the fact that the narcissistic component of the child's instinctual life is normally stronger than the part which is concerned with object relations, even though these are much the easier to observe and consequently more likely to occupy our attention.

We cannot leave the subject of superego formation without some discussion of the modifications of it and accretions to it which occur in later childhood, in adolescence and even to some extent in adult life. Each of these additions and alterations results from an identification with an object of the child's or adult's environment, or, rather, with the moral aspect of such an object. At first, such objects are exclusively people whose role in the child's life is similar to that of his parents. Examples of such persons are teachers, religious instructors, and domestic servants. Later on the child may introject persons with whom he has no personal contact and even historical or fictional characters. Such identifications are particularly common in prepuberty and in adolescence. They mold the individual's superego in the direction of conformity with the moral standards and ideals of the social groups of which he is a member.

When we stop to think of the very considerable differences that are found among the moral codes of various social groups, we realize what a great part of the adult superego is the result of these later identifications. Changes may even occur in the superego during adult life, as happens for instance as the result of a religious conversion. However, the original nucleus of the superego which was formed during the oedipal phase remains always the firmest and most effective part. As a result, the prohibitions against incest and parenticide are the parts of most persons' morality which are the most thoroughly internalized, or, conversely, the least likely to be transgressed. Other superego prohibitions are much more likely to be transgressed if there is a particularly favorable opportunity or a particularly strong temptation.

We wish now to discuss certain aspects of the role which the superego plays in the functioning of the psychic apparatus once it has been formed. We may say in general that after the oedipal phase is over it is the superego which initiates and enforces the defensive activities of the ego against the impulses of the id. As the child in the oedipal period feared that he would be castrated by his parent and repressed or repudiated his oedipal wishes in order to avoid the danger, so the child or adult in the postoedipal period unconsciously fears his introjected parental images, that is, his superego and controls his id impulses in order to avoid the danger of his superego's displeasure. Disapproval by the superego thus takes its place as the final one of the series of danger situations to which the ego reacts with anxiety which we discussed in Chapter IV (Freud, 1926). To repeat and complete the list from that chapter, the first such danger situation, chronologically speaking, is loss of the object, the next is loss of the object's love, the third is the fear of castration or of analogous genital injury, and the final one is disapproval by the superego. As the reader will remember, these various danger situations do not successively *disappear* as the next one emerges. It is rather that each in turn plays the chief role as the source of anxiety and as the occasion for the ego to employ defensive measures against whatever id impulses precipitate the danger situation or threaten to do so.

Disapproval by the superego has some consequences which are conscious and hence familiar to us and others which are unconscious and therefore have been made apparent only as the result of psychoanalytic investigation. For example, we are all familiar with the painful feeling of tension which we call guilt or remorse, and we have no hesitation in connecting it with the operation of the superego. However, there are other equally familiar psychic phenomena whose relation to the superego is less obvious, though equally close. Thus, as Freud (1933) pointed out, the commonest cause of painful and apparently unwarranted feelings of inferiority is disapproval by the superego. For practical purposes such feelings of inferiority are the same as feelings of guilt. This is obviously a point of considerable clinical importance, since it tells us that a patient who has considerable feelings of inferiority or lowered self-esteem is probably unconsciously accusing himself of some misdeed, regardless of what reason he may consciously give to account for his feelings of inferiority.

Just as disapproval of the ego by the superego gives rise to feelings of guilt and inferiority, so may feelings of joy or happiness and self-satisfaction be the result of the superego's approval of the ego for some behavior or attitude on the part of the ego which the superego particularly approved. Such a "virtuous" glow, like its opposite, a sense of guilt, is a familiar phenomenon. The two opposite feelings or states of mind are readily comparable to the states of mind of the small child who is either praised and loved, or scolded and punished by his parents for his behavior. In other words, the conscious feelings which result from the approving or disapproving attitude of the superego in later life are easily understood when we realize that the superego is the introjected parental images and that throughout life the relationship between ego and superego is very similar to the relationship between a small child and his parents.

There are two features of the operation of the superego which are ordinarily unconscious in adult life and which show very clearly its connection with the mental processes of those early periods of childhood in which the superego takes it origin. The first of these is the talion law and the second is the lack of discrimination between wish and deed.

Lex talionis means very simply that the punishment for a misdeed or crime is to have the malefactor suffer the same injury as he inflicted. This is expressed most familiarly in the Biblical demand of "an eye for an eye, and a tooth for a tooth." It is a concept of justice which is a primitive one in two senses. The first sense is that it is a concept of justice which is characteristic of historically old or primitive social structures. This fact is undoubtedly of great importance, but it does not concern us at present. The second sense, which does concern us, is that the talion law is essentially the little child's concept of justice. The interesting and unexpected thing about it is the degree to which this concept persists unconsciously into adult life and determines the functioning of the superego. The unconscious penalties and punishments which the superego imposes are found on analysis to conform in many instances to the talion law, even though the individual has long since outgrown this childish attitude as far as his conscious mental life is concerned.

As for the lack of discrimination between wish and deed, it is a commonplace of psychoanalytic investigation that the superego threatens punishment for the one nearly as severely as for the other. It is clearly not merely the doing something that is forbidden by the superego, it is the wish or impulse itself that is interdicted or punished, as the case may be. We believe that this attitude of the superego is a consequence of the fact that a child of four or five, or younger, distinguishes between his fantasies and his actions much less clearly than he does in later life. He is in large part dominated by the belief that "wishing makes it so" and this magical attitude is perpetuated by the unconscious operations of the superego in later life.

Another feature of the unconscious operation of the superego is that it may result in an unconscious need for expiation or self-punishment. Such a need for punishment, in itself unconscious, can ordinarily be discovered only by psychoanalysis. However, once one knows that such a thing exists and is on the lookout for it, one sees evidence of its presence much oftener than one might think. For example, an opportunity, as prison psychiatrist, to read the official records of the ways in which felons are caught is very instructive in this regard. The criminal's own unconscious desire for punishment is frequently a most important aid to the police. The criminal often unconsciously provides the clues that he himself knows will lead to his being discovered and captured. To analyze a criminal is ordinarily not possible, of course, but in some cases the mere facts of the record are sufficient to make matters clear.

For instance, a sneak burglar operated successfully for over a year in the following way. He frequented lower middle-class, tenement districts where entrance to any apartment could easily be effected from a rear porch or stairway. By keeping watch during the middle of the morning he could wait until the housewife in a particular apartment was out shopping and he would then force an entry into the vacant flat. He left no fingerprints and took nothing but cash, which of course the police had no way of tracing. It was obvious that this burglar knew just what he was doing and for months the police were quite unable to interfere with his activities in any substantial way. It seemed as though only bad luck could put an end to his career. Suddenly he changed his habits. Instead of taking only cash, he stole some jewelry as well, pawned it for a relatively small sum in a nearby pawnshop, and was in the hands of the police within a few days. On many previous occasions he had left untouched jewelry which was just as valuable as that which he finally stole precisely because he knew that it was quite impossible for him to dispose of stolen goods without the police tracing it to him sooner or later. The conclusion seems inescapable that this criminal unconsciously arranged for his own arrest and imprisonment. In view of all we know at present about the unconscious workings of the mind, his motive for doing so was an unconscious need to be punished.

Of course the need for punishment need not be connected with actual misdeeds, as in the instance just described. It may as well be a consequence of fantasies or wishes, whether conscious or unconscious ones. Indeed, as Freud (1915c) pointed out, a person's criminal career may begin as the result of a need for punishment. That is to say, an unconscious need for punishment which stems from repressed oedipal wishes may result in the commission of a crime for which punishment is certain. Such a person is often referred to as a criminal from a sense of guilt.

However, we must add that an unconscious need for punishment need not necessarily result in criminal actions which will be punished by some legal authority. Other forms of suffering or self-injury may be unconsciously arranged for instead, such as failure in career (the so-called "fate-neurosis"), "accidental" physical injuries, and the like.

We can readily understand that a superego which insists on self-punishment or self-injury becomes itself a danger from the point of view of the ego. It will not surprise us, therefore, to learn that the ego may employ against the superego defensive mechanisms and other defensive operations which are entirely analogous to those which it regularly employs against the id. Perhaps the following example will serve to clarify what we mean by this.

A man with strong voyeuristic tendencies in childhood grew up to be a strong and active supporter of an anti-vice society in adult life. In this connection he was especially zealous in the detection and prosecution of dealers in obscene pictures. Since his activities in this connection involved his continually looking for pictures of naked men and women, it is easy to see that they offered ready opportunity for the unconscious gratification of his voyeurism. This comment, however, is made from the point of view of the defensive struggle or conflict between the id and the ego rather than from that of conflict between ego and superego. From the latter point of view we may say two things. In the first place, the feeling of guilt that would have been conscious in childhood as a consequence of looking at naked bodies was not apparent when he looked at naked pictures in adult life. His ego had succeeded in barring any guilt feeling from consciousness and had instead projected it onto others. It was then *other* people who were guilty of voyeurism, or, more exactly, who were bad and should be punished for their voyeuristic wishes and actions. In addition, our subject's ego had established a reaction formation against his sense of guilt, so that instead of any conscious sense of guilt he felt consciously superior and particularly virtuous in connection with his absorbing interest in ferreting out and discovering pictures of naked bodies.

Defenses on the part of the ego against the superego are a regular and important part of normal mental functioning.

They may also play an important role in many cases of mental illness, so that they are often of considerable practical importance in clinical work (Freud, 1923; Fenichel, 1939).

There is an important connection between the superego and group psychology which Freud (1921) pointed out in a monograph on the subject. Certain groups at least are held together by virtue of the fact that each of the members of the group has introjected or identified with the same person, who is the leader of the group. The consequence of this identification is that the image of the leader becomes a part of the superego of each of the members of the group. In other words, the various members of the group have in common certain superego elements. The will of the leader, his commands and precepts thus become the moral laws of his followers. Although Freud's monograph was written long before the beginning of Hitler's rise, his analysis of this aspect of group psychology explains very well the extraordinary alterations that were effected by Hitler's influence in the moral standards of the millions of Germans who were his followers.

A similar mechanism is presumably involved in the case of religious groups or sects. In these instances also the various members of the group have a common morality, that is, common superego elements, which are derived from identification with the same god or spiritual leader. Here the god plays the same role, psychologically speaking, as the leader or hero does in the nonreligious group. This comes as no surprise, of course, in view of the close relationship that we know existed quite consciously in peoples' minds between gods and heroes even among such highly civilized people as the Romans of the empire, who deified their emperors as a matter of course.

Perhaps we may conclude our discussion of the superego by restating the essentials of its origin and nature. It arises as a consequence of the introjection of the parental prohibitions and exhortations of the oedipal phase and throughout life its unconscious essence remains the prohibition of the sexual and aggressive wishes of the oedipus complex, despite the many alterations and additions it undergoes in later childhood, in adolescence, and even in adult life.

SUGGESTED READING

FREUD, S., The Ego and the Id. *Standard Edition*, Vol. 19, pp. 3–66, 1961. Also New York: Norton, 1961.

FREUD, S., The Passing of the Oedipus-Complex. *Standard Edition*, 19, pp. 172–179, 1961.

CHAPTER VI

PARAPRAXES AND WIT

In this chapter and in the two which follow it we shall apply to certain of the phenomena of human mental life the knowledge of the functioning of the mind which we have gained from our discussions so far. The phenomena which we have chosen for this purpose are, first, the slips, mistakes, omissions and memory lapses with which all of us are familiar and which Freud (1904) grouped together as the psychopathology of everyday life; second, wit; third, dreams; and fourth and last, the psychoneuroses. These topics have been selected because they are among what might be called the classic topics of psychoanalytic theory. They have been the objects of study for many years, first by Freud and later by other psychoanalysts, with the result that our knowledge about them is reasonably extensive and reliable. In addition, the subject of the psychoneuroses is of very great practical importance, since these mental illnesses are the principal object of psychoanalytic therapy.

We shall start with the *psychopathology of everyday life.* This includes slips of the tongue, slips of the pen, slips of memory, and many of the mishaps of life which we ordinarily attribute to chance and call accidents. Even before Freud's systematic investigations of these phenomena there was some vague awareness in the popular mind that they were purposeful, rather than chance occurrences. For example, there is an old proverb which says, "A slip of the tongue betrays the true state of the mind." Moreover, not all such slips were *treated* as accidental. Even before Freud's day if Mr. Smith forgot Miss Jones' name, or called her Miss Robinson "by mistake," Miss Jones would ordinarily react to it as to an *intentional* slight or sign of disinterest, and Mr. Smith would be unlikely to be looked upon with favor by her. To go a step further, if a subject "forgot" a rule of etiquette in addressing his royal master, he was punished despite his plea that the forgetting was accidental. The authority in question *attributed* intent to his actions even though he himself was unaware of any. In quite the same way, some 300 years ago, when a Bible was printed in which one of the commandments of the decalogue was accidentally printed, "Thou shalt . . . ," instead of "Thou shalt not . . . ," the printer was as severely punished as though he had consciously intended to be sacrilegious. However, by and large, such phenomena were attributed either to chance or, by those who were superstitious, to the influence of evil and malicious spirits, like the printers' devils, who took type that the printer had set correctly and tormented the poor man by mixing it up and introducing all kinds of mistakes into it. It was Freud who first seriously and consistently maintained the view that slips and related phenomena are the result of a purposeful and intentional action of the individual involved, although the intent is unknown to the actor himself, or, in other words, is unconscious.

The simplest to understand of these slips, or parapraxes, as they are sometimes called, is that of forgetting. Such slips are most often the direct consequence of repression, which the reader will remember is one of the defense mechanisms of the ego which were discussed in Chapter IV. One can observe it in its most simple and obvious form on occasion during the course of a psychoanalysis, when it sometimes happens that a patient forgets from one minute to the next something which he considers important and which he consciously wants to remember. In such cases the motive for forgetting may also be apparent. Though the specific details of motivation may vary from case to case, it is basically the same in all such cases, that is, to prevent the possibility of the development of anxiety or guilt, or both.

As an example, it had just been made clear to an analytic patient that he had for years kept himself from feeling frightened and ashamed of certain aspects of his sexual behavior with the help of an elaborate system of rationalizations. At the same time the patient became aware of how much fear and shame were really associated with his sexual behavior in his own mind, although he did not by any means experience these emotions fully or even very strongly at that time. He was very much impressed by this new insight, which he felt was of great importance in the understanding of his neurotic symptoms, as indeed it was. A minute or two later, as he was talking about how valuable this insight was, he suddenly realized that he could no longer remember what it was and that all that had been said during the previous five minutes had been forgotten!

This example illustrates rather dramatically the usually unsuspected capacity of the human mind for forgetting, or, more pecisely, for repressing. It is clear that the same forces within the patient's mind which had successfully prevented the emergence of shame and fear over his sexual behavior during the course of many years were also responsible for the prompt repression of his newly won insight that his behavior really did frighten and shame him. We might add that in this case the ego's repressive countercathexes were directed rather against the superego than against the id. That is, the patient's ego repressed the recent auditory memories and thoughts which it feared would lead to the further emergence of feelings of shame and of the fear of being sexually abnormal. In other cases, of course, the countercathexes are directed primarily against the id.

It may seem to the reader that the example we have just

given is exceptional rather than typical and that "ordinary" cases of forgetting to do something one had intended to do or of forgetting a familiar name or face may be quite different. It is easy to see why the patient in our example forgot what he did, but why should one forget something that there is "no reason" to forget?

The answer is that the reason in most cases is an unconscious one. It can usually be discovered only by means of the psychoanalytic technique, that is, with the full cooperation of the person who did the forgetting. If his cooperation can be enlisted and if he is able to say freely and without conscious selection or editing all of the thoughts which occur to him in connection with the slip, then we shall be in a position to reconstruct its intent and motivation. Otherwise we must depend on chance to put us in possession of enough of the facts to permit us to guess more or less accurately at the "meaning" of the slip, that is, at the unconscious motives which produced it.

For instance, a patient could not think of the name of an acquaintance who was quite familiar to him when the two met in a social gathering. This episode of forgetting would have been quite impossible to understand without the patient's own associations to it. As he talked about it, it developed that the name of his acquaintance was the same as that of another man whom he knew and toward whom he had strong feelings of hatred which made him feel very guilty as he spoke about them. In addition he mentioned that the acquaintance was crippled, which reminded him of some of his wishes to hurt and injure the namesake whom he hated. With this information from the patient's associations, it was possible to reconstruct what had happened when his memory had failed him. The sight of his crippled acquaintance had unconsciously reminded him of the other man who bore the same name and whom he hated and wished to maim or injure. In order to avoid becoming conscious of his destructive fantasies, which would have made him feel guilty, he repressed the name which would have made the connection between the two. In this case, therefore, repression was instituted to prevent the entrance into consciousness of destructive fantasies which constituted a part of the id and which would have led to guilt had they become conscious.

In the examples which we have just given the disturbance or "slip" of memory was the consequence of the operation of a defense mechanism, namely repression. Since the motivation of the repression, as well as its actual operation, were both unconscious, the subject was himself at a loss to account for his lapse of memory and could only attribute it to ill luck, fatigue, or whatever other excuse he might prefer. Other slips may be the consequence of somewhat different mental mechanisms. The causation of all of them is similar, however, in the respect that it is *unconscious*.

For example, a slip of the tongue or slip of the pen is often the consequence of a *failure* to repress completely some unconscious thought or wish. In such cases the speaker or writer expresses what he would have unconsciously liked to say or write, despite his attempt to keep it hidden. Sometimes the hidden meaning is openly expressed in the slip, that is to say, it is clearly intelligible to the listener or reader. On other occasions the result of the lapse is not intelligible and the hidden meaning can only be discovered from the associations of the person who made the slip.

As an illustration of a slip whose meaning is clear we may cite the following. An attorney was boasting of the confidences he received from his clients and wished to say that they told him "their most intimate troubles." Instead, however, what he actually said was, "their most interminable troubles." By making the slip he revealed to his listener what he was desirous of hiding, that is the fact that sometimes what his clients told him of their troubles bored him and made him wish that they would talk less about themselves and not take up so much of his time.

The reader may perhaps conclude from this example that if the meaning of a slip is clear, the unconscious thought or wish that it reveals is one which is not very strenuously repressed and, on the contrary, that it was only temporarily unconscious in the speaker's mind and could be admitted to consciousness by him with relatively little disturbance in the way of fear or guilt. In fact, this is by no means the case. For instance, a patient may unwittingly call his wife his mother during the first interview with his therapist. When confronted with this slip he can make nothing of it. Indeed he points out at length and in detail how unlike his mother his wife actually is. It is only after many months of analysis that the patient is able to admit to consciousness that in fantasy his wife represents the mother whom he longed to marry at the height of his oedipus complex many years before. In such a case a slip reveals clearly an id content against which the ego has for many years maintained an extremely strong countercathexis.

We should add that no matter how clear a slip may *seem* to be, the listener's or reader's interpretation of its unconscious meaning can never be more than a conjecture as long as it remains unsupported by the associations of the person who himself made the slip. To be sure, the conjecture may be so solidly buttressed by confirmatory evidence, such as knowledge of the circumstances in which the slip occurred and of the subject's personality and life situation, as to seem irrefutable. Nevertheless, in principle the meaning of any slip can be firmly established only by the subject's associations.

This dependence on the subject's associations is obvious and absolute in the case of those written or spoken slips which are *not* immediately intelligible. In them, an unconscious mental process interferes with what the subject wishes to say or write in such a way as to result in the omission, insertion, or distortion of one or more syllables or words with an apparently senseless result. Among those who are neither wholly ignorant nor completely informed concerning Freud's explanation of these phenomena, such slips are often considered to be exceptions to his statement that slips have a meaning. Such people speak of intelligible slips as "Freudian" ones and of unintelligible slips as "non-Freudian" ones. In fact, however, the use of the proper technique of investigation, that is, of the psychoanalytic method, will reveal the nature and significance of the unconscious mental processes underlying an unintelligible slip as well as it does those which underlie an intelligible one.

The occurrence of slips of the tongue or pen is often attributed to fatigue, inattention, haste, excitement, or the like. The reader may ask whether such factors were considered by Freud to play any role in the causation of slips. The answer to this question is that he assigned to them a purely accessory or adjuvant part in the process. He considered that such factors might, in certain instances, facilitate the interference of unconscious processes with the conscious intent to say or write a particular word or phrase, with the result that a slip then occurs which would not have occurred if the subject had not been tired, inattentive, in a hurry, etc. He believed that the main role in the production of a slip is played by the subject's unconscious mental processes, however. To illustrate his point he used the following analogy. If a man was held up and robbed on a dark and lonely street, we should not say that he was robbed by the darkness and loneliness. He was robbed by a robber, who was, however, helped by darkness and loneliness. In this analogy the robber corresponds to the unconscious mental processes which were responsible for the slip, while the darkness and loneliness correspond to such factors as fatigue, inattention, etc. If we

wish to use more formal language, we may say that the unconscious mental processes in question constitute the necessary condition for a slip in all cases. In some cases they may
be a sufficient condition as well, while in other cases they
may be insufficient in themselves and may perhaps require
the assistance of such general factors as we have been discussing in order to interfere with the subject's conscious intent to a sufficient degree to produce a slip.

No discussion of slips of the tongue or pen would be complete without some mention of the part played in their construction by the operation of the primary process. For instance, in talking about the interest which he had had as a
youth in physical culture, a patient made a slip and said,
"physible culture," instead. When his attention was called to
his mistake, it occurred to him that "physible" sounded like
"visible." From there his associations led to the unconscious
wish to show his naked body to others as well as his wish to
see them naked in turn. These wishes had been an important,
though unconscious factor in his interest in physical culture.
However, the point to which we wish to call particular attention at the moment is the *form* of the slip which was produced by the momentary interference of the patient's unconscious exhibitionistic and voyeuristic wishes with his
conscious intent to say the word, "physical." What resulted
was a sort of hybrid word that combined "physical" and
"visible." The two words were condensed into one, contrary
to all the linguistic rules which characterize secondary
process thinking.

The reader will remember, from our discussion in Chapter
III of the modes of thought that we called the primary and
secondary processes, that one of the characteristics of primary process thinking is the tendency to condensation. It is
just this characteristic which we consider to be responsible
for the combination of "physical" and "visible" into "physible."

In other slips one will find evidence of the other characteristics of primary process thinking: displacement, representation of the whole by a part, or vice versa, representation by
analogy, representation by the opposite, and symbolism in
the psychoanalytic sense. Any one of these characteristics, or
several of them at once may determine the form of a slip.

We should add at this point that the participation or operation of primary process thinking is by no means limited to
slips of the tongue or pen. Although it is likely to be most
obvious in these, it occurs as often and is as important in the
other parapraxes as well. For example, in the case of the man
who forgot the name of his acquaintance, which we cited on
page 139, the reader will remember that one reason for the
lapse of memory was that the acquaintance was crippled,
which reminded the subject of an unconscious and guilty
desire to maim another man of the same name. In fact the
acquaintance had an arm which was shortened and partially
paralyzed as the result of an injury sustained at the time of
birth. On the other hand, what the subject unconsciously
wished to do to his acquaintance's namesake was to cut off
his penis. In this case, therefore, the acquaintance's brachial
deformity symbolized castration, an example of primary
process thinking.

Let us now consider the class of parapraxes which are
ordinarily referred to as accidental mishaps, whether the
mishap occurs to oneself or to another as the result of one's
own "carelessness." We must make it clear at the outset that
the only accidents with which we are here concerned are
those which the subject caused by his own actions, although
he had, of course, no *conscious* intention to do so. A mishap
which is beyond the subject's control is of no interest to us in
our present discussion.

It is often easy to decide whether the subject was responsible for the mishap under consideration, but it is by no
means always such a simple matter to do so. For example, if

we are told that someone was struck by lightning during an electrical storm, we should ordinarily be quite confident that the mishap was truly accidental and could not possibly have been unconsciously intended by the victim. After all, who can tell where lightning will strike? However, if we learn that the victim was sitting under a tall, solitary tree next to a heavy, steel chain that dangled from one of the branches to within a few feet of the ground, then we might well begin to wonder whether the victim was or was not aware, before the accident, of the relatively great danger that a person in such a situation will in fact be struck by lightning. If we then discover that this was well known to the victim and if, having recovered from his mishap, he honestly disclaims any conscious intent to endanger his life, we must conclude that this particular victim of lightning was deliberately, though unconsciously, trying to get it to strike him. In the same way, an automobile accident may be due to a purely mechanical failure and have nothing whatever to do with the driver's unconscious intent, or it may, on the other hand, have been either directly caused or made possible by unconsciously intentional acts of commission or omission by the driver.

The reader may ask whether we propose the view that every mishap that *could* have been caused or facilitated by an unconscious intent on the part of the subject was in fact so caused. Is there to be *no* room left for human imperfection? Are we to assume, for instance, that no one would ever have an automobile accident unless he unconsciously wanted to?

The answer to this question is, in principle, an unequivocal one. Insofar as a foreseeable mishap is caused by a "human imperfection" in the performance of some action or other, we assume that it was unconsciously intended by the performer of that action. It is true, of course, that fatigue, boredom induced by monotony, and other, similar factors may increase the frequency of such mishaps to a greater or less extent, but we are here in the same position as that which we took with respect to slips of the pen or tongue. The necessary condition for a mishap of this sort, which is often a sufficient condition as well, is an unconscious intent to produce it. Fatigue, boredom, etc., are merely accessory or adjuvant factors.

If the reader now asks how we can be so *sure* that mishaps within the control of the subject were in fact unconsciously produced by him, our answer must be that this conclusion is a generalization which has been made on the basis of those cases of such mishaps which have been accessible to direct study. Here again, as in the case of other parapraxes, direct study means the application of the psychoanalytic technique. If the subject's cooperation can be obtained, his associations will lead to an understanding of his unconscious motives for causing the mishap that seemed at first glance to be quite accidental. It happens not infrequently that, in the course of the analysis of such a mishap, the subject recalls that he knew for a moment that the "accident" was going to happen, just *before* he performed the action that produced it. Obviously, he could know such a thing before the fact only if he intended that it should happen. This partial awareness of intent is usually repressed, that is, forgotten, during or just after the mishap and is only restored to conscious memory if the mishap is analyzed. Thus, without analysis the subject himself usually is quite convinced of the purely accidental nature of the mishap that in fact he himself intentionally caused.

Naturally it is in the course of psychoanalytic therapy that the opportunity arises most often for studying such mishaps directly, as opposed to merely speculating about them in a more or less convincing way on the basis of external, circumstantial evidence. Most of our examples will consequently be drawn from this source, though such mishaps are by no means more frequent in the lives of psychoanalytic patients than they are in the lives of other persons.

On one occasion a patient, while driving to work, was making a left turn at a fairly busy intersection. Because of the number of pedestrians who were crossing, he had slowed to a speed of about five miles an hour when he suddenly struck an elderly man with his left, front fender and knocked him to the ground. As far as the patient was aware when he first told the story of the mishap, he had not seen the man at all. Later, however, he was able to recall that he was not surprised when he felt his car hit something. In other words, he was dimly aware of his unconscious intent to strike the man with his fender at the moment of the "accident." On the basis of his associations to the various circumstances of what had happened it was possible to discover that the chief, unconscious motive for the mishap was the patient's wish to destroy his father. In fact, his father had been dead for a number of years, but the wish was one which had been most active during the patient's oedipal phase, had been energetically repressed at that time and had lived on in his id thenceforth. We can understand that this wish was displaced in the way that is characteristic for the primary process onto an unknown, elderly man who was in the path of the patient's car and who therefore became the victim of what was apparently an accident. It is understandable also that despite the fact that the victim sustained no injuries and that the patient himself was fully insured, he nevertheless felt both frightened and guilty to a degree that was considerably out of proportion to the actually trivial nature of the accident. Knowing the unconscious motives which led to his knocking the man down, we can realize that it was these motives which were the more important sources of the patient's subsequent guilt and fear. In other words, his reaction to the accident was only apparently a disproportionate one. It was quite in proportion to his repressed wish to destroy his father.

Another example, which is so trivial that it hardly deserves to be called a mishap, is one which we mentioned in Chapter I. In that case a young man, driving to his fiancée's home on the morning of his wedding, stopped at a green traffic light and was not aware of his mistake until after it had changed to red. In this case the driver's associations led to the discovery of unconscious feelings of reluctance to go ahead with his marriage which were chiefly due to the guilt and fear connected with certain unconscious sexual fantasies of a sadistic and incestuous, that is, oedipal nature.

In the first of the two examples which we have just given the mishap was due to inadequate or incomplete repression of a hostile, id impulse. The id impulse in question escaped in part from repression, as it is often expressed in psychoanalytic writings. In the second example the parapraxis was the result of either a defense against certain id impulses or of a superego prohibition directed against them, or even, perhaps, of both, since in this instance it is not easy to distinguish with certainty between the two.

Unconscious activity of the superego frequently plays an important part in causing parapraxes of this sort. Many mishaps are unconsciously intended to result in loss or self-injury. In the motivation of such cases a large role is played by an unconscious need for punishment, for sacrifice, or for making restitution for some previous act or wish. All of these motives belong to the superego, as the reader will remember.

As an example of such motivation we may cite the following case. The patient of our first example one day drove the right front wheel of his car against the corner of a curbstone while attempting to park with such force as to tear the sidewall of the tire beyond repair. It is uncommon for an experienced driver to have such an accident and this one was all the more surprising because it occurred at the curb in front of the patient's own house, where he had parked many times before without incident. However, his associations furnished the explanation. At the time of the mishap he was returning from a visit to his grandfather's house on the morning after the latter had died following an illness of several months. Unconsciously the patient felt guilty as a result of his grandfather's death because of his own hostile wishes toward the old man, wishes that were to a considerable degree the counterparts of similar, unconscious wishes toward his own father. He smashed the tire on his own car to satisfy the unconscious demand of his superego that he be punished for having, in his unconscious fantasy, willed his grandfather's death.

Sometimes such a mishap combines both the crime and the punishment. We may suspect, for instance, that in the example just given, some repressed fantasy of smashing his father achieved a displaced or symbolic gratification in the patient's action of smashing his car against the curb. In this particular example, as it happened, the patient's associations did not point in that direction, so that we are left with no more than a suspicion or conjecture. However, in other cases, there is no doubt of the fact that crime and punishment are both contained in a single action.

For instance, a patient, while driving her husband's car, stopped so suddenly in traffic that the car behind her crumpled one of the rear fenders of the car she was in. The analysis of this mishap revealed a complicated set of unconscious motives. Apparently three different, though related ones were present. For one thing, the patient was unconsciously very angry at her husband because of the way he mistreated her. As she put it, he was always shoving her around. Smashing up his car was an unconscious expression of this anger, which she was unable to display openly and directly against him. For another thing, she felt very guilty as a result of what she unconsciously wanted to do to her husband in her rage at him and damaging his car was an excellent way to get him to punish her. As soon as the accident happened, she knew she was "in for it." For a third thing, the patient had strong sexual desires which her husband was unable to satisfy and which she herself had strongly repressed. These unconscious, sexual wishes were symbolically gratified by having a man "bang into my tail," as she put it.

We shall not attempt to list and illustrate all of the various types of parapraxes that might be distinguished from one another, since the causes and underlying mechanisms are the same for all, or at least are very similar. It is interesting to note that it is not easy to draw a sharp line of distinction between parapraxes and so-called normal psychic events. For instance, a slip of the tongue is certainly very different from a metaphor that has been consciously and deliberately sought for. But then there are metaphors, or other figures of speech, that appear in conversation without their having been consciously sought for. They bob up spontaneously, so to speak, sometimes to the speaker's delight, sometimes to his dismay, and sometimes without any particular reaction except that of routine acceptance by him as part of "what he wanted to say." Thus we see that although the deliberately chosen metaphor and the slip of the tongue are easy to separate, there are intermediate cases. How to separate the unwelcome metaphor which the speaker then retracts with "Oh, no. That isn't what I meant," from the slip of the tongue? In the same way, we should certainly classify it as a parapraxis if an individual took a wrong turn during a familiar walk and found himself heading away from his consciously intended destination. However, sometimes one varies a familiar walk, without consciously planning to do so, by taking a less familiar route to get to the same destination. Shall we call that a parapraxis? Or again one may find that he has changed his favorite route without any particular, conscious thought about it, so that what was once the customary way to go is now the unusual way. Where do we draw the line here between the parapractic and the normal?

The fact is that there is no sharp distinction to be drawn. The differences are of degree, not of kind. Unconscious motives and impulses which arise from the id and from the unconscious parts of the ego and of the superego play a role in producing and shaping so-called normal psychic events no less than they do in producing parapraxes. In the former case, however, the ego is able to mediate among the various unconscious influences so as to control them and to combine them in a harmonious way with one another as well as with the factors arising from the external environment with the result that what then emerges into consciousness appears to be a single, integral whole rather than what it really is, that is, a composite of many, different tendencies from several, different sources. In the case of the parapraxes, on the other hand, the ego has not been as successful in thoroughly integrating the various mental forces which are unconsciously active at the moment when the parapraxis occurs, with the result that one or several of these forces independently achieve some degree of motor expression. The more nearly successful the ego's integrative activities, the more nearly "normal" the psychic result. Contrariwise, the less successful the integrative activities, the more obviously parapractic the result.

If we try now to summarize our understanding of the parapraxes of everyday life, we shall say that they are caused by some degree of failure of the ego to integrate into a harmonious whole the various forces which are active within the mind at a particular time. The unconscious, psychic forces which more or less resist integration and which achieve some degree of direct, independent influence over thought or behavior in a parapraxis stem sometimes from the id, sometimes from the ego, sometimes from the superego, and sometimes from two or all of these together. An observer can occasionally make a shrewdly accurate guess as to the specific nature of these unconscious forces on the basis of external evidence alone. However, in most cases the subject's active cooperation in the application of the psychoanalytic method is necessary in order to discover what unconscious forces have been at work. Moreover, even in those cases where it has been possible to make a convincing guess, it is only by the application of the psychoanalytic method that one can be sure whether his guess was correct and complete or not.

We wish to turn now to a discussion of *wit*. Like the parapraxes, wit is a familiar phenomenon of everyday life to which Freud turned his attention quite early in the course of his psychoanalytic investigations (Freud, 1905a). He succeeded in demonstrating both the nature and the importance of the unconscious mental processes that are a part of the formation and the enjoyment of witticisms and advanced a theory which explained the source of the psychic energy which is discharged in laughter when the witticism is a "good" one.

Freud demonstrated that in every witticism primary process thinking plays an essential part. This he did by a most ingenious technique. He restated the witticism in the *language* of the secondary process without changing its content in any way, whereupon the wit had entirely disappeared. What was left after the restatement might be interesting, wise, bitter, cynical, or conventionally improper, but it was no longer witty.

For example, let us take the well-known, witty, political epigram that says, "A liberal is a man with both feet planted firmly in mid-air." It may not be apparent at first glance that primary process thinking is utilized to a high degree in this statement, but let us see what happens if we restate its content in strictly secondary process language. If we do so, our epigram becomes something like this, "A liberal tries to be firm and practical, but is really neither," which is a critical, but no longer a witty remark.

Now that we have restated our epigram in language which belongs exclusively to the mode of the secondary process, we see at once that in the original form of the epigram its serious meaning is expressed in a mode characteristic of the primary rather than the secondary process. That is to say, the original form conveys explicitly to the reader via secondary process thinking only an image or concept of a man, labeled "a liberal," who is standing firmly in mid-air. It is by way of analogy that the reader or listener understands that "a man with his feet planted firmly" means, "a firm or decisive man" and that "a man standing in the air" means "an impractical and indecisive man." In addition, the original form of the epigram lacks entirely the explanatory and connective words which appear in the restatement, namely, "tries to be" and "but is really." As the reader will remember from Chapter III, representation by analogy and the tendency toward an extreme simplification of syntax, with the omission of connectives and explanatory words, are characteristics of primary process thinking.

Other witticisms naturally exemplify various other characteristics of primary process thinking, such as displacement, condensation, representation of the whole by a part, or vice versa, the equivalence of opposites, and symbolism in the specifically psychoanalytic sense of the word. In addition, since wit is primarily a verbal phenomenon, one sees particularly often in the analysis of witticisms the ways in which words may be used in primary process thinking. For example, parts of different words may be joined together to form a new word which then has the meaning of both the original words. This we may consider to be the process of condensation as applied to words. Again, a part of a word may be used to represent the whole, or the meaning of a word may be displaced to another word which ordinarily means something quite different from the first word, but which resembles it in sound or appearance. All of these characteristics of the primary process are included in what we call "plays on words." The best-known of such playing with words for pleasure is punning, which is proverbially referred to as the lowest form of wit. In fact, however, despite this slur on their value, puns are present in many excellent witticisms.

We may recall the fact that from a developmental point of view the primary process is the mode of thought which is characteristic of childhood and that it is only gradually displaced by the secondary mode as the individual grows older. From this point of view we may say that an activity like wit involves for *both* author and audience the partial and temporary reinstatement of the primary process as the dominant mode of thought, or, in other words, a partial and temporary ego regression. In the case of wit it is the ego itself which initiates the regression, or at least encourages it. Kris (1952) has referred to such processes as regressions in the service of the ego and as controlled regressions, in order to differentiate them from the various types of pathological regressions which may occur in uncontrollable fashion and very much to the detriment of the ego's functional efficiency, or even of its very integrity.

To summarize our exposition thus far, we may say that the author of a witticism, by means of a partial regression, expresses an idea according to the primary process. The resulting image or concept is then put into the language of the secondary process, that is, it is expressed in words. Conversely, the audience understands the witticism by a temporary regression to primary process thinking. The reader must understand that these regressions take place quite automatically and without attracting the attention of either author or audience.

For instance, in the case of the example we used above,

the author of the epigram, whoever he may have been, wished to convey in a witty way the idea that a liberal tries to be firm and practical, but is really neither. By means of a partial regression to primary process thinking this thought was expressed by the idea of a man standing in the air with his feet held firmly. This idea, expressed in words, constituted the witticism. Vice versa, the listener or reader comprehends the author's meaning via the primary process, in consequence of a partial regression of his own.

So much for the formal characteristics of wit. They constitute, as Freud showed by many examples, a necessary condition for a witticism, since if they are removed, the quality of wit disappears as well. However, as Freud also showed, these formal characteristics rarely suffice to produce the impression of very considerable wit by themselves alone, although there are exceptions to this statement. For example, complex and multiple puns may be judged witty by many people simply by reason of their technical or formal excellence. They are not "just puns," they are extremely clever puns by reason of their form alone and hence deserve the adjective "witty." The following verse may serve as an illustration of this point.

> There was a young man named Hall
> Who died in the spring in the fall.
> 'Twould have been a sad thing
> If he'd died in the spring,
> But he didn't, he died in the fall.

Moreover, a remark may achieve the impression of considerable wit by virtue of the fact that the audience is very ready to be amused. As every wit or raconteur knows, once an audience is laughing heartily, almost anything will suffice to produce more laughter, even something that the same audience would have greeted without a smile if it had been in a sober mood. In the same way, the audience's alcoholic intake will often seem to increase a speaker's wit. Conversely, to a person who is "not in the mood" for it, nothing whatever appears to be witty.

However, these exceptions, if indeed the reader will agree that they are exceptions, are of but minor significance. By and large the formal characteristics which we have described are a necessary, but not in themselves a sufficient condition for wit. The content is important as well, as Freud pointed out. Characteristically the content consists of hostile or sexual thoughts which are more or less firmly defended against by the ego at the time when the witticism is either made or heard. In this connection, the word "sexual" is used in the psychoanalytic sense. That is to say, it is intended to include the oral and anal components of sexuality as well as the phallic and genital ones. The *technique* of wit generally serves to effect the release or discharge of unconscious tendencies that would otherwise not be permitted expression, or at least not as complete expression.

To illustrate this we may offer the following, very witty remark, which was current in the 1930's, when it was attributed to a famous wit of the time: "If all the girls at the Yale prom were laid end to end, I wouldn't be a bit surprised." The *content* of this witticism clearly is, "I wouldn't be a bit surprised if all the girls at the Yale prom had sexual intercourse while they were there." To express this content so directly in a social gathering would be likely to arouse some degree of superego condemnation in the minds of the audience. They would probably consider both the author and the remark vulgar and would experience no pleasure in connection with whatever sexual fantasies or wishes may have been stirred in their minds by what they heard. On the other hand, when the same content is conveyed in a witty way, superego condemnation is much more likely to be avoided and the sexual excitement is more likely to be accompanied by pleasure than by discomfort. In other words, the *technique* of wit permits a certain amount of sexual gratification that would otherwise be unattainable under the circumstances.

In the same way, if we return to our epigram about the liberal, we see that by using the technique of wit the author is able to heap more scorn on the heads of the liberals whom he despises than he would feel sure of being able to do directly with the full approval of his audience. Indeed, with the help of the primary process he is able to sound as though he were paying liberals a compliment rather than reviling them, until the very last word of his sentence. Here again, from the audience's point of view, impulses which would otherwise have been forbidden can achieve a degree of gratification or pleasurable discharge. In this case, of course, the impulses in question are hostile ones.

It is the pleasure derived from these otherwise forbidden impulses, whether they be hostile, sexual, or both, which contribute the major share to the enjoyment of a witticism. To be really good, a witticism must be more than clever, it must have a "point." Except perhaps for the connoisseur of wit, formal excellence is hardly ever a satisfactory substitute for content or meaning. In other words, the pleasure derived from the technical part of the witticism is rarely as great as that which results from the escape of some forbidden impulse from the pressure of the ego's defenses against it.

However, despite the disparity in amount, we must recognize that in fact the pleasure of wit arises from two separate sources. The first of these is the regressive substitution of the primary for the secondary process of thinking which we have seen to be the necessary condition for wit. We may reasonably assume that the pleasure derived from this regression is a special case of the pleasure that comes in general from reverting to childish behavior and throwing off the restraints of adult life. The second source of pleasure, as we have said, is the consequence of the release or escape of impulses that would otherwise have been checked or forbidden. Of the two, the latter is the one which is the source of the greater pleasure, while the former is the one which is essential in achieving the effect which we call wit.

The reader will recognize that the theoretical discussion contained in the last few paragraphs has been formulated in subjective terms, that is to say, in terms of the experience of pleasure. In his monograph on wit, Freud tried to go a step further and to account for the laughter and pleasure which accompany wit on the basis of the discharge of psychic energy.

His formulation was as follows. The substitution of the primary for the secondary process in itself results in a certain saving of psychic energy which is then available for immediate discharge in the form of laughter. A much greater amount of psychic energy, however, is made available by the temporary abrogation of the ego's defenses as a result of which the otherwise forbidden impulses of which we spoke above are momentarily released. Freud suggested that it was specifically the energy which the ego ordinarily expended as a countercathexis against these impulses which is suddenly and temporarily freed in wit and is therefore available for discharge in laughter.

We may conclude this chapter by comparing what we have learned about wit with what we have learned about the parapraxes. That there are similarities between the two classes of phenomena is clear. In both there is a momentary emergence of otherwise unconscious tendencies and in both primary process thinking characteristically plays a significant or essential role. However, in the case of the parapraxes the emergence of an otherwise unconscious tendency is due to the temporary inability of the ego either to control it or to integrate it in normal fashion with the other psychic tendencies which are active within the mind at the same time. A parapraxis occurs *despite* the ego. In the case of wit, on the other hand, the ego either produces or willingly permits a temporary and partial regression to primary process thinking and thus encourages the momentary abrogation of its defensive activities which allows otherwise unconscious impulses to emerge. The ego *produces* or *welcomes* wit. A further difference seems to be that the unconscious tendency which emerges temporarily in a parapraxis may derive from id, ego, or superego, whereas in wit the emerging, hitherto unconscious tendency is regularly an id derivative.

SUGGESTED READING

FREUD, S., The Psychopathology of Everyday Life. *Standard Edition*, Vol. 6, 1960. Also, New York: Norton, 1965.

FREUD, S., Jokes and their Relation to the Unconscious. *Standard Edition*, Vol. 8, 1960.

CHAPTER VII

DREAMS

The study of dreams occupies a particular place in psycho-analysis. *The Interpretation of Dreams* (Freud, 1900) was as revolutionary and as monumental a contribution to psychology as the *Origin of Species* was to biology a half century earlier. As late as 1931 Freud himself wrote, in a foreward to the third edition of Brill's translation of *The Interpretation of Dreams*, "It contains, even according to my present-day judgment, the most valuable of all the discoveries it has been my good fortune to make. Insight such as this falls to one's lot but once in a lifetime." Moreover, his success in understanding dreams was of immense help to him during the early years of this century, at a time when his professional work was of necessity carried on in complete isolation from his medical colleagues. In that difficult time he was struggling to understand and to learn how to treat successfully the neuroses from which his patients suffered. As we know from his letters (Freud, 1954) he was often discouraged and sometimes even in despair. Yet however discouraged he might be, he was able to take courage from the discoveries which he had made about dreams. There he knew that he was on firm ground and this knowledge gave him the confidence that he needed in order to go forward (Freud, 1933).

Freud was certainly right in valuing his work on dreams so highly. In no other phenomenon of normal psychic life are so many of the unconscious processes of the mind revealed so clearly and made so accessible to study. Dreams are indeed a royal road to the unconscious reaches of the mind. Yet even this does not exhaust the reasons for their importance and value to the psychoanalyst. The fact is that the study of dreams does not simply lead to an understanding of unconscious mental processes and contents in general. It leads particularly to those mental contents which have been repressed, or otherwise excluded from consciousness and discharge by the defensive activities of the ego. Since it is precisely the part of the id which has been barred from consciousness that is involved in the pathogenic processes which give rise to neuroses and perhaps to psychoses as well, one can readily understand that this characteristic of dreams is still another, very important reason for the special place that the study of dreams occupies in psychoanalysis.

The psychoanalytic theory of dreams may be formulated as follows. The subjective experience which appears in consciousness during sleep and which, after waking, is referred to by the sleeper as a dream is only the end result of unconscious mental activity during sleep which, by its nature or its intensity, threatens to interfere with sleep itself. Instead of waking, the sleeper dreams. We call the conscious experience during sleep, which the sleeper may or may not recall after waking, the *manifest dream*. Its various elements are referred to as the *manifest dream content*. The unconscious thoughts and wishes which threaten to waken the sleeper we call the *latent dream content*. The unconscious mental operations by which the latent dream content is transformed into the manifest dream we call the *dream work*.

It is of the utmost importance to keep these distinctions clearly in mind. A failure to do so constitutes the greatest source of the frequent confusion and misunderstandings that arise concerning the psychoanalytic theory of dreams. Strictly speaking, the word "dream" (in psychoanalytic terminology) should only be used to designate the total phenomenon of which the latent dream content, the dream work, and the manifest dream are the several, component parts. In practice, in the psychoanalytic literature, "dream" is very often used to designate "manifest dream." Usually when this is done it leads to no confusion if the reader is well acquainted with the psychoanalytic theory of dreams already. For example, the statement, "The patient had the following dream," when followed by the verbal text of the manifest dream, leaves no doubt in the mind of the informed reader that the word "dream" is intended to mean "manifest dream." However, it is essential for the reader who is not yet fully at home in the field of dream theory to ask himself what the author meant by the unqualified word "dream" whenever he encounters it in the psychoanalytic literature. There is another term which in practice appears in the literature and in discussion and which it is convenient to define here. This is the phrase, "the meaning of a dream," or, "a dream means." Properly speaking the meaning of a dream can signify only the latent dream content. In our present discussion we shall try to keep our terminology precise in order to avoid the possibility of misunderstanding.

Having defined the three component parts of a dream, let us proceed to a discussion of that part which we believe initiates the process of dreaming, namely of the latent dream content. This content is divisible into three major categories. The first category is an obvious one. It comprises nocturnal sensory impressions. Such impressions are continually impinging on the sleeper's sense organs and at times some of them take part in initiating a dream, in which case they form part of the latent content of that dream. Examples of such sensations are familiar to all of us. The sound of an alarm clock, thirst, hunger, urinary or fecal urgency, pain from an injury or disease process, or from the cramped position of some part of the body, uncomfortable heat or cold, all can be a part of the latent dream content. In this connection it is important to bear two facts in mind. The first is that most nocturnal sensory stimuli do not disturb sleep, even to the extent of participating in the formation of a dream. On the contrary, the vast majority of the impulses from our sensory apparatus are without discernible effect upon our minds during sleep. This is true even of sensations which in our waking state we should evaluate as rather intense. There are persons who can sleep through a violent thunderstorm without either waking or dreaming, despite the fact that their hearing is quite normally acute. The second fact is that a disturbing sensory impression during sleep can have the effect of waking the sleeper directly, without any dream, at least as far as we can tell. This is particularly obvious in those situations in which we are sleeping "with one ear cocked," or "with one eye open," as happens for example with parents when a child in the family is sick. In such a case the parent will often waken immediately at the first disturbing sound from the child, however slight its intensity.

The second category of the latent dream content comprises thoughts and ideas which are connected with the activities and the preoccupations of the dreamer's current, waking life and which remain unconsciously active in his mind during sleep. Because of their continued activity they tend toward waking the sleeper, in the same way as impinging sensory stimuli during sleep tend to do. If the sleeper dreams instead of waking, these thoughts and ideas act as part of the latent dream content. Examples are innumerable. The include the whole variety of interests and memories which are ordinarily accessible to the ego, with whatever feelings of hope or fear, pride or humiliation, interest or repugnance which may accompany them. They may be thoughts about an entertainment of the night before, concern about an unfinished task, the anticipation of a happy event in the future, or whatever else one might care to imagine that is of *current* interest in the sleeper's life.

The third category comprises one or several id impulses

which, at least in their original, infantile form, are barred by the ego's defenses from consciousness or direct gratification in waking life. This is the part of the id which Freud called "the repressed" in his monograph on the structural hypothesis of the psychic apparatus (Freud, 1923), although he later favored the view, now generally accepted by psychoanalysts, that repression is not the only defense which the ego employs against id impulses which are inadmissable to consciousness. Nevertheless, the original term, "the repressed," continues in current usage to designate this part of the id. With this understanding, therefore, we may say that the third category of the latent dream content in any particular dream is an impulse, or impulses, from the repressed part of the id. Since the most important and far-reaching of the ego's defenses against the id are those which are instituted during the preoedipal and oedipal phases of the child's life, it follows that id impulses from those early years are the chief content of the repressed. Accordingly, that part of the latent dream content which derives from the repressed is generally childish or infantile, that is to say, it consists of a wish appropriate to and stemming from early childhood.

As we can see, this is in contrast to the first two categories of the latent dream content, which comprise, respectively, *current* sensations and *current* concerns. Naturally in childhood the current and the childish may coincide. However, as far as dreams of later childhood and adult life are concerned, the latent content has two sources, the one in the present and the other in the past.

We naturally wish to know what is the relative importance of the three parts of the latent content and whether all three are to be found in the latent content of every dream. As to the first question, Freud (1933) declared unequivocally that the *essential* part of the latent content is that which comes from the repressed. He believed that it is this part which contributes the major share of the psychic energy necessary for dreaming and that without its participation there can be no dream. A nocturnal sensory stimulus, however intense it may be, must, as Freud expressed it, enlist the aid of one or more wishes from the repressed before it can give rise to a dream and the same thing is true of the concerns of waking life, however compelling may be their claim on the sleeper's attention and interest.

As to the second question, it follows from our answer to the first one that one or more wishes or impulses from the repressed are an essential part of the latent content of every dream. It also appears to be the case that at least some concerns from current, waking life are a part of every latent dream content. Nocturnal sensations, on the other hand, are not demonstrable in the latent content of every dream, although they play a conspicuous role in some dreams.

We wish now to consider the relationship between the latent dream content and the manifest dream, or, to be more specific, the elements or content of the manifest dream. Depending on the dream, this relationship may be very simple or very complex, but there is one element that is constant. The latent content is unconscious, while the manifest content is conscious. The simplest possible relationship between the two, therefore, would be that the latent content become conscious.

It is possible that this does happen occasionally in the case of sensory stimuli during sleep. For example, a person may be told in the morning, after waking, that fire engines passed the house during the night while he was asleep and he may then recall that he heard a fire siren in his sleep. However, we should probably be inclined to look on such an experience as a borderline or transitional experience between ordinary, waking perception and a typical dream rather than to classify it as a true dream. We might even suspect that the sleeper awoke momentarily when he heard the sirens, although we must admit that this cannot be more than an assumption on our part.

In any case, for our present purposes we shall do better to confine ourselves to a consideration of phenomena which are unquestionably dreams. Of these, it is the dreams of early childhood which most often offer us examples of the simplest relationship between latent and manifest content. For one thing, in such dreams we need not distinguish between infantile and current concerns. They are one and the same. For another thing, there is not as yet any clear distinction to be made between the repressed and the rest of the id, since the very little child's ego has not yet developed to the point of having erected permanent defenses against any of the impulses of the id.

Let us take as an example the dream of a two-year-old whose mother had just returned from the hospital with a new baby. On the morning after his mother's return he reported a dream with the following manifest content: "See baby go away." What was the latent content of this dream? Ordinarily this is something that we can determine only from the dreamer's associations, that is by the use of the psychoanalytic method. Naturally, a two-year-old child cannot understand or consciously cooperate in such an undertaking. However, in this case we can justifiably take the child's known behavior and attitude toward the new baby, which were hostile and rejecting, as the equivalents of associations to the manifest content of the dream. If we do so, we can conclude that the latent content of the dream was a hostile impulse toward the new baby and a wish to destroy or get rid of it.

Now what is the relationship between the latent and the manifest content of the dream in our example? The answer seems to be that the manifest content differs from the latent one in the following respects. First, as we have already said, the former is conscious and the latter, unconscious. Second, the manifest content is a visual image, while the latent content is something like a wish or impulse. Finally, the manifest content is a fantasy which represents the latent wish or impulse as gratified, that is, it is a fantasy which consists essentially of the gratification of the latent wish or impulse. We may say then that in the case we have chosen as an example, the relation between the latent and the manifest dream content is that the manifest dream is a conscious fantasy that the latent wish has been or is being gratified, expressed in the form of a visual image or experience. Consequently, the dream work in this example consisted of the formation or selection of a wish-fulfilling fantasy and its representation in visual form.

This is the relationship that obtains between the latent and the manifest dream content in all of the dreams of early childhood, as far as we know. Moreover, it is the basic pattern for this relationship which is followed in the dreams of later childhood and of adult life as well, even though in these more complex dreams the pattern is elaborated and complicated by factors which we shall discuss shortly.

First, however, we note that the process of dreaming is in essence a process of gratifying an id impulse in fantasy. We can better understand now how it happens that a dream makes it possible for a sleeper to keep on sleeping instead of being wakened by a disturbing, unconscious mental activity. It is because the disturbing wish or impulse from the id, which regularly forms a part of the latent content of the dream, is gratified in fantasy and in that way loses at least some of its urgency and hence some of its power to waken the sleeper.

Conversely, we understand that the fact that the manifest dream is regularly a wish fulfillment is due to the nature of the latent content, which after all is the initiator of the dream as well as its principal source of psychic energy. The id element which plays this role in the latent content can only press constantly for gratification, since this is the very nature of the instinctual drives of which it is a derivative. What happens in a dream is that a partial gratification is achieved by means of fantasy, since full gratification through appropriate action is rendered impossible by the state of sleep. Since motility is blocked, fantasy is used as a substitute. If we express the same idea in terms of psychic energy, we shall say that the cathexis which is attached to the id element in the latent content activates the psychic apparatus to carry out the dream work and achieves partial discharge via the wish-fulfilling, fantasy image which constitutes the manifest dream.

At this point we must take account of the obvious fact that the manifest content of most of the dreams of later childhood and of adult life is not at all recognizable as a wish fulfillment on first, or even on second glance. Some dreams, indeed, have as their manifest content images which are sad or even frightening, and this fact has been cited repeatedly in the past fifty years as an argument to disprove Freud's assertion that every manifest dream is a fantasied wish fulfillment. How can we understand this apparent discrepancy between our theory and the obvious facts?

The answer to our question is a very simple one. As we have said, in the case of the dreams of early childhood the latent dream content gives rise, via the dream work, to a manifest dream which is a fantasy of the satisfaction of the impulse or wish which constitutes the latent content. This fantasy is experienced by the dreamer in the form of sensory impressions. The same obvious relationship between the latent and the manifest dream content is sometimes found in a dream of later life. These dreams closely resemble the simple ones of early childhood. However, it is more often the case that the manifest content of a dream of later life is the *disguised* and *distorted* version of a wish-fulfilling fantasy, experienced predominantly as a visual image, or a series of visual images. The disguise and distortion are often so extensive that the wish-fulfilling aspect of the manifest dream is quite unrecognizable. Indeed, as we all know, the manifest dream is sometimes a mere hodgepodge of apparently unrelated fragments and seems to make no sense whatever, much less to represent the fulfillment of a wish. At other times the disguise and distortion are present in such high degree that the manifest dream is actually experienced as frightening and unwelcome, rather than retaining the pleasurable character that we should expect a wish-fulfilling fantasy to have.

It is the dream work which creates the disguise and distortion which are such prominent features of the manifest dreams of later childhood and of adult life. We are interested to know what processes are involved in the dream work and how each of them contributes to disguising the latent content so that it is no longer recognizable in the manifest dream.

Freud was able to show that there are two principal factors to be considered in connection with the dream work and one subsidiary one. The first principal factor, which is, indeed, the very essence of the dream work, is that it is a translation into the language of the primary process of those parts of the latent content which are not already expressed in that language, followed by a condensation of all of the elements of the latent content into a wish-fulfilling fantasy. The second principal factor consists of the defensive operations of the ego, which exercise a profound influence on the process of translation and fantasy formation, an influence which Freud likened to that of a news censor with wide powers to suppress objectionable items. The third, subsidiary factor is what Freud called secondary revision.

Let us consider each of these factors in turn. In the first place, as we have said, the dream work consists of the translation into primary process thinking of that part of the latent dream content which is originally expressed according to the secondary process. This would ordinarily include what we have called the concerns and interests of current life. Moreover, as Freud pointed out, this translation occurs in a certain way. As he put it, there is a regard for the possibility of expressing the result of the translation in the form of a plastic, visual image. This regard for plastic representability, of course, corresponds to the fact that the manifest dream content consists principally of such images. A similar regard for plastic representability is exercised consciously in some activities of normal, waking life, as for example in charades and in composing cartoons and rebuses.

Another consideration that doubtless affects this process of translation in the dream work is the nature of the latent dream elements which are already in primary process language, that is, essentially, the memories, images, and fantasies associated with the wish or impulse from the repressed. In other words, the dream work will tend to translate the current concerns of waking life into terms or images that stand in as close a relationship as possible to the material which is connected or associated with the repressed. At the same time, of the several, or even, perhaps, of the many fantasies of gratification which are associated with the repressed impulse, the dream work chooses that one which can most easily be brought into connection with the translated current concerns of waking life. All of this is a necessarily clumsy way of saying that the dream work effects as close an approximation as possible among the various latent dream elements in the course of translating into primary process language those parts of the latent content that need translating, while at the same time creating or selecting a fantasy which represents the gratification of the impulse from the repressed that is also a part of the latent content. As we said in the previous paragraph, all of this is done with regard to visual representability. In addition, the process of approximation which we have just described makes it possible for a single image to represent several latent dream elements simultaneously. This results in a high degree of what Freud called "condensation," which is to say that, at least in the vast majority of cases, the manifest dream is a highly condensed version of the thoughts, sensations and wishes which make up the latent dream content.

Before we proceed to a discussion of the part played in the dream work by the ego's defenses, we may pause to ask whether that part of the dream work which we have already discussed is responsible for any part of the disguise and distortion which we have said characterizes most manifest dreams and, if so, how great a role it plays in this direction.

It is understandable that expressing concerns of waking life in the language of the primary process should result in a considerable degree of distortion of their meaning and content. However, the reader may well ask why this psychic operation should have the effect of rendering its end result unintelligible to the dreamer. After all, the person who *composes* a cartoon, a charade, or a rebus can understand the meaning of its images, despite the fact that the meaning has been expressed in the language of the primary process. In fact, the meaning of these creations is grasped by many persons other than the composer himself. Moreover, ideas which are expressed in the language of the primary process are intelligible to us in other situations, as for example in the case of witticisms, as we saw in Chapter VI. Why then should a manifest dream be unintelligible, simply because it contains ideas which are expressed via the primary process?

One part of the answer to this question would appear to be the following. Wit, cartoons, rebuses, and even charades, are all composed with a special requirement, namely that they be intelligible. They must communicate a meaning to an actual or potential audience if they are to be "good." A manifest dream, on the other hand, is subject to no such restriction. It is merely the end result of a process which aims at the fantasied gratification of a wish, or, alternatively expressed, at the discharge of enough of the psychic energy associated with the latent dream content to prevent this content from awakening the sleeper. It is not surprising, therefore, that the manifest dream is not generally immediately comprehensible even to the sleeper himself.

However, the second of the principal factors which we have mentioned as participating in the dream work plays much the more important role in disguising the latent dream content and making the manifest dream unintelligible. This second factor, as the reader will remember, is the operation of the defenses of the ego. We may note in passing that Freud's first description of this factor long preceded his formulation of the structural hypothesis concerning the psychic apparatus, of which the terms "ego" and "defenses" are a part. For that reason he had to devise a name for the factor in question and the one that he chose, as we said above, was "the dream censor," a most apt and evocative term.

In order to understand clearly the operation of the ego's defenses in the process of the formation of the manifest dream, we must first recognize that it affects the different parts of the latent dream content to different degrees. The part of the latent content consisting of nocturnal sensations is ordinarily subject to no defensive operations of the ego, unless, perhaps, we should consider that the ego attempts to deny all such sensations in consequence of its wish to sleep. However, we are really not certain whether this attitude of the sleeper toward nocturnal sensations is an ego defense in the usual meaning of the term and we may safely leave it out of consideration for the purposes of our present discussion.

In marked contrast to nocturnal sensations, the part of the latent dream content which consists of wishes or impulses from the repressed is directly opposed by the defenses of the ego. We know indeed that this opposition is a long-standing and essentially permanent one and that its presence is the reason for our speaking of "the repressed." We have no difficulty, therefore, in understanding that the ego's defenses tend to oppose the appearance of this part of the latent dream content in the conscious, manifest dream, since they are permanently opposed to its appearance in consciousness in waking life as well. It is the opposition of the defenses of the ego to this part of the latent content of the dream which is principally responsible for the fact that the manifest dream is so often incomprehensible as such and quite unrecognizable as a wish-fulfilling, fantasy image.

The remaining part of the latent dream content, that is, the current concerns of waking life, occupies a position with respect to the ego's defenses which is intermediary between those of the two parts which we have just discussed. Many of the concerns of waking life are unobjectionable to the ego except, perhaps, as potential disturbers of sleep. Some are even considered by the ego to be pleasurable and desirable. However, there are other current concerns which are directly unpleasurable to the ego as sources of either anxiety or guilt. During sleep, therefore, the ego's defense mechanisms attempt to bar from consciousness these sources of unpleasure. The reader will remember from our discussion in Chapter IV that it is unpleasure, or the prospect of unpleasure, that calls into action the ego's defenses in general. In the case of such latent dream elements as we are presently discussing, we believe that the strength of the ego's unconscious opposition to them is proportional to the intensity of the anxiety or guilt, that is, of unpleasure, which is associated with them.

We see then that the ego's defenses strongly oppose the entry into consciousness of the part of the latent dream content which derives from the repressed and oppose more or less strongly, as the case may be, various of the concerns of waking life which are also a part of the latent content. However, by definition, the unconscious thoughts, strivings and sensations which we call the latent content of the dream do in fact succeed in forcing their way into consciousness, where they appear as a manifest dream. The ego cannot prevent this, but it can and does influence the dream work so that the manifest dream is unrecognizably distorted and consequently unintelligible. Thus the incomprehensibility of most manifest dreams is not due simply to the fact that they are expressed in the language of the primary process with no regard for intelligibility. The major reason for their incomprehensibility is that the ego's defenses *make* them that way.

Freud (1933) called the manifest dream a "compromise formation," by which he meant that its various elements could be thought of as compromises between the opposing forces of the latent dream content, on the one hand, and those of the defenses of the ego, on the other. As we shall see in Chapter VIII, a neurotic symptom is likewise a compromise formation between an element of the repressed and the defenses of the ego.

Perhaps a simple example might be helpful at this point. Let us assume that the dreamer is a woman and that the part of the latent dream content deriving from the repressed is a wish, originating in the dreamer's oedipal phase, for a sexual relationship with her father. This might be represented in the manifest dream, in accordance with an appropriate fantasy from that period of life, by an image of the dreamer and her father fighting together with an accompanying feeling of sexual excitement. However, if the ego's defenses oppose such an undisguised expression of this oedipal wish, the sexual excitement may be barred from consciousness, with the result that the manifest dream element becomes merely an image of fighting with father, with no attendant sexual excitement. If this is still too close to the original fantasy to be tolerated by the ego without anxiety or guilt, the image of the father may fail to appear, and instead an image may appear in which the dreamer is fighting with someone else, for example, with her own son. If the image of fighting is still too close to the original fantasy, it may be replaced by some other physical activity, as, for example, dancing, so that the manifest dream element is that of the dreamer dancing with her son. Even this may be objectionable to the ego, however, and instead of the manifest dream element just described there may appear in the dream an image of a strange woman with a boy who is her son, in a room with a polished floor.

We should really end this series of examples with the words "and so on," since the possibilities for disguising the true nature of any element of the latent dream content are, for practical purposes, infinite in number. In fact it is the balance between the strength of the defenses and that of the latent dream element which will determine how closely or how distantly related is the manifest to the latent dream, that is, how much disguise has been imposed on the latent dream element during the dream work. Incidentally, in the example given in the previous paragraph, the reader should understand that each of the manifest dream images which were described is a separate possibility which might appear in a particular dream under the proper circumstances. The example is *not* intended to imply that, in a particular dream, manifest content "A" is tried first, then, if the ego will not tolerate "A," "B" is substituted, if not "B," then "C," and so forth. On the contrary, depending on the balance of forces between the defenses and the latent dream element, either "A" or "B" or "C," etc., will appear in the manifest dream.

As might be expected, our example did not exhaust, or even suggest, the variety of "compromise formations" that are possible between defense and latent content. Anything approaching a complete list of such possibilities would be quite beyond the scope of the present chapter, but there are a few important or typical ones that we should mention. For one thing, things that belong together in the latent content may appear in widely separated parts of the manifest content. Thus, the dreamer of the example which we gave above might have seen herself fighting with someone in one part of the manifest dream, while her father was present in quite a different part. Such disruptions of connections are common results of the dream work.

Another common "compromise" phenomenon is that a part, or even all, of the manifest dream is very vague. As Freud pointed out, this invariably indicates that the opposition of the defenses to the corresponding element or elements of the latent dream is very great. True, the defenses were not quite strong enough to prevent the part of the manifest dream in question from appearing in consciousness altogether, but they were strong enough to keep it from being more than half or vaguely conscious.

The affects or emotions which belong to the latent dream content are also subjected to a variety of vicissitudes by the dream work. We have already illustrated the possibility that such an emotion, which in the case of our example was sexual excitement, might not appear in the manifest content at all. Another possibility is that the emotion may appear with greatly diminished intensity or somewhat altered in form. Thus, for instance, what was rage in the latent content may appear as annoyance, or as a mild dislike in the manifest content, or may even be represented by an awareness of *not* being annoyed. Closely related to the last of these alternatives is the possibility that an affect belonging to the latent dream content may be represented in the manifest dream by its opposite. A latent longing may therefore appear as a manifest repugnance, or vice versa, hate may appear as love, sadness as joy, and so on. Such changes represent a "compromise," in Freud's sense of the word, between the ego and latent content and introduce an enormous element of disguise into the manifest dream.

No discussion of affects in dreams would be complete without including the particular affect of anxiety. As we mentioned earlier in the course of this chapter, some of Freud's critics have attempted to disprove his statement that every manifest dream is a wish fulfillment on the basis that there exists a whole class of dreams in which anxiety is a prominent feature of the manifest content. In the psychoanalytic literature these dreams are usually called anxiety dreams. In nonanalytic literature the most severe of them are referred to as nightmares. The most extensive psychoanalytic study of the latter is that by Jones (1931). In general we may say of anxiety dreams that they signal a failure in the defensive operations of the ego. What has happened is that an element of the latent dream content has succeeded, despite the efforts of the ego's defenses, in forcing its way into consciousness, that is, into the manifest dream content, in a form which is too direct or too recognizable for the ego to tolerate. The consequence is that the ego reacts with anxiety. On this basis we can understand, as Jones pointed out, that oedipal fantasies appear in the manifest content of the classical nightmare with relatively little disguise and that, indeed, sexual gratification and terror are not infrequently present together in the conscious or manifest portion of such dreams.

There is another class of dreams which is closely related to anxiety dreams and which are often referred to as punishment dreams. In these dreams, as in so many others, the ego anticipates guilt, that is, superego condemnation, if the part of the latent content which derives from the repressed should find too direct an expression in the manifest dream. Consequently the ego's defenses oppose the emergence of this part of the latent content, which is again no different from what goes on in most other dreams. However, the result in the so-called punishment dreams is that the manifest dream, instead of expressing a more or less disguised fantasy of the fulfillment of a repressed wish, expresses a more or less disguised fantasy of punishment for the wish in question, certainly a most extraordinary "compromise" among ego, id, and superego.

At this point we must pose a question which may already have occurred to the reader. We have said that in dreams an unconscious wish or impulse from the repressed appears in consciousness, though more or less disguised, as the wish-fulfilling fantasy image which constitutes a manifest dream. Now, by definition, this is precisely what an impulse belonging to the repressed cannot do. That is to say, we have defined "the repressed" as comprising those id impulses, with their directly associated fantasies, memories, and so forth, which the ego's defenses permanently bar from direct access to consciousness. How then can the repressed appear in consciousness in a dream?

The answer to this question lies in the psychology of sleep (Freud, 1916b). During sleep, perhaps because the path to motility is effectively barred, the strength of the ego's defenses is considerably diminished. It is as though the ego said, "I don't have to worry about these objectionable impulses. They can't do anything as long as I'm asleep and stay in bed." On the other hand, Freud assumed that the drive cathexes at the disposal of the repressed, that is, the strength with which they push toward becoming conscious, is not significantly reduced during sleep. Thus sleep tends to produce a 'relative weakening of the defenses vis-à-vis the repressed, with the result that the latter has a better chance of becoming conscious during sleep than during waking life.

We should realize that this difference between sleep and waking life is one of degree rather than one of kind. It is true that during sleep an element of the repressed has a *better chance* of becoming conscious than it has during waking life, but, as we have seen, in many dreams the ego's defenses introduce or compel such a high degree of distortion and disguise during the dream work that the access of the repressed to consciousness is hardly a very direct one in those cases. Conversely, under certain circumstances, elements of the repressed may gain fairly direct access to consciousness during waking life. For example, in Chapter VI, the case of the patient who "accidentally" knocked down an old man with his car at a busy intersection illustrates how an oedipal impulse from the repressed may momentarily control behavior and thus achieve rather direct expression even during waking life. Since other phenomena which illustrate the same point are by no means rare, it is clear that we cannot directly contrast sleep and waking life in this respect. However, the fact remains that by and large the repressed will appear in a manifest dream more directly than it is apt to do in the conscious thought or behavior of waking life.

As we have said there is still another process, much less important than the two which we have discussed so far, which contributes to the final form of the manifest dream and which may add to its lack of intelligibility. This process might well be considered to be the final phase of the dream work, although Freud (1933) preferred to separate the two. He called this final process secondary revision. By it he meant the attempts on the part of the ego to mold the manifest dream content into a semblance of logic and coherence. The ego attempts, as it were, to make the manifest dream "sensible" in just the same way as it tries to "make sense" of whatever impressions come within its domain.

We wish now to say a few words about a characteristic of the manifest dream to which we have already referred several times and which, on a purely descriptive level, is its most typical feature. This is the fact that a manifest dream nearly always consists chiefly of visual impressions. Indeed, it not infrequently consists exclusively of such impressions. However, other sensations may be perceived as part of the manifest dream as well.[1] Next in frequency to visual sensory

---

[1] The reader will note that we are referring here to sensory experiences which are consciously perceived by the dreamer as a part of the manifest dream and *not* to whatever nocturnal sensations may be a part of the latent dream content.

experiences in the manifest dream come auditory ones and occasionally any of the other modalities of sensation may appear in the manifest dream. It is also by no means rare for thoughts, or fragments of thoughts to appear as parts of the manifest dream in later life, as, for example, when a dreamer reports, "I saw a man with a beard and I knew he was going to visit a friend of mine." Nevertheless, when such thoughts do appear in a manifest dream they nearly always occupy a position in it which is distinctly subordinate to that of the sensory impressions.

As we all know from our own experience, the sensory impressions of a manifest dream command full credence while we are asleep. They are just as real to us as our waking sensory perceptions. In this respect these elements of the manifest dream are comparable to the hallucinations which are often present as symptoms in cases of severe mental illness. Indeed, Freud (1916b) referred to dreams as transient psychoses, though there is no doubt that dreams are not in themselves pathological phenomena. The problem therefore arises of accounting for the fact that the end result of the dream work, that is, the manifest dream, is essentially a hallucination, albeit a normal, sleeping one.

In his first formulation of the psychology of the dream, Freud (1900) explained this characteristic of the manifest dream in terms of what we noted in Chapter III is often called the topographic theory of the psychic apparatus. According to that theory the normal course of psychic discharge is from the perceptual end of the apparatus to the motor end, where the psychic energy involved is discharged in action. This formulation was undoubtedly based on the model of the reflex arc, where the course of the nerve impulse is from sense organ, through central neurones, and out along the motor pathway. Freud proposed that, since motor discharge is blocked in sleep, the path taken through the psychic apparatus by the psychic energy of the dream is necessarily *reversed*, with the result that the *perceptual* end of the apparatus is activated in the process of psychic discharge and consequently a sensory image appears in consciousness, just as it does when the perceptual system is activated by an external stimulus. It is for this reason, according to Freud's original explanation, that a sensory image in a manifest dream appears to be real to the dreamer.

In terms of the present-day psychoanalytic theory of the psychic apparatus, the so-called structural hypothesis, we should formulate our explanation of the fact that the manifest dream is essentially a hallucination about as follows. During sleep many of the ego's functions are more or less suspended. As examples, we have already mentioned the diminution in the ego's defenses during sleep and the nearly complete cessation of voluntary motor activity. What is important for our present argument is that during sleep there is also a marked impairment in the ego's function of reality testing, that is, in its ability to differentiate between stimuli of internal and of external origin. In additon to this, there also occurs in sleep a profound regression in ego functioning to a level characteristic of very early life. For example, thinking is in the mode of the primary rather than of the secondary process and is even largely perverbal, that is, it consists largely of sensory images which are primarily visual ones. Perhaps the loss of reality testing is also merely a consequence of the far-reaching ego regression that occurs during sleep. In any case, during sleep there is both a tendency for thinking to be in preverbal, largely visual images and inability on the part of the ego to recognize that these images arise from inner rather than from outer stimuli. It is as a result of these factors, we believe, that the manifest dream is essentially a visual hallucination.

One easily observable fact that speaks in favor of the explanation which is based on the structural hypothesis as opposed to the simpler explanation based on the topographic hypothesis is the following. During many dreams, the capacity to test reality is not entirely lost. The dreamer is aware to some extent even while he is dreaming that what he is experiencing is not real, or is "only a dream." Such a partial preservation of the function of reality testing is difficult to reconcile with the explanation based on the topographic hypothesis. It is, however, perfectly compatible with the one based on the structural hypothesis.

This concludes what we have to say about the psychoanalytic theory of the nature of dreams. We have discussed the three parts of a dream, that is, the latent content, the dream work, and the manifest content, and have tried to indicate how the dream work operates and what factors influence it. In practice, of course, when one attempts to study an individual dream, one is confronted by a manifest content and has then the task of ascertaining in some way what the latent content might be. When the task is completed successfully and we are able to discover the latent content of a dream, we say that we have interpreted the dream or discovered its meaning.

The task of interpreting dreams is pretty well limited to psychoanalytic therapy, since it generally requires the application of the psychoanalytic technique. We shall not discuss dream interpretation here because it is, in fact, a technical procedure and is properly a part of psychoanalytic practice rather than of psychoanalytic theory.

SUGGESTED READING

FREUD, S., The Interpretation of Dreams. *Standard Edition*, Vols. 4 and 5, 1953. Also, New York: Basic Books, 1955.
FREUD, S., Fragment of an Analysis of a Case of Hysteria. *Standard Edition*, Vol. 7. The analysis and synthesis of the first dream, pp. 64–93. 1953.

FREUD, S., New Introductory Lectures on Psycho-Analysis. *Standard Edition*, Vol. 22, Chapter 1, Lecture XXIX, 1964. Also in: *Complete Introductory Lectures on Psychoanalysis*. New York: Norton, 1966.

ARLOW, J. A. & BRENNER, C., *Psychoanalytic Concepts and the Structural Theory*. New York: International Universities Press, 1964, Chapter 9.

CHAPTER VIII

PSYCHOPATHOLOGY

Psychoanalytic theories concerning mental disorders have changed and developed in the course of the past sixty years just as the theories of the drives and of the psychic apparatus have done. In this chapter we shall sketch this development from its origins to the present and discuss in a general way the fundamentals of the psychoanalytic theory of mental disorders as it exists at the present time.

When Freud first began to treat mentally sick patients, psychiatry was barely past its infancy. The diagnostic term, dementia praecox, had only just been introduced into the psychiatric literature; neurasthenia was the favorite label for most of the conditions which we should today call psychoneuroses; Charcot had recently succeeded in showing that hysterical symptoms could be removed or induced by hypnosis; and the neuropathic constitution was believed to be the prime cause of all mental sickness, ably abetted by the unnatural strains and tensions caused by the frenzied tempo of civilized, that is, of industrialized, urban life.

The reader will recall from Chapter I that the first condition to which Freud turned his attention was hysteria (Breuer and Freud, 1895). Following a suggestion of Breuer's, he treated several cases of hysteria by a modified form of hypnotic therapy which was called the cathartic method. On the basis of their combined experience he concluded that hysterical symptoms were caused by unconscious memories of events which had been accompanied by strong emotions that for one reason or another could not be adequately expressed or discharged at the time the actual event had occurred. As long as the emotions were blocked from normal expression, the hysterical symptom would persist.

In essence, therefore, Freud's initial theory of hysteria was that the symptoms were the result of psychic traumata, presumably in individuals who were congenitally or hereditarily neuropathic. As he himself remarked (Freud, 1906), this was a purely psychological theory of etiology. On the other hand, as a result of his early experiences with another group of mentally ill patients, whom he diagnosed as neurasthenics, he evolved a quite different theory concerning the etiology of this condition, which he considered to be exclusively the consequence of unhygienic sexual practices (1895).

These practices were of two kinds and each kind, according to Freud, resulted in a different syndrome, or set of symptoms. Excessive masturbation or nocturnal emissions comprised the first group of pathogenic, sexual abnormalities. They produced symptoms of fatigue, listlessness, flatulence, constipation, headache, and dyspepsia. Freud proposed that the term "neurasthenia" be henceforth limited to this group of patients alone. The second type of sexual noxa was any sexual activity which produced a state of sexual excitement or stimulation without an adequate outlet or discharge, as, for example, coitus interruptus, or love making without sexual gratification. Such activities resulted in states of anxiety, most typically in the form of anxiety attacks, and Freud proposed that such patients be diagnosed as anxiety neurosis. He made it clear, even as late as 1906, that he considered the symptoms of neurasthenia and of anxiety neurosis to be consequences of the somatic effect of disturbances in sexual metabolism and that he believed the conditions themselves to be biochemical disturbances analogous to thyrotoxicosis and adreno-cortical deficiency. In order to emphasize their special character, he proposed that neurasthenia and anxiety neurosis be grouped together as *actual* neuroses, as opposed to hysteria and obsessions, which he proposed be called *psycho*neuroses.

The reader will note that the classifications which Freud proposed were based primarily on etiology and not simply on symptomatology. Indeed, he specifically mentioned (Freud, 1898) that a case should be diagnosed as neurasthenia *only* when the typical symptoms were accompanied by a history of excessive masturbation or emissions, since without such a history they must be due to a different cause, as, for example, general paresis (syphilitic meningo-encephalitis) or hysteria. It is important to emphasize this fact for the reason that even today the usual psychiatric classifications of mental disorders which are not the consequence of disease or injury of the central nervous system are on the basis of their symptomatology. These are what are known as descriptive classifications and in psychiatry as in any other branch of medicine, descriptive classifications of diseases or disorders are of relatively little value, since proper treatment depends in most instances on a knowledge of the *cause* of the symptoms rather than of their nature, and the same symptoms in two different patients may have quite different causes. It is therefore worth while noting that from the very early years of his work with mentally ill patients Freud attempted to go beyond a purely descriptive classification and to set up categories of mental disorders which resembled one another in having a common cause, or, at the very least, a common, underlying, mental mechanism. Moreover, an interest in etiology and in psychopathology, rather than merely in descriptive symptomatology, has continued to characterize the psychoanalytic theory of mental disorders to the present time.

From about 1900 on, Freud's major clinical interest was in

those mental disorders which he called the psychoneuroses and the other, so-called actual neuroses practically ceased to be objects of his study. However, in his monograph on anxiety (Freud, 1926) he reasserted his conviction that the classification of anxiety neurosis was a valid one (he did not mention neurasthenia) and that it was caused by sexual excitement without adequate gratification. He no longer maintained that anxiety neurosis was essentially a biochemical, endocrine disturbance, though. Instead he attributed the appearance of anxiety, which constituted the principal symptom of the neurosis and which gave it its name, to a purely psychological mechanism. He assumed that the drive energies which should have been discharged in a sexual climax, but which were not so discharged, created a state of psychic tension which eventually became too great to be mastered by the ego, with the result that anxiety developed automatically, as we described in Chapter IV.

It is somewhat difficult to say what the consensus of psychoanalysts is today about neurasthenia and anxiety neurosis as Freud described them. They are discussed as genuine entities in the standard textbook on clinical psychoanalysis (Fenichel, 1945), yet they are rarely mentioned in the periodical literature of psychoanalysis and there have been no case reports since Freud's original description. It seems fair to say that in practice, at any rate, the category of the actual neuroses has ceased to be a significant part of psychoanalytic nosology.

The case is quite otherwise with respect to the category of the psychoneuroses. Freud's early theories concerning these disorders underwent a steady expansion and revision that continued over a period of some thirty years. These changes in theoretical formulation were always the result of fresh information concerning their psychopathology which resulted from the psychoanalytic treatment of patients, a method of treatment which, by its very nature, is at the same time the best method that has yet been devised for the observation of the functioning of the mind.

The changes and additions came thick and fast in the early years. The first was the recognition of the importance of psychic conflict in the production of psychoneurotic symptoms. The reader will recall that Freud's conclusion from his work with Breuer was that hysterical symptoms and, we may add, obsessional ones as well, were caused by a forgotten event of the past whose concomitant emotion had never been adequately discharged. He soon added to this the formulation, based on further observation and reflection, that for any psychic event or experience to be pathogenic it must be repugnant to the individual's ego to such a degree that the ego tried to ward it off, or to defend itself against it (Freud, 1894 and 1896). The reader must realize that, although the words "ego" and "defend" or "defense" are the same *words* as those which Freud used thirty years later in formulating the structural hypothesis of the psychic apparatus, they meant something quite different in this early formulation. At that time, "ego" meant the conscious self and in particular the ethical and moral standards of the conscious self, while the word "defense" had rather the meaning of conscious repudiation than the very special significance that was assigned to it in the later theory and that we discussed in Chapter IV.

Freud considered this formulation to hold good for cases of hysteria, obsessions, and, as he put it, for "many phobias," and he proposed therefore to group such cases together as "defense neuropsychoses." We can see here another instance of Freud's constant effort to establish an etiologically based system of classification rather than one which was based merely on the description of morbid mental symptoms. This tendency is particularly clear in the present instance, since at that time Freud believed some phobias, as, for example, agoraphobia, and some obsessions, as, for example, doubting mania, to be symptoms of anxiety neurosis proper and to be due, therefore, to the inadequate discharge of sexual excitement, with a resultant disturbance of the body's sexual metabolism, rather than to any purely psychological mechanism such as a defense against a repugnant experience.

The next addition to Freud's formulations concerning the psychopathology of the psychoneuroses was the result of his experience that his pursuit of the forgotten, pathogenic event regularly led back to an event in the patient's *childhood* which concerned his *sexual* life (Freud, 1896, 1898). He therefore proposed the hypothesis that these mental illnesses were the psychic consequence of a sexual seduction in childhood by an adult or an older child. On the basis of his experience he further suggested that if the patient had taken an active role in the pathogenic, or, as it came to be called, the traumatic, sexual experience of childhood, his later, psychoneurotic symptomatology was obsessional. If, on the other hand, his role in the traumatic experience had been a passive one, his later symptoms were hysterical. It is this theory, which postulates a particular, psychically traumatic event of childhood as the usual cause of psychoneurotic symptoms in later life, that is so beloved by writers for Hollywood, Broadway, and the "best seller" lists. To be sure, in such fictional versions the additional, theoretical requirement that the traumatic experience be a sexual one is usually ignored, in deference to the several watchdogs of our public morals.

Freud never abandoned the idea that the roots of any psychoneurosis of later life lie in a disturbance of the sexual life of childhood, and indeed this concept remains to the present time the cornerstone of the psychoanalytic theory of these conditions. However, Freud was soon forced to recognize that in many instances the stories which his patients told him of having been sexually seduced in childhood were, in fact, fantasies rather than real memories, even though the patients themselves believed them to be true. This discovery was at first an overwhelming blow to Freud, who castigated himself as the credulous dupe of neuropathic patients and who, in his despair and shame, was nearly ready to abandon his psychoanalytic researches altogether and to return to the respectable fold of the local medical society from which those researches had ostracized him. It was one of the great triumphs of his life that his despair was short-lived, that he was able to re-examine his data in the light of his new knowledge, and that instead of abandoning psychoanalysis he made an immense step forward by recognizing that, far from being limited in childhood to exceptional, traumatic events like seductions, sexual interests and activities are a normal part of human psychic life from earliest infancy on (Freud, 1905b). In a word, he formulated the theory of infantile sexuality which we discussed in Chapter II.

As a result of this discovery the importance of purely accidental, traumatic experiences in the etiology of the psychoneuroses was relatively diminished and the importance of the patient's sexual constitution and heredity as an etiological factor was relatively increased. Freud assumed, in fact, that constitutional and experiential factors both contributed to the etiology of the psychoneuroses and that in some cases the one was predominant and in some cases the other (Freud, 1906). This remained his view throughout his life and it is the opinion which is generally accepted by psychoanalysts today. We should add, however, that although psychoanalytic observations since 1906 have added greatly to our knowledge of those etiological factors which are experiential, the very nature of such observations has precluded their adding substantially to our knowledge of constitutional factors. Recent studies of child development (cf. Fries, 1953) have been aimed at elucidating the nature of such constitutional factors, but as yet they are hardly beyond the exploratory stage.

The discovery that infantile sexuality is a normal phenomenon also led to other new and interesting concepts. For one thing, it led to a narrowing of the gap between the normal and the psychoneurotic. For another, it gave rise to a formulation concerning the origins of the sexual perversions and their relation to both the normal and the psychoneurotic. Freud's formulation was that in the course of development of the normal individual some of the components of infantile sexuality which we discussed in Chapter II were repressed, while the remainder were integrated at puberty into adult sexuality. As such they played a recognizable role in sexual excitement and gratification, but one which was secondary to the role of the genital organs themselves. Common examples are kissing, looking, fondling, and smelling. In the development of those individuals who later became psychoneurotic, the process of repression went too far. The excessive repression presumably created an unstable situation, so that in later life, as the result of some precipitating event, the repression failed and unwanted, infantile, sexual impulses escaped from repression, at least in part, and gave rise to psychoneurotic symptoms. Finally, in the development of those individuals who became sexual perverts, there was an abnormal persistence into adult life of some component of infantile sexuality, as, for example, exhibitionism or anal erotism. As a result, the pervert's adult sexual life was dominated by that particular component of infantile sexuality, instead of by the normal, genital wishes (Freud, 1905b and 1906).

The reader will note two points about these formulations. The first is that they already express the idea that repression is as characteristic of normal as of abnormal psychic development. This is an idea to which we referred repeatedly in Chapter IV, not only with respect to repression, but with respect to the other defense mechanisms of the ego as well. The second point is that the concept of a repressed impulse escaping from repression to create a psychoneurotic symptom is very similar to the concept which we discussed in Chapter VII of an impulse from the repressed during sleep escaping from the ego's defenses sufficiently to produce a manifest dream.

Freud, of course, was well aware of this similarity and in accordance with it he proposed the formulation that a psychoneurotic symptom, like a manifest dream, was a compromise formation between one or more repressed impulses and those forces of the personality which opposed the entrance of such impulses into conscious thought and behavior. The one difference was that the latent, instinctual wish of a dream might or might not be a sexual one, whereas the repressed impulses which produced neurotic symptoms were always sexual.

Freud was also able to show that psychoneurotic symptoms, like the elements of a manifest dream, had a meaning, that is to say, a latent or unconscious content. Such symptoms could be shown to be the disguised and distorted expressions of unconscious, sexual fantasies. This led to the formulation that a part or all of the sexual life of a psychoneurotic patient was expressed in his symptoms.

So far we have traced the development of Freud's ideas concerning mental disorders up to 1906. Such was the genius of the man and such the fruitfulness of the psychoanalytic method, which he had devised and which he used as a technique of investigation, that his theories at that time already contained all of the major elements of our present-day formulations, either fully developed or in the bud. As we have seen, he began his studies with the concepts that were current in the psychiatric thought of the time, according to which mental disorders were diseases of the mind which had nothing in common with normal mental functioning, that were classified on a descriptive, symptomatic basis, and whose causes were either frankly admitted to be unknown or were attributed to such vague and general factors as the tensions of modern living, mental strain or fatigue, and a neuropathic constitution. By 1906 he had succeeded in understanding the psychological processes underlying many mental disorders to a degree which was sufficient to permit him to classify them on the basis of their psychology, or, if you will, of their psychopathology, rather than of their symptomatology. Moreover, he had recognized that there is not a wide gulf between the normal and the psychoneurotic, but that, on the contrary, the psychological differences between them are ones of degree rather than of kind. Finally, he had made a beginning toward a psychological understanding of characterological disturbances, as exemplified by the sexual perversions, and had realized that these psychic disorders, too, were related to the normal, rather than sharply and qualitatively distinct from it.

The studies of Freud which followed 1906, as well as the later studies of others, served essentially to add to and revise his theories of that time concerning the psychopathology of mental disorders with respect to many important details. They did not, however, lead to changes in principle or in fundamental orientation. Analysts today still direct their attention to the psychological causes of a symptom rather than to the symptom itself, they still think of these causes in terms of psychic conflict between instinctual and anti-instinctual forces, and they still view the phenomena of human mental functioning and behavior as ranging from the normal to the pathological in much the same way as the spectrum of an incandescent solid ranges from red to violet, with no sharp line separating one color from the next. Indeed, we know today that some, at least, of what Freud called psychoneurotic conflicts and symptoms are present in every so-called normal individual. Psychic "normality" can only be defined arbitrarily in relative and quantitative terms. Finally, and in particular, analysts still look to infancy and childhood for the events and experiences which are either directly responsible for mental disorders in later life or at the least cooperate in their development.

In terms of modern psychoanalytic theory, what we refer to clinically as *mental disorders can best be understood and formulated as evidences of malfunctioning of the psychic apparatus to various degrees and in various ways.* As usual, we can best orient ourselves if we adopt a genetic, or developmental approach.

From what we have said in Chapters II-V it is clear that there are many possibilities for trouble in the course of the early years of childhood, when the various parts or functions of the psychic apparatus are actually in the process of developing. For example, if the infant is deprived of normal, physical handling and stimulation by a maternal figure during the first year of life, many of its ego functions will fail to develop properly and its capacity to relate to and deal with its external environment may be impaired to such an extent as to make it feeble-minded (Spitz, 1945). Then, too, even after the first year of life the development of necessary ego functions may be marred by a failure to develop the necessary identifications, owing either to excessive frustration or to overindulgence, with the result that the ego is unable to perform to best advantage its essential task of mediating between the id and the environment with all that this implies in the way of controlling and neutralizing the drives, on the one hand, and of exploiting to the full the opportunities for pleasure which the environment can afford, on the other.

If we look at the same difficulties from the point of view of the drives, we can readily understand that they must be suitably controlled, but not excessively so. Too little control of the drives will result in an individual who is unfit or unable to be a member of the society to which man ordinarily belongs. On the other hand, excessive suppression of the drives will lead to results that in their way are just as undesirable. If the sexual drive is suppressed too much and particularly if this happens too early, the result is likely to be an individual whose capacity for enjoyment is seriously impaired. If the aggressive drive is the one which is unduly controlled, then the individual will be unable to hold his own in what we consider to be normal competition with his fellows. In addition, because the aggression which cannot be expressed toward others so often turns against the self, he may become more or less overtly self-destructive.

It is also possible for the normal processes of superego formation to go awry. That is to say, the complex, psychological revolution which puts an end to the oedipal period may miscarry in some way, and in consequence the superego may be overly harsh, unduly lenient, or an inconsistent mixture of the two.

In fact all of these possibilities are real ones which do occur. Of course, in our outline of them we have been overly schematic. For example, if the drives are too little controlled, this naturally means that there are corresponding deficiencies in the functions of the ego and superego. On the other hand, if control of the drives is too rigid, then presumably the ego is too fearful and the superego too harsh.

As we said in Chapter III, many of the ego's interests, that is, many of the activities it chooses as outlets for drive energy and sources of pleasure, are selected on the basis of identification. However, there is another factor which may sometimes be of even greater importance than identification in the selection of a particular activity of this sort. The choice in such cases is determined primarily by an instinctual conflict. Thus, for example, a child's interest in modeling or painting may be determined by a particularly urgent conflict over the desire to smear with feces rather than by the need or desire to identify with a painter. Similarly, scientific curiosity may derive from an intense, sexual curiosity in early childhood, and so on.

The two examples which we have just given are ones that

we naturally consider to be favorable as far as the individual's development is concerned. They are examples of that
outcome of instinctual conflict which we discussed in Chapter IV under the heading of sublimation. However, it may
happen that an instinctual conflict is resolved, or at least
stilled, by a restriction or inhibition of ego activity rather
than by an enlargement of it such as is found in sublimation.
A simple example of this is furnished by the inability of an
otherwise bright child to learn arithmetic, because to do so
would have been to compete with an older sibling who was
gifted in that particular direction. The self-imposed inhibition on his own intellectual activity protected him from some
of the painful feelings arising from his jealous rivalry with
his brother.

Such restrictions of ego interests or activities may be of
little consequence in an individual's life, or they may, on the
other hand, be extremely deleterious. It is not rare, for example, that an individual unconsciously shuns success in his life
work as resolutely as the child in our last example shunned
arithmetic and for essentially the same reason, that is, to put
an end once and for all to an instinctual conflict that would
otherwise be intensely unpleasurable. In addition, severe ego
restrictions often serve to satisfy a superego demand for punishment or penance. Moreover, to complicate matters even
further, not all ego restrictions which arise from instinctual
conflicts get the child into trouble with his environment, as
an inability to do arithmetic would be likely to do. For instance, a small child's exemplary behavior may be a self-
imposed, desperate attempt to win love from his surroundings rather than to continue to suffer the unpleasure of being
in violent conflict with them. Is this good or bad for the child
and how does it differ from "normal" good behavior?

The same sorts of questions arise in connection with the
regressions and fixations that may occur either in the sphere
of the ego or of the id or of both. For example, in a particular

individual the resolution of the oedipus complex may be accomplished only at the expense of a partial regression of his instinctual life to an anal level, with the result, let us say, that he remains for the rest of his life with an unusually great interest in his own anal processes and products as well as a tendency to collect and hoard whatever he can lay his hands on. As we said in Chapter II, such instinctual regressions usually proceed to a previous fixation point and we believe that the fixation actually facilitates the regression. In our example, we have assumed that the subject's anality was regressive. In another case it might instead be due to a fixation, with essentially the same end result. As another example, this time in the sphere of the ego, there may be a partial regression, as a result of the oedipal conflicts, of the ego's relationship to objects, so that thereafter the objects of his environment are important to him only in so far as they gratify his desires with the result that no object has any permanent or very lasting cathexis. In this example as in our first one, the same result may in another case be the consequence rather of fixation than of regression.

Such ego restrictions, as well as such fixations and regressions of both the ego and the id as those which we have just described, produce character traits which we shall tend to call normal if they do not interfere unduly with the individual's capacity for pleasure and his ability to avoid severe conflicts with his environment, while we shall tend to call them abnormal if they do interfere with pleasure to a great extent and do bring him into severe conflict with his environment. Here again we must emphasize that there is no sharp dividing line between the normal and the abnormal. The distinction is purely a pragmatic one and the choice of where to make it is necessarily an arbitrary decision. For instance, we consider that the formation of the superego is a normal consequence of the severe, instinctual conflicts of the oedipal phase, yet it is certainly accurate to characterize one aspect of superego formation as a permanent imposition of certain inhibitions or restrictions on both ego and id in order to put an end to the danger situation arising from the oedipal conflicts.

From a purely theoretical point of view we could avoid the accusation of arbitrariness simply by considering all of the possibilities that we have discussed in the last several paragraphs as different ways in which the psychic apparatus may develop and function, without attempting to characterize any as either normal or abnormal. However, the clinician, who is consulted by persons in distress or in serious conflict with their environment, must risk being called arbitrary and must make a division somewhere between what he considers to be normal and not a reason for either concern or treatment and what he considers to be pathological and worthy of both concern and treatment. As we have already said, the distinction between what is normal and what is pathological among the patterns of development and functioning of the psychic apparatus which we have been discussing in the past few pages tends to be made on the basis of how much the individual's capacity for pleasure is restricted and how seriously impaired is his ability to adapt to his environment. As for terminology, when a pattern of psychic functioning of the sort we have been discussing is considered to be abnormal, it is usually labeled a character disorder or a character neurosis in clinical parlance. Such a label, then, ordinarily refers to a type of functioning of the psychic apparatus which is considered to be sufficiently disadvantageous to the individual to be called pathological, but which represents, nevertheless, a relatively fixed and stable equilibrium within the psyche which developed, as any intrapsychic equilibrium must do, from the interaction between the various forces within the psyche and those influencing it from without during the course of growth.

The various, so-called character disorders, or character

neuroses vary considerably in their responsiveness to treatment. In general, the younger the patient and the more discomfort he suffers from his particular character trait or character structure, the more likely is therapy to be effective. We must confess, however, that we have as yet no very precise or very reliable prognostic criteria for such cases.

We come now to the type of disturbance of functioning of the psychic apparatus with which Freud became familiar as a result of his early studies of hysteria and the other "defense neuropsychoses." In such disturbances the following sequence of events occurs. First comes a conflict between ego and id during early childhood, characteristically during the oedipal or preoedipal phase. This conflict is solved by the ego in the sense that the ego is able to set up some stable and effective method of checking the dangerous drive derivatives in question. The method is usually a complex one, involving both defenses and ego alterations such as identifications, restrictions, sublimations, and, perhaps, regression. Whatever the method, it works satisfactorily for a longer or shorter period of time until some subsequent event, or series of events, destroys the equilibrium and makes the ego apparatus unable any longer to control the drives effectively. Whether the precipitating circumstances act by reinforcing and strengthening the drives or by weakening the ego is of no consequence as far as we know. What is important is that the ego be *relatively* weakened sufficiently to impair its ability to control the drives. When this happens, the drives, or, to be more exact, their derivatives, threaten to irrupt into consciousness and to be translated directly into overt behavior despite the ego's efforts to contain them. An acute conflict thus arises between ego and id with the ego at a relative disadvantage and a compromise formation results of the sort with which we are familiar from Chapter VII. This compromise is called a psychoneurotic symptom. It is also frequently called a neurotic symptom, even by Freud himself in his later writings, despite the fact that it has nothing to do with his concept of the actual neuroses, corresponding instead to what he called the psychoneuroses.

In the type of psychic malfunctioning which we have just described, then, there is a failure of the ego's defenses, whatever the precipitating reasons, as a result of which the ego can no longer adequately control id impulses which had previously been effectively mastered by the ego. A compromise formation results which unconsciously expresses both the drive derivative and the ego's reaction of defense and of fear or guilt to the danger which is represented by the partial breakthrough of the drives. Such a compromise formation is called a neurotic or a psychoneurotic symptom and, as Freud pointed out many years ago, it is highly analogous to a manifest dream or dream element.

A few examples may help to illustrate what we mean. Let us take first a case of vomiting in a young woman. On analysis it developed that the patient had an unconscious, repressed wish to be impregnated by her father. The wish and the countercathexis against it originated during the oedipal period of the patient's life. The relatively stable solution which she was able to achieve for this and other oedipal conflicts in childhood functioned satisfactorily until her parents divorced and her father remarried when she was in her twenties. These events reactivated her oedipal conflicts and disturbed the intrapsychic equilibrium which had been established years before with the result that the forces of her ego could no longer control her oedipal wishes adequately. In this case, one of the compromise formations that resulted was the symptom of vomiting. The symptom represented unconsciously the gratification of the repressed, oedipal wish to be impregnated by father, as though the patient were demonstrating by her vomiting, "See, I'm a pregnant woman with morning sickness." At the same time the suffering caused by the vomiting and the anxiety which accompanied it were the expression of the ego's unconscious fear and guilt, which were associated with the wish in question. In addition, the ego was able to maintain a sufficient degree of repression so that the infantile content of the wish did not become conscious. The patient had no conscious knowledge of the fact that her vomiting was part of a fantasy of being pregnant, much less of having been made pregnant by her father. In other words, the dysfunction of the psychic apparatus which gave rise to the symptom of vomiting afforded a discharge of the drive energy with which the wish was cathected, but a discharge which was substantially distorted and disguised by the defensive operations of the ego and which gave rise to unpleasure rather than to pleasure. We should add that psychoneurotic symptoms are commonly "overdetermined," that is, that they ordinarily stem from more than one such unconscious conflict between id and ego. In the present case, for example, the wish expressed by the fantasy, "Mother is dead or gone and I have taken her place," as well as the guilt and fear arising from it, also contributed to the symptom which we have described.

Another example is that of a young man with the following symptom. Whenever he left the house, he had to make sure that all of the floor and table lamps had been disconnected. The frightening fantasy that served as a rationalization for this behavior was that if the lamps were not disconnected, there might be a short circuit while no one was home and the house might burn down. Here again the original conflict was an oedipal one. However, in this case the solution of the oedipal conflict was never a very stable one and the ego's defenses and regulatory mechanisms failed with the onset of the psychic storms of puberty, so that compromise formations, or psychoneurotic symptoms, were conspicuous in his psychic functioning from that time forward.

In the course of analysis it appeared that this young man's symptom had the following unconscious or latent content.

Unconsciously the patient wished to take his father's place with his mother. In his unconscious fantasy this would be accomplished in the following way: the house would burn down, his father would be crushed by the loss of the house, would take to drink, and would be unable to work, so that the patient would have to take his place as the head of the house. In this case the irruption of the id wish is represented by two facts: (1) the frequent preoccupation with that part of the fantasy of displacing his father which was permitted to remain conscious, that is, that the house would burn down, and (2) the fact that in his rounds before leaving the house the patient would plug the lamps *in* as well as unplug them, thus expressing his desire to *make* the house burn down, despite his conscious preoccupation with the necessity for preventing this disaster. On the other hand, the ego's part in the symptom is equally clear: undoing, repression, anxiety, and guilt.

A third example is that of a young man with a pathological fear of cancer. Here again the infantile conflict was an oedipal one, while the precipitating factor was the patient's successful completion of professional school and the early prospect of marriage, both of which meant to him unconsciously the gratification of dangerous, oedipal fantasies. The patient's symptom expressed the unconscious, oedipal fantasy of being a woman and being loved and impregnated by his father. The expectation or fear of being mortally ill, which formed the one part of his symptom, symbolized the fantasy of being castrated and hence female, while the idea that something was growing inside his body, which formed the remainder of his symptom, expressed the fantasy that he had been impregnated and that a baby was growing inside him. At the same time his ego maintained as best it could its lifelong defenses against these frightening oedipal wishes. They remained repressed, at least in their original, infantile form. It was only a distorted version of them, unrecognizable to the patient himself, which reached his consciousness. He had no conscious knowledge of any desire to be a woman or to have a baby by his father. However, despite his best defensive efforts, it was not possible for him to avoid anxiety altogether. Even in their disguised forms his oedipal wishes made him anxious. Thus, worry about sickness and death were a part of his symptom also (see below).

Freud coined two terms in connection with the formation of psychoneurotic symptoms. They are, respectively, the primary and secondary gain of illness, or of symptom formation. Let us see now what Freud meant by saying that an actual gain or advantage somehow accrued to the individual as a result of symptom formation.

Freud considered that the primary gain of this process consists in the fact that there is at least partial instinctual discharge, i.e., at least partial gratification of one or more wishes of instinctual origin, without the overwhelming guilt, anxiety, or both that had previously prevented the patient from achieving even the partial gratification which accompanies a psychoneurotic symptom. This may seem a strange thing to say in view of the fact that anxiety so frequently accompanies neurotic symptoms and may indeed be such a prominent part of them, but the paradox is more apparent than it is real. Freud conceived of it in this way. The relative weakness of the ego threatens to permit the irruption into consciousness of the full, infantile content of the id impulse. If it occurred, this would be accompanied by the full, infantile guilt and terror that originally were produced by the impulse in question. By permitting a partial, disguised emergence of the drive derivative via the compromise formation which we call a psychoneurotic symptom, the ego is able to avoid some or all of the unpleasure which would otherwise develop. Here we see how similar a psychoneurotic symptom is to that other compromise formation which we called a manifest dream. In the manifest dream the ego is likewise unable to avoid the emergence into consciousness of an impulse from the repressed, but by permitting the impulse a fantasied gratification or discharge which is adequately disguised and distorted, the ego can avoid the unpleasure of experiencing anxiety or of being awakened.

As seen from the side of the id, therefore, a psychoneurotic symptom is a substitute gratification for otherwise repressed wishes. As seen from the side of the ego, it is an irruption into consciousness of dangerous and unwanted wishes whose gratification can be only partly checked or prevented, but it is at least preferable to and less unpleasurable than the emergence of those wishes in their original form.

The secondary gain is merely a special case of the ceaseless efforts of the ego to exploit the possibilities for pleasurable gratification which are available to it. Once a symptom has been formed, the patient who suffers from it may discover that it has some advantages as well as its obvious drawbacks. To take an extreme example, the combat soldier in wartime who develops an anxiety state has a realistic advantage over his fellows: he is evacuated to the rear, where the danger of being killed is less. To be sure, such an example is not the best, though so obvious on the surface, since the development of the anxiety state itself may be unconsciously influenced by the knowledge that it will lead to removal to safety. However, there are many cases in which there is no question of such a possibility and in which the neurosis comes to have a certain value to the individual only after its development.

From the point of view of the theory of psychoneurotic symptoms the secondary gain is not nearly as important as the primary gain. From the point of view of their treatment, however, it may be very important, since a high degree of secondary gain may result in the fact that the patient unconsciously prefers to keep his neurosis rather than to lose it, since his symptoms have become valuable to him. The treatment of severe obesity, for example, is always a difficult matter, but it becomes impossible if the patient is a fat lady in a circus, who makes her living from her illness.

In the examples which we gave of the formation of psychoneurotic symptoms we did not include one which illustrated the possibility, which we have mentioned earlier, that one of the ego's defenses may be a regression, both of the ego functions and of the drives. Once again, from a theoretical point of view, regression is but one of the many defensive maneuvers which the ego may employ. However, from the point of view of its practical consequences, it is a particularly serious one. The greater the degree of regression, by and large, the more serious is the symptomatology which results, the poorer is the outlook for successful treatment, and the greater is the likelihood that the patient will require hospital care.

Another point which we wish to make about the type of malfunctioning which may result from a failure of the ego's defenses is this. Those malfunctionings which we speak of as psychoneurotic symptoms are ordinarily those which are felt by the individual's ego to be alien to it, unpleasurable, or both. The young man who had to check all the lamps before he could leave the house, for instance, didn't *want* to do so. On the contrary, he couldn't help himself. He *had* to check them. His symptom, in other words, was perceived as alien by his ego and at the same time as unpleasant. On the other hand, the young woman who vomited did not feel her symptom as alien to herself. There was no question in her mind that it was *her* stomach that felt sick, just as would have been the case if her nausea had been due to an acute infection. However, her symptom was distinctly unpleasant.

Now there are compromise formations which result from a failure to establish or maintain a stable method of controlling the drives owing to a relative weakness of the ego which are neither ego alien nor unpleasurable. The most severe and obvious of these are many cases of sexual perversion and addiction. Two observations are in order about such cases. In the first place, they are obviously intermediate between what we have chosen to call character disorders and what we have chosen to call psychoneurotic symptoms and cannot be sharply differentiated from either. In the second place, the instinctual gratifications which constitute the perversion or addiction as the case may be are used by the ego in a defensive way to keep in check other drive derivatives whose emergence and gratification is too dangerous to the ego to be permitted. These compromise formations, from the point of view of the ego, are examples of the use of one drive derivative to help in the control of another and in this sense they are similar to the defense mechanism of reaction formation, which we discussed in Chapter IV. The reader will note that this represents a considerable emendation of Freud's original statement that a sexual perversion is the reverse of a neurosis, to which we referred earlier in the present chapter (Freud, 1905b).

It would be beyond the scope of our presentation to discuss in detail what specific, intrapsychic conflicts and compromise formations give rise to the variety of symptoms which are clinically referred to as hysterical, obsessional, phobic, manic-depressive, schizophrenic, perverse, and so forth. It has been our aim rather to give to the reader some understanding of the general, fundamental, theoretical formulations which are common to all of these clinical subdivisions, or which may be used for the purpose of making broad, psychopathological distinctions among them. Above all, we have tried to make clear the fact that there is no sharp or indisputable distinction to be made between what we consider normal and what we consider pathological in the realm of mental functioning. What we call normal and what we call pathological are to be understood as the consequence of differences in the functioning of the psychic apparatus from individual to individual—differences which are of degree rather than of kind.

SUGGESTED READING

FREUD, S., Introductory Lectures on Psycho-Analysis, part 3. *Standard Editon*, Vol. 16, 1963. Also in: *Complete Introductory Lectures on Psychoanalysis.* New York: Norton, 1966.

DEUTSCH, H., *Psychoanalysis of the Neuroses.* New York: Anglobooks, 1952.

FENICHEL, O., *The Psychoanalytic Theory of the Neuroses.* New York: Norton, 1945.

CHAPTER IX

PSYCHIC CONFLICT AND NORMAL MENTAL FUNCTIONING

In the previous chapter we focused our attention primarily on those consequences of psychic conflict that are classed as pathological. In this chapter we shall concentrate on the other end of the psychic spectrum. We shall consider aspects of personality development which, though intimately related to psychic conflict, are nevertheless to be classed as normal rather than as abnormal.

We have already noted that the difference between what is normal in this area and what is pathological is in fact a difference of degree. It is not a qualitative difference. Thus it is impossible, except on a purely arbitrary basis, to distinguish sharply between one consequence of psychic conflict which is marginally abnormal and another which is marginally normal. The range of the normal and the range of the abnormal shade into one another like the colors of a rainbow.

On the other hand, there are many consequences of psychic conflict which are unquestionably normal. One often has an opportunity for observing such normal phenomena when one analyzes a neurotic patient. It is in the course of analysis that one may discover some of the complex origins and the unconscious meaning of normal phenomena as one could never do if the individual were not in analysis. On the basis of such analytic experience we shall, in the present chapter, attempt to illustrate the relation between mental conflict and such normal aspects of personality development as character traits, choice of vocation, choice of a sexual partner, etc. We shall also discuss other aspects of normal mental life which are demonstrably related to psychic conflict, but where data from individual psychoanalyses are less satisfactory or less abundant, such as fairy tales, myths, legends, religion, morality, etc. In these latter instances our conclusions will be based in part on experiences with individual patients in analysis and in part on what psychoanalysis can say about human nature in general.

Psychoanalytic interest in traits of character was from the first concerned with their relation to childhood instinctual wishes. Freud (1908a) pointed to a relationship between the vicissitudes of anal erotism in childhood and orderliness, parsimony, and stubbornness in later life, as well as to a similar relationship between childhood phallic wishes and later ambition. Other psychoanalysts followed Freud's lead in this respect. As a result, there developed a nomenclature of character types which derived from the connection which could often be observed between character traits and a particular phase of libidinal development. Analysts spoke of oral, anal, and phallic characters or character traits. Clinical experience with many patients substantiated Freud's original impression that the character traits mentioned above are very often derived from the anal wishes and conflicts of early childhood. The term "anal" has also been applied to individuals who are characteristically messy, dirty, and untidy for the same reason. Self-assurance, optimism, and generosity, as well as their opposites, have been described as oral character traits on a similar basis, while ambition and a need for recognition and applause have been labeled phallic.

This classification is on the basis of drives—in particular, of the libidinal drive. It reflects the emphasis on the drive aspect of mental life which characterized the first phase in the development of psychoanalytic psychology. It was only gradually that a fuller knowledge developed of the complexity of the path that leads from the instinctual wishes of childhood, and the conflicts to which they give rise, to the mental life and behavior of adults. In the examples to follow, an attempt is made to indicate both how complicated this path can be and how individual life experiences help to shape the final outcome.

Our first example is a woman in her mid-twenties in whose life style the character trait of charitable generosity was very conspicuous. She came to analysis because of rather severe neurotic symptoms. In the course of her analysis it turned out that her charity was just as closely related to her childhood conflicts as were her neurotic symptoms, yet it is properly classified as a normal character trait, since it was a source of pleasure to the patient, was not self-injurious, and was socially acceptable. The pertinent facts are as follows.

Beginning very early in childhood the patient had been separated from her mother for prolonged periods of time. The circumstances of these separations made it very clear that even when they were together, the patient's relationship with her mother must have been most unsatisfactory and frustrating for the patient. Her intensely ambivalent ties to her mother and the conflicts they engendered were of principal importance in every aspect of the patient's neurotic symptomatology. In addition, they were the principal determinants of her charity. From a very early age she was the protector of her younger siblings, babes as forlorn as herself and as exposed as she was to their mother's unpredictable moods and behavior. Though she was only slightly older than the others—they were all born within a few years—she championed them, argued their causes, tried to shield them from punishment, and solaced them in distress, as though she were herself their mother rather than their sister. She acted to them as a "good" mother should behave to her children. In her adult life she experienced and lived out the same urge to help the poor, mistreated "little people" of our great world. She was passionately devoted to such charitable work, to which she gave generously of her time, her effort, and her money. Coupled with her generosity to the oppressed was an equally strong contempt and hatred for the oppressors—for the establishment. Those she succored were unconsciously equated with herself and her siblings as children. Those she hated were unconsciously equated with her mother as she had been to them in their childhood. By her anger at the oppressors of the weak she took the revenge she had longed to take on her mother when she was a child. By her generosity to the helpless she unconsciously gave to herself and to her siblings a dependable, devoted mother, rather than the self-centered, undependable mother she had had in fact. Thus, the patient's lifelong yearning for a loving, dependable mother, together with her hatred and desire for revenge, were major determinants of the importance to her of the particular type of charitable work that interested her as an adult. Other charities had little appeal for her. When she gave to them, she did so in a perfunctory way that contrasted sharply with her fervent devotion to the favorite objects of her loving generosity. Here, then, is an example of a normal character trait which clearly derives from the patient's early childhood instinctual needs and frustrations.

The second example is that of a thirty-year-old male patient who was characteristically cheerful, pleasant, sensible, and cooperative. Like the first patient, he had considerable neurotic difficulties in life, but in the particular respects just mentioned, he behaved like the ideal stereotypes of what, in fact, he was: the product of a well-bred, highly moral, upper middle-class family and of the best schools. "Good manners" were as natural to him as breathing, one would say, and if it weren't for what came out in his analysis, one would be inclined to attribute his "natural" good manners to the fact that he had been taught good manners from the time he was a baby. It was clear, moreover, that this aspect of his personality was a normal character trait by any definition. It was socially acceptable, and far from causing the patient himself either pain or distress, his pleasant, good-natured, common-sense approach to life often served him very well. He had his moments of worry or discouragement from time to time, as everyone does when failure or danger threaten, but with him these emotions never lasted very long. He would quickly adopt the sensible attitude that what can't be cured must be endured, that one is better off if one is cheerful than if one complains, and that if one "gets on with it" and keeps at what he's supposed to be doing, things will surely work out satisfactorily in the end. "A philosopher, a second Aesop," you will say. Yet, in fact, it was not a talent for philosophy, but rather the grim realities of his childhood that had so reinforced the conventional virtues of his cultural milieu that they had become for him a vitally important, indeed, a necessary part of his personality.

At the age of nine years the patient had been suddenly threatened with the prospect of losing the person who was to him the most important adult member of his family. For three days he was acutely and profoundly depressed. Then, fortunately, the danger of loss passed. But never permanently, as far as he was concerned. The possibility of abandonment remained ever present in his mind. He reacted to it in two different ways. The first was to assure, by his behavior, that it would never happen. The second, to prepare himself for the time when it would inevitably happen, so that he would not be helpless and overwhelmed when it did. The first set of reactions had basically to do with warding off wishes and behavior of instinctual origin. Prior to the threatened loss the patient had been a hot-tempered boy with occasional temper tantrums. Never again. From that time until he entered analysis he could recall but one occasion when he felt really angry. His sexual activities were also curtailed, though by no means as drastically. He became a very *good* boy, in other words, who no longer showed the faults of sexual and aggressive behavior that he had been sure had occasioned the threat of desertion which he had experienced at age nine. The second set of reactions consisted essentially of an identification with the adult whose loss he feared. He became, like that adult, cheerful, sensible, practical, and optimistic in an unquestioning sort of way. He became able "to take care of himself" by means of this identification, and later he did so in the literal sense when he left home for boarding school in early adolescence. In this case, as in the previous one, it is clear that there is a close connection between psychic conflict and trauma in childhood and a normal, useful character trait of later childhood and adult life. The patient's even temper, good manners, and cheerful optimism were not just the result of his upbringing. They were strongly motivated by the conviction that ill temper or misbehavior would result in his being deserted again, as he had almost been when he was nine. In addition, they were a result of his identification with the adult he nearly lost at that time. In other words, these particular normal and adaptively useful character traits were as intimately connected with the patient's childhood trauma and conflict as were his neurotic symptoms. Their motivation arose from the same sources.

We have already noted, in Chapter V, the importance of the mechanism of identification in the formation of the superego during the oedipal period. Superego formation is a subject to which we shall return later in this chapter. At the moment we wish to emphasize that not all identifications of the oedipal period are related to superego formation. Some, for example, arise as an expression, only slightly disguised, of the child's sexual and competitive wishes. It is common for a small boy to have a conscious wish to be just like his father he so admires and envies, and it is not rare for such a wish to persist into adult life, so that the son becomes in various ways a psychological replica of his father. The same is often conspicuously true in the relationship between a mother and daughter. In such cases parent and child may have similar gestures, identical facial expressions, the same way of walking, of talking, of laughing, the same manner of reserve or of ebullience when in company, etc. In fact, what passes for physical resemblance between parent and offspring is sometimes not a physical resemblance at all, but a behavioral one. It is the result, not of hereditary physical characteristics, but of psychologically determined traits, that is, of unconscious identifications which arose during childhood, often as an expression of the child's wish to *be* the parent with whom he is identified in these various ways.

Children's admiration and envy are not directed exclusively toward their parents, though as we know, these are their principal objects. They have similar feelings, often very intense, toward siblings, feelings which may play a considerable role in a child's instinctual life and in the conflicts and compromise formations which result therefrom. Such was the case with a young woman who had a considerable avocational interest in music. She enjoyed listening to music, was well educated musically for an amateur, and had studied the cello for several years, an instrument which she enjoyed playing, without ever achieving great proficiency. In all of this she imitated, not her mother, but her older sister, a woman who was an accomplished professional musician. Their father prized his older daughter's musical ability and achievements very highly. Since childhood it had seemed to my patient that her sister was their father's favorite because of her musical talent, and she herself studied music in imitation of her sister, with the hope of rivaling her in his affections. The subsequent development of this patient's musical interest was such that it must be classed as normal. It was a pleasurable, subordinate part of her life, as music is to most music lovers in our society. Yet there is no doubt that the patient's interest in music grew out of her oedipus complex, i.e., out of her childhood rivalry with her sister for her father's love. In addition, it could be observed during the patient's analysis that even in adult life her musical activities had still an unconscious oedipal significance. On one occasion, for example, she reported a dream in which she was playing in an orchestra. Her associations led to memories of a musician with whom she had been in love a number of years before, and who, she had recently heard, had become the conductor of a well-known orchestra. He was, she said, not at all like her father either in age or in physical appearance, yet he had always reminded her of him. Perhaps it was because he used the same toilet water as an after-shave lotion. Thus, it was clear, from her associations, first, that the latent content of her dream was an oedipal wish for a sexual union with her father, and, second, that this wish was expressed in disguised form by a fantasy (dream) of "making music" with a man whom she had loved "long ago." Music still retained, unconsciously, its original, oedipal significance for her.

One can observe very much the same relationship between the instinctual life of childhood and such normal features of adult life as choice of vocation or choice of a sexual partner. It is difficult to give satisfactory examples from one's practice with respect to choice of vocation because of the risk of professional indiscretion. Even abbreviated and diguised examples may, however, suffice to carry to the reader at least some sense of conviction concerning the correctness of the assertion we are attempting to illustrate.

A forty-year-old obstetrician was the oldest of six siblings. Like himself, all of his brothers and sisters were born in the farmhouse where the patient lived during his childhood. Each delivery was a major event, an event about which he was intensely curious, but which he was never permitted to witness, though witnessing animal births was a common-place experience from his earliest years. His childhood sexual curiosity was an important factor in determining this patient's life work. In addition to satisfying his curiosity, his choice of profession served other purposes that were also unconscious. For one thing, it gratified his desire to be superior to his father, who was always deferential and submissive to the physician who attended the patient's mother during her frequent confinements. For another, it reinforced his defenses against the rage he felt with each pregnancy against his mother and against the new baby. As an obstetrician he was kind and beneficent to mothers and babies, not murderously angry and correspondingly guilty, as he had been in childhood. Finally, as an obstetrician, he felt competent and self-confident whenever a new baby was born, instead of insignificant and helpless, as he had felt when he was a boy.

Another physician, a man in his mid-thirties, had been separated from his mother for several weeks when he was in his fourth year because she was hospitalized for a major surgical procedure. Among the principal consequences for the patient's life that resulted from this experience with his decision to become a physician—in fact, a surgeon, a doctor who "cuts 'em up," as he thereafter told anyone who asked him what he was going to be when he grew up. The ambivalence to his mother is obvious and was amply confirmed in the course of his analysis in his later years. To be a surgeon meant, on the one hand, to be with his mother rather than separated from her, to cure her, and to be her hero. At the same time, it meant to hurt and punish her for her infidelity in leaving him.

A third patient, who came for analysis in his late twenties, was a labor negotiator. As with the patient just mentioned, a major trauma of this patient's childhood was an enforced separation from his mother at an early age. He was sent away to boarding school when he was only six years old. The ostensible reason for his exile was that his parents had quarreled and separated. The patient had many neurotic difficulties in later life, but he was conspicuously successful as a labor negotiator. He was tireless in his efforts to resolve differences between the two sides of any labor dispute in which he was involved, and he was usually successful in avoiding an open rupture between the two parties. It was his conscious contention that there are no differences between the parties to a dispute that can't be satisfactorily resolved if the parties will only sit down at a table and talk to one another. In this case the patient's separation from his parents had given rise to an intense longing that they stop fighting and reunite so that he could be with them again, especially with his mother. Throughout his life he worked to keep people together so that they wouldn't separate, as his parents had done, and make the workers figuratively homeless as he had literally become when he was six. Again, a childhood trauma resulted unconsciously in a useful vocational choice in adult life.

When one turns to a consideration of the relationship between the instinctual life of childhood and the later choice of a sexual partner, one is faced with an embarrassment of riches. The connections between the two are so manifold and so intimate that the chief difficulty lies in giving some indication of their complexity. To establish their mere existence is hardly necessary. Nor should this be surprising. One need only recall that in the case of each individual the first sexual objects are those of childhood. All subsequent sexual objects are later editions of the childhood ones. And this is true for normal or mildly neurotic individuals quite as much as for severely neurotic ones. An example or two will suffice to illustrate what can be amply confirmed by even relatively superficial observation.

A young man fell in love with and married a woman, who,

as he himself consciously recognized at the time, resembled himself in such physical characteristics as complexion, height, and physiognomy. He had no idea, however, that this physical resemblance was one of the reasons he was attracted to her. It was only later, when he was in analysis, that he became aware that the fact that they looked so like sister and brother was unconsciously sexually exciting to him. Unconsciously she represented for him a sister to whom he had been closely attached in childhood. As a child he fantasied being married to his sister and being the father of her children. As a man, he unconsciously lived out this fantasy with a woman who looked as though she were his sister. It was interesting to note, as one impressive consequence of his unconscious fantasy that his wife was his sister, that during the first several months of his analysis he frequently referred to his wife by his sister's name, an error he never noticed unless his analyst called it to his attention.

Another patient's choice of a sexual partner was influenced in a more complex way by her childhood relationship with her older sister. When they were little girls, their closest male playmate was a little boy who lived next door. The patient's sister and he were so fond of one another that it was common talk that when they grew up they would marry. The patient felt excluded by her two playmates and was jealous of them, just as was the case in her relationship to her parents. In later childhood the sisters saw little of their former neighbor, since the two families moved to different neighborhoods. Many years later, when the patient was in late adolescence, circumstances reunited the three young people. This time the patient made a conscious effort to get the young man to prefer her to her sister while the latter was away at college. She was successful in accomplishing her aim, but rebuffed his sexual advances, preferring to be, instead, "good friends." She then fell in love with and married a close friend of the young man whom she had just won away from her sister, a friend who was himself engaged to be married to another young woman at the time the patient met him. Thus the patient, in her adult life, successfully accomplished in her love life what she had keenly desired as a little girl: to be the successful, rather than the unsuccessful woman in a family triangle. In the process she took revenge on the man who had in childhood preferred her older sister to herself: she threw him over for another man. Her unconscious triumph over both her sister and her playmate was complete.

As one reviews these examples, one is struck by the powerful and long lasting effect that childhood instinctual wishes have on mental life. They can determine the choice of career, the course of one's adult sexual life, one's hobbies, one's mannerisms, peculiarities, etc. In many instances it is more precise to say that these effects do not result directly from the instinctual wishes and conflicts themselves, but rather from the fantasies which arise from them. Thus the last patient lived out a fantasy of being sexually preferred over her older sister—a Cinderella fantasy, one might say. The young man who looked like his wife's brother also lived out a childhood fantasy. So did the obstetrician, the surgeon, and the labor negotiator. In each case a fantasy which arose from the instinctual wishes of childhood and the fears related to them became a major driving force, though an unconscious one, in the patient's life.

The examples given so far are from clinical practice. In each instance the psychoanalytic method could be applied. In each, the individual was a patient who cooperated by telling as fully and freely as he could his thoughts, his associations, and the details of his past and present life, even details too intimate or too distressing to tell anyone else. Consequently there is a considerable degree of reliability to the conclusions that have been offered concerning the relationship between psychic conflict, often unconscious, of childhood origin on the one hand, and the conscious thoughts, wishes, and behavior of adult life on the other. In most of the discussion that follows similar conclusions will be offered, but they will be conclusions which are not based entirely on data derived from the use of the psychoanalytic method in individual therapeutic analyses. We shall make allowance for this fact by limiting ourselves for the most part to formulations that seem amply warranted by such data as are available, and by pointing from time to time to the nature of the difficulties that result when one does not have access to data which only the psychoanalytic method is, as yet, able to supply.

Among the consequences of childhood instinctual fantasies are daydreams and stories of all kinds: fairy tales, myths, legends, and literary productions at every level of sophistication and excellence. Fairy tales and similar stories are usually the first that interest a child. Their perennial popularity suggests that they deal with themes which are of nearly universal appeal to small children, and so they do. They deal in a very direct way with the themes of childhood instinctual life, primarily with the themes of the oedipal period. In nearly every fairy tale there is a young hero or heroine who triumphs over and kills a wicked old villain, also either male or female, and who marries a beautiful youth or damsel, living happily ever after. Every story has its own variations, but the basic pattern remains the same. Each variation has its special interest for a particular child. The story of Cinderella, for example, appeals especially to younger sisters. In the Cinderella story it is the despised younger sister who marries the prince, becomes a queen, and takes revenge on her horrid mother and older sisters. It may be noted at this point that the problem of guilt over oedipal wishes has always to be dealt with in fairy stories. Since these are stories for little children, and for simple, childlike adults, simple devices suffice to set at rest the guilty consciences of the audience. The hero or heroine is always good, often mistreated, like Cinderella, and the rival is always a mean, vicious, despicable person who thoroughly deserves his ill fortune. In addition, as in many versions of Cinderella, it is not her real sisters and mother whom she bests, but step-relatives she is not supposed to love anyhow.

Another very popular fairy story is Jack and the Beanstalk, or, as it is alternatively and more honestly called, Jack the Giant Killer. In Cinderella, the themes of love and marriage receive principal attention. In Jack, the emphasis is on parricide and castration, with just enough disguise to make the story exciting and pleasurable to a child, rather than frightening. In the story the giant whom Jack first robs of his magic possessions and then kills is not Jack's father, but a vile cannibal, who would eat Jack up if a silly woman didn't save him. In some versions the giant had himself killed Jack's real father, so Jack is a pious avenger, not a parricide, and the magic possessions originally belonged to Jack's father, so Jack is quite justified in stealing them back from the horrid, bad giant, who is the *real* thief and murderer.

And so it goes from one fairy tale to the next. The cast of characters is always the hero (heroine) and his (her) father, mother, sisters, and brothers. The hero and his friends are always good, his rivals are always bad. The ending is always "happy," i.e., victory for the hero, death for his rival(s), and sexual union (marriage) between hero and beloved, with a promise that they will have lots of children and will "live happily forever after." Eternally fascinating for children; of little interest, as literature, for adults. However, when they are read by adults, not for their intrinsic value as literature or entertainment, but rather for the insight they give into the mind of the child, into his hopes, his wishes, his passions, his ambitions and his fears, then fairy tales are very interesting reading indeed. They afford the reader a useful mode of access to many of the features of the instinctual mental life of childhood and, hence, of the unconscious mental life of later years.

Myths and legends spring from the same source as fairy tales. It is true that their purpose is different in certain essential respects. For one thing they are for adults, not for children. Consequently, they are psychologically more complex. They are more realistic in the sense that they reflect much more than do fairy tales an adult's view of the complexity of man's environment and his relative helplessness in the face of it. They are also more realistic in the sense that they attempt to explain the origin of man's environment, its nature, and its mode of functioning. They are not intended to be simple entertainment, as are fairy tales. They are serious attempts at cosmology and are, therefore, the precursors of scientific theories. Nevertheless, they are, like fairy tales, basically derived from the instinctual life of childhood: from its passions, fears and conflicts.

For example, the Homeric version of the Greek myths that were, presumably, current shortly after 1,000 B.C., portrays gods and goddesses as a large family, living in a palace on a mountain top, with a father, Zeus, a mother, Hera, and many children. Incest, jealousy, fighting, and intrigue are as common on Homer's Olympus as they are in any child's oedipal fantasies, but murder is impossible, because all the gods are immortal, and since Zeus is the strongest, he is always the victor or final arbiter. The Homeric myth precludes parricide. It never ends in tragedy for the father.

In other myths, however, including many Greek ones, the theme of parricide is expressed directly. The father god meets the same fate as the giant in the fairy tale of Jack the Giant Killer. He is killed, castrated, and often eaten by his children, frequently with their mother's help, and the children take over his power, only to be destroyed in turn by their offspring. In the story of Oedipus himself, as told by

Euripides about 500 B.C., the young hero unwittingly slew his father, married his mother, and finally blinded himself as a punishment for his awful, though unintentional crime. It was the fact that the story of Oedipus expresses the themes of incest, parricide, castration, and remorse so directly that led Freud to coin the phrases "oedipus complex" and "oedipal phase" of development.

If we turn from classic Greek mythology to Judaeo-Christian myths, we find the same relationship to the instinctual life of childhood in the latter as we did in the former. The principal hero of the Old Testament is Moses, the law giver, i.e., the representative of God's will on earth. Moses, (reared as) an Egyptian prince, rebelled against the Egyptian king, defeated him, and became a king with a people and a kingdom of his own. As we have seen, this theme of rebellion and parricide arises from the rivalry, the hate, and the envy which little boys feel toward their fathers during the oedipal phase of development. But, as we noted in Chapter V, the attitude of a child toward his parents during the oedipal period is ambivalent. It is compounded of both love and hate for each parent, however much the proportion of each emotion may vary. In the story of Moses, the loving feelings of a little boy for his father, and his longing for his father to love him, are clearly apparent in Moses' relationship with his divine father, God. Moses is depicted as serving God faithfully and punishing those who would rebel against him by worshiping other gods. In a word, Moses is thoroughly identified with and submissive to God.

This attitude toward God has been such an integral part of western religious tradition that it is taken for granted by anyone reared in that tradition. The fact is, however, that it is by no means a universal feature of religious myths in general. Even in the Moses story, there is a hint of rebellion against God, some minor disobedience for which Moses was punished by never being allowed to enter the promised land of

Canaan. In the main, however, Moses is portrayed as God's devoted and beloved servant. His rebellion is supposed to have been only against a lesser father, the Pharaoh.

In the Christ story, the elements of the ambivalent relationship between father and son are also portrayed in a complex and disguised way. As in the Moses story, the principal, explicit emphasis is on the love of son for father and his submission to his father's wishes. Jesus and his father, God, are represented as so closely identified that they are actually one and the same. The hero never rebels. On the contrary, he is so obedient to his father's will that he permits his father to have him killed, after which Jesus and God, son and father, are lovingly united forever. The themes of parricide and incest appear in the story, but only peripherally, as it were. They are not attributed to the hero as motives or wishes of his own. On the contrary, it is bad men, Jews and Romans, who crucify the young God Jesus. It is they who commit parricide, not the hero, who is, in fact, himself their victim. As for incest, it is only hinted at by the idea that the hero, Jesus, was killed because of man's original sin, the sin that Adam and Eve committed of having sexual relations with one another in the garden of Eden, despite the express prohibition of their father, God.

Our discussion of religious myths has brought us to the topic of religion as a whole. There is probably no aspect of societal life which is of greater psychological interest than is religion. In particular, one can readily observe its connections with those aspects of mental functioning which are our special interest here: the unconscious motives and conflicts that derive from the instinctual life of childhood.

A small child's family—his parents and siblings—are essentially his whole world. His sexual and aggressive impulses toward the members of his family give rise to the wishes and conflicts that characterize the mental life of childhood: to passionate love, to violent jealousy, to rage, to terror, to remorse, to urgent efforts to control his frightening impulses and to placate and appease his parents, who seem to him to be both omniscient and omnipotent. Religion makes of the whole world a new version of a small child's family, a family in which the believer is a child, and Gods and priests are his parents. Like his parents, they will tell him how he should behave, what he should or should not wish for, and they will answer his questions about the world, especially about how the world began, which every adult wants to know, just as every little child wants to know how his little world began, i.e., how he was made, and where he and other babies come from. As Freud (1933) noted, religion serves a threefold function for its believers. It offers them a cosmology, a code of behavior, and a system of rewards and punishments, the same functions which their parents fulfilled in their childhood.

As one would expect, the relationship of believer to God bears the stamp of its origin, for it is psychologically similar in many respects to the relationship between child and parent. One can observe the same ambivalence, the same mixture of love and hate, of submission and defiance, and the same admixture of sensual elements, despite every effort to eliminate them. These features of religious belief and observance are apparent on an individual basis, so to speak, in any patient in analysis for whom religion plays an important psychological role. In addition they are discernible in their institutionalized form in religious rites themselves. Often one has only to view a rite naïvely, as a child would, only to take the words and actions that constitute the rite literally, rather than allegorically, in order to perceive its unconscious relationship to childhood wishes and fears.

As an illustration of this we may consider the closely related rites of mass and communion, which have been practiced as the central elements of religious worship by a majority of Christians for about 1500 years. Communicants are told that, by magic, bread and wine have been turned into God's flesh and blood, which they are invited to eat and drink. One cannot imagine a clearer, more direct expression of a parricidal wish. To be sure, the emotional attitudes of rebellion against father and of triumph over him are explicitly denied. This is not a rebellion, it is obeying God's command. It is not a triumph, it follows on the confession of sin, penance and fasting, and is consciously thought of as a way of becoming morally good, like God, by eating his sacred flesh and blood. Nevertheless, the words are very clear: here are your Father's flesh and blood; you, his children, will eat the one and drink the other. At the same time, the rite serves as a reminder of Jesus' submission to mutilation and death in order to win his Father's love. The words of the communion service remind the communicants of Jesus' death on the cross, which is praised as a model of submission to the will of God, the father of all men. Communicants are told that they, too, should submit willingly to whatever fate befalls them, because, whatever it is, it is their Father's wish, and they should obey his wish faithfully, just as Jesus did, even if it means for them suffering, mutilation, and death. If they are obedient like Jesus, God will love them and take them, as he took Jesus, to live with Him in heaven forever. This religious belief (dogma) bears a striking resemblance to fantasies which we know from psychoanalytic practice to be common among boys in the oedipal stage of development. The oedipal boy often fantasies being a girl, which to him means being castrated, i.e., physically mutilated, as one way of winning his father's forgiveness and love and of sharing in his father's power. The related adult belief, institutionalized in religious practice and teaching, promises divine paternal love to all who will be like God's submissive and mutilated son, Jesus.

These examples are intended to illustrate what only a monograph could prove, namely, that however much one religion may seem to differ from another, they are all the same in one major respect. They all reflect in a variety of ways the fact that they derive from early childhood conflicts over incest and parricide, over love, jealousy, and hate, over homosexual and heterosexual wishes, over castration fears, penis envy, remorse and self-punishment. In every religion the believers are unconsciously children, their Gods and priests are unconsciously their parents—parents whom they both love and hate, fear and despise, obey and defy, worship and destroy. The history of each social group determines many features of its religious beliefs and practices. This is something that sociologists and historians without knowledge of the findings of psychoanalysis have shown repeatedly. What psychoanalysis can add is that, regardless of a group's history, no matter whether it is primarily agrarian, or primarily food gathering, settled or migratory, warlike or peaceful, the religion of every group deals with the unconscious conflicts which stem from the instinctual wishes and fears of early childhood.

We should not leave the subject of religion without at least a few words about morality. As we noted earlier, every religion contains a moral code, i.e., a system of rewards for conforming to prescribed behavior and of punishments for transgressing. In every religion there are "thou shalts" and "thou shalt nots." How are these societal exhortations and prohibitions related to the prohibitions and exhortations of each individual, to each individual's superego, whose formation and operation we described in Chapter V?

In most organized societies at the present time, morality is represented as a desirable consequence of religious faith. In terms of the teachings of Christianity, for instance, the argument would run as follows: if a child is taught to fear and to love God, and to identify with Jesus on the cross, then he will obey God's moral laws and will grow up to be a good person. In other words, religious faith is credited with the power to make people morally good. As far as we know, this is believed in every society, certainly in every civilized one. Despite the widespread acceptance of this belief, however, the data derived from the application of the psychoanalytic method, i.e., from therapeutic psychoanalyses, indicate clearly that it is not true. In fact, individual morality—individual superego formation—comes first. It is a precursor of religious education, not a consequence of it. The moral sense of an individual is mainly shaped by the conflicts of instinctual life in early childhood, particularly in the oedipal period, and it carries the stamp of those conflicts whatever may happen later on. It persists as such throughout later life, though to a considerable extent unconsciously. It is a strange but true fact that one does not know all of one's own moral code, not even all the most important parts of it. One often feels guilty about actions that one consciously believes to be morally good, actions that society approves or applauds. One often habitually does what one consciously considers immoral, what society condemns.

The fact is that psychoanalytic data substantiate, and afford a scientific explanation for the observation which critics of religion have often made, namely, that no creed, no catechism, no commandments carved in stone can or do make a person moral. Morality is an individual matter. It is a consequence of superego formation, and it derives from the violent passions and the overwhelming fears which are part of the instinctual life of childhood, not from Sunday School lessons. It is the particular experience of each individual that is of major importance, that is dynamically decisive, when it comes to morality. In a very real sense it is correct to say that the moral code of any religion is generated by the childhood wishes and conflict of its believers, quite as much as its myths and legends are.

At the same time, one must recognize that this is not the whole story of the relationship between individual and societal morality. It is an important part of the story, to be sure, a part which represents a specifically psychoanalytic contribution, but it is only a part. Every religion represents, among other things, an effort to assuage the anxiety of its believers and at the same time to permit them some degree of instinctual gratification. Its moral code does this by offering answers to the question, "What must I do so that the Gods (my parents) will love and protect me rather than hate and punish me for my sexual and murderous wishes and actions?" These answers are offered to each growing child by its elders, indeed, by its own parents, as a ready-made solution for the child's instinctual conflicts. It is a solution his parents have found acceptable and useful, and which they prescribe for him in his turn. If a moral code is a satisfactory solution in this sense of the word for all or most of the members of a society, it is viable. If not, it is altered in one way or another until it is satisfactory. Failing that, it is discarded altogether and is replaced by some other system of beliefs and practices. For an individual to conform more or less to any moral code offered him by society, or, for that matter, for him to believe in any religion, he must find in it a workable solution for his unconscious conflicts, conflicts which stem from the instinctual wishes of his childhood.

In recent times religion as a social institution has been on the decline. In a general way this decline may be attributed to the psychological impact of the scientific and technological developments of the past three centuries. Galileo, more than any other single man, initiated the events that led finally to just the consequences which the church hoped to prevent by forcing him to recant and then holding him prisoner for the rest of his life. However, it took a long time for the progress of science to affect the religious beliefs of mankind to any great degree. As recently as 1915 every government in the world espoused some religious belief. There was not a single one that was officially atheistic. At present the governments of two of the most populous countries in the world, China and the Soviet Union, condemn all religions. So do the governments of many smaller countries. More than one quarter of the world's population live in these countries. What has happened to the religious belief of these one-billion human beings? There is no doubt that some have consciously clung to one religion or another, but hundreds of millions of them are consciously in agreement with their political and intellectual leaders, with their rulers and their teachers, that all religions are factually incorrect, that their gods are nonexistent, that their assurances of a life after death are illusory, whether they are a hope of paradise or a threat of hell, and that their cosmologies are but the charming myths of primitive, unscientific, ignorant people, however poetically gifted they may have been. If religion comes from so deep a source in mental life as psychoanalysts say that it does, it seems impossible that it could simply disappear without some substitute taking its place. Surely the unconscious consequences of the instinctual conflicts of childhood, which have motivated people to participate in organized religious beliefs and practices for countless centuries, must be as strong among inhabitants of China and the Soviet Union as they are in the rest of the world's inhabitants. What are their manifestations in an atheistic, irreligious society?

The answer seems to be that politics occupies the same psychological position in those countries as religions do elsewhere. It serves many of the same major functions for each individual. Instead of religious processions and festivals for believers to participate in, there are political ones. Instead of religious icons, there are political banners and pictures. Instead of ancient gods or divine beasts, there are Marx and Lenin. Instead of priests, there are political leaders who command obedience, love, and reverential awe. In addition, there is a strong moral trend in socialist or communist teaching. As is the case with most religions, one is "good" if one conforms or believes, "bad" if one does not. Moreover, there is a promise, sometimes only implicit, but sometimes quite explicit, that the advent of socialism will bring with it a kind of heaven on earth, the equivalent of the stereotyped, fairy tale ending, ". . . and they lived happily ever after."

It should be clearly understood that what has just been said about the psychology of politics in China and the Soviet Union is not intended to discredit either the economic and political theories of socialism or its ideal goal of economic plenty for all. Indeed, if it is true that imitation is the sincerest form of flattery, all of the major capitalist countries have only the highest praise for the socialist ideal of social justice. Without exception they offer to their citizens the same promise of material prosperity and security for all. All the previous paragraph is intended to propose is that, in irreligious societies, the unconscious trends which otherwise are expressed in religious practices and beliefs have made a kind of religion of politics and politicians. One should add that such a development was neither intended nor foreseen. The reformers who were the architects and the leaders of the revolutions that created the irreligious societies of today had no conscious desire to have those societies become themselves a kind of religion. Quite the contrary. Such an idea would have been abhorrent to them. Nevertheless, this is what seems to have happened.

Moreover, to a certain extent this is not something new in societal organization. From the most ancient times men have tended to deify their rulers. In Egypt and in the valley of the Tigris and Euphrates Rivers, where the first empires we know of arose, king, high priest, and god were one and the same. Even after the birth of rationalism in the golden age of Greece, Aristotle's pupil, Alexander, was deified, as were countless other Greek and Roman rulers who succeeded him. It seems strange to us to think of a living person who claims to be a god and who is considered to be one by others. "Barbaric," we say. "Pagan. How different from us!" Yet is it *so* different? Until very recently most of the world was ruled, at least in name, by men and women who claimed to have been selected for the position of king or queen by God himself. To rebel against such a ruler, to be less than wholly submissive to him, was to disobey God. It was a crime against religion. Even yet, the conservative faithful consider the Pope (in Italian, *il Papa* = father), who is officially bishop of Rome, to be the direct representative of God on earth, a position which is surely not far removed, psychologically speaking, from that of a living deity—not the equal of one of the great Gods, to be sure, but still like them, though on a smaller scale.

In fact, analytic experience with individual patients has made it quite clear that anyone who is looked up to as older and as being in a position of superior wisdom, authority, or ability can and does unconsciously represent a parent. Religious and atheistic political regimes are by no means unique in this respect. Any bureaucracy, indeed, is not just imposed from above. It is supported from below as well, and the attitude of the humble toward their rulers in any society has one of its unconscious roots in their respective oedipal wishes and conflicts. The president of a republic is unconsciously viewed as a father no less than God is, or a dictator, or a divinely annointed king, or an imperial demigod. The difference seems to lie in the forcefulness with which a particular society or social organization insists *in reality* that one person, or a relatively few people, do indeed possess the attributes with which small children regularly endow their parents: that they are so wise as to be omniscient, so strong as to be omnipotent, and so good as to be without sin or flaw. That to love and obey them is to be good, i.e., to be deserving of love and reward in return, while to fail to love and obey is to be bad and to deserve whatever punishment they measure out.

The closer any religious organization or political system approaches such criteria, the more obviously is it an adult reproduction of the mental life of childhood, a time of life consciously forgotten by most adults, but one which is still active unconsciously and which impels them to repeat their childhood throughout their lives in countless ways. As far as politics and religion are concerned, the trend toward duplication of the childhood family situation in the institutions of the adult world is an unmistakable one, a trend observable in society today no less than in the societies of fifty centuries ago.

Let us turn at this point from the topic of religion to the closely related, more general topics of magic and superstition. In this age of science, the word "magic" usually connotes entertainment consisting of tricks and feats of ledgerdemain which merely *pretend* to contradict one's commonsense, pragmatic knowledge of the world. Serious adults don't really believe that a magician actually has supernatural powers, that he can really and truly saw a woman in two and make her whole again before their eyes. Only children are fooled by such tricks, we think. Still, in societies or in social groups where faith in science has not supplanted faith in magic to the same extent as it has in our own, even adults do seriously attribute special powers to certain persons, whether they are called sorcerers, witches, or holy men and women. Even in our own society, where a belief in magic, miracles, or sorcery has become so unfashionable that few educated persons would admit to it, the fact is that horoscopes are still eagerly consulted by many and faith healers flourish. Nor should one be surprised at this. It is only recently, as historical time is to be reckoned, that *dis*belief in magic has spread among a fairly wide segment of the population. It is true that a few great philosophers took a rational view of the world, as opposed to a magical one, as long ago as the fifth century B.C. in ancient Greece, but only a few. The vast majority of their contemporaries and nearly all of their successors for many centuries continued to believe in magic as men have always done. Even now, when science and rationalism are so highly regarded, magical thinking and magical beliefs still flourish. Perhaps they always will. In any case, they are certainly important enough and widespread enough to warrant our paying some attention to them.

Magic and superstition are most simply defined as consequences of a belief that one's thoughts and words can influence, can even control other persons and the objects in one's environment. As psychoanalysts have discovered, all children go through a phase during which they firmly believe this to be the case. "The omnipotence of thought" is a phrase which appears frequently in psychoanalytic literature. To a certain extent small children are justified in this belief, since each child, as he learns to speak, discovers that he has simultaneously acquired a control over his environment that is literally magical, as we have just defined the term. Now that he can, for the first time, say what he is thinking to his mother or father, they will do or get for him what he wants. As in the Arabian Nights, no sooner said than done! In addition, children's wishes are much stronger, at least relatively, than are the wishes of adults. They give rise to fantasies, which to the child are very real. If the harsh facts of the real world about him are at odds with his wishful daydreams, a child is much more apt than is an adult to ignore the unpleasant reality and to insist that what he wishes were true is indeed true. Only gradually does each child learn to distinguish external fact from wishful fancy, to test reality, as psychoanalysts say (cf. Chapter IV). Moreover, even when an individual's ability to test reality is well developed, the tendency to think magically, as children habitually do, still persists in all of us more or less, and in most of us, rather more than less.

Still another feature of childhood thinking plays an important part in magic and superstition. All the objects of a child's environment are at first assumed by the child to have thoughts, feelings, and wishes just as he himself does. All nature is animate until experience, and his parents, tell him otherwise. Traces of this belief persist in areas of adult life other than magic. Some systems of religious belief, for example, are strongly animistic. Animistic beliefs also play a part in representational art, i.e., in sculpture and painting, and in literary productions, particularly in poetry.

To repeat, magical or superstitious beliefs and practices depend on omnipotence of thought, especially of wishful fantasies, and on an animistic view of nature. They are often obviously related to one or another aspect of the instinctual wishes of childhood, although this relationship is characteristically an unconscious one. We have already remarked that magic plays a large role in religion, although it is by no means restricted to religion. As for superstition, it has often been observed that one man's religion is another's superstition. To a nonbeliever, any religion is, by definition, mere superstition. Its sacred character is inseparable from faith in it.

Children after the age of six or so are invariably attracted by all sorts of magic and superstition. A common superstition among urban children is that it is "bad luck" to step on a crack of a sidewalk. Such children will make a more or less strenuous effort, half in fun, half seriously, to avoid the cracks when walking on a sidewalk. If one wished to be certain of the unconscious meaning of this superstition to a particular child, one would have to apply the method of psychoanalysis to that child. One would have no way of knowing in advance whether the meaning would be the same or different for two or more such children. It is quite conceivable that the same superstition and the same magical ritual could have different meanings for different children, rather than the same for each. However, other evidence is available which suggests that there is a common meaning, at least in many cases, and which justifies a guess as to its general nature.

There is a ditty these children sometimes sing as they walk along a sidewalk. Its words are:

> Step on a crack,
> Break your mother's (or father's) back.
> Step on a line,
> Break your father's (or mother's) spine.

In addition, the same children sometimes run along in great glee, stepping, or jumping, on *all* the cracks and shouting the same ditty.

It seems that a reasonable conclusion to draw from the evidence just outlined is that these are children whose hostile, even murderous wishes concerning their parents have been but recently repressed. In the ditty they are expressed directly enough for the listener to recognize them quite readily. When the children jump up and down on the cracks they are expressing the same wishes in gleeful play, but in a more disguised form. Without the accompanying words, one would be unable to guess with any degree of assurance what was the unconscious meaning of the play. In order to explain the superstition, one must assume that the hostile wishes in question arouse guilt. Thus the unconscious thought, "I ought to be punished for having such bad wishes about mother (or father)," gives rise to the conscious superstition, "If I step on a crack [which has the unconscious, symbolic meaning of gratifying the bad wishes], something bad will happen to me." In order to avoid punishment (consciously, "bad luck"), the child uses magic: he avoids the cracks and thus forces fate to give him "good luck." The unconscious idea has nothing magical about it. If put into words, it would be, "I'm being good, mama (or papa), so I know you won't punish me, as you would if I were bad to you." This is a perfectly realistic idea, reflecting a child's experience and expectation. In the conscious superstition and magic ritual, however, his parent has become an omnipotent, omniscient "fate," whose good will can be assured by behavior (not stepping on cracks) which has no realistic, practical value whatever. Its value derives solely from the child's unconscious thought, from the equation in the child's mind between stepping on a crack and gratifying his hostile wishes about his parent. The magic depends on thought, in this case, on thoughts about childhood wishes and fears, rather than on experience with the real world.

Another common superstition concerns the number thirteen. The belief that thirteen is an unlucky number is so widespread that many buildings have no floor marked "13," lest people refuse to go there, theater seats are numbered so as to avoid "13," etc. Here again, one can make a guess concerning the probable, general significance of this widespread superstition even without having analyzed patients who share it.

Interestingly enough, this is a Christian superstition. In its original form, it was a belief that it is bad luck for thirteen people to sit at table. The reason given is that there were thirteen at the last supper: Christ and his 12 apostles. Another, closely related Christian superstition has it that Friday is unlucky, since that was the day of the week on which Christ was crucified. A combination of the two superstitions has it that Friday the 13th is particularly unlucky.

One can understand why a pious Christian would be saddened by a reminder of the crucifixion, but why the superstition that thirteen brings bad luck? From our previous example we may anticipate that it is somehow related to unconscious guilt over Christ's crucifixion. However, let us begin our attempt to elucidate matters by considering the original form of the superstition: if thirteen people dine together, something bad will happen. Perhaps one will die, is one form the superstition takes. Superficially this looks like an example of faulty reasoning, or of poor statistical analysis, perhaps. The idea is that because Christ was arrested and crucified after a meal at which thirteen people sat together, if one believes the Gospels, the same thing or something similar is likely to happen any time thirteen are at table. So likely, in fact, that one had best avoid such a dinner party. Any other number is much safer for the participants. The fact that non-Christians have not observed such a correlation is of no consequence. Thirteen at table is bad luck.

In fact, however, it is only the conscious reasoning that is faulty in this, as in any superstition. The last supper was the first communion. Here is the description in Matthew, 26. "Jesus took bread and blessed it and brake it and gave it to the disciples and said, 'Take, eat; this is my body.' And he took the cup and gave thanks, and he gave it to them, saying, 'Drink ye of it, for this is my blood . . .' "

It is clear, therefore, that at the last supper Christ's disciples ate his flesh and drank his blood; their food was God himself. Once more we are dealing with a childhood instinctual wish: to kill and devour one's father. Thus, to be thirteen at table symbolizes for a Christian an unconscious childhood wish to kill and eat his father, a wish fraught with guilt and fear. Unconsciously, the superstitious Christian, like the children in our previous example, is telling his father that he is a good son, who does *not* want to do such a bad thing as to kill and eat him, something he would expect to be punished for if he tried to do it. By avoiding the action which symbolizes the gratification of his bad wish, he can avoid retribution ("bad luck") as well.

It is interesting to speculate about the unconscious meaning of "13" to the many who fear it will bring bad luck without having the least knowledge of the origin of the superstition and of its relation to the last supper, or even to Christ. Whatever one is feeling guilty about unconsciously can give rise to a consciously inexplicable, or irrational, expectation of misfortune, an expectation which one may try to allay magically. We may assume, therefore, that whoever feels strongly about the likelihood that "13" or any other omen will bring him bad luck, is probably unconsciously guilty about something. Why a particular individual is more frightened by one bad omen than another, is a question that can be satisfactorily answered only on an individual basis, that is, by applying the analytic method to that individual. It may be of interest to note that psychoanalysts have frequently observed in their clinical practice that in patients who are consciously preoccupied with counting or with similar rituals involving numbers, such activities are a result of unconscious preoccupation with masturbation and with the fantasies associated with masturbation. One cannot say that such a connection is invariable, but it seems to be frequent.

Omens and fortunetelling in general are an important part of superstitious belief. The magician, the astrologer, and the fortuneteller are closely associated in the popular mind. In many societies, past and present, they have occupied important and respected positions in the community. Fortunetellers generally fulfill a double function. They predict the future, and they advise the community or the individual whether now is or is not a good time to undertake a particular project, whatever the project may be: a love affair, a business venture, or a foreign invasion. Almost any natural phenomenon may be used to make the desired prediction: the stars, the flight of birds, an eclipse of moon or sun, the liver of an animal, the lines on one's palm, or the leaves in a cup of tea. In any case, the superstitious belief is that whoever, or whatever "power" has made the stars move, the birds fly, or the sun cease to shine, has done so to tell each of us what he may or may not do without fear of punishment now, as well as how he will be favored in the future. On the basis of what we know of unconscious mental life, it seems reasonable to conclude that this belief, like a religious adult's belief in God, derives from children's attitudes to their parents. In childhood it is one's parent who tells one what one may or may not do. If one disobeys one's parents, one expects to be punished. In childhood it is also one's parents who are responsible for the future, who hold in their hands the power to gratify one's wishes or to frustrate them and to bring one's hopes and plans to grief. The superstitious believer in omens and fortunetellers is unconsciously still a child, it seems, who adopts an attitude of submissive obedience to his parents, eager to learn their will and to obey it in order to deserve their love and their help. As one would predict if one accepts this explanation, astrologers and fortunetellers, who are the representatives in real life of the "powers" believed to guide one's destiny, are themselves usually older men and women, often very old ones, just as one's parents seem to be when one is a small child.

As we have noted, believers in religion, astrology, and the like, manifest an obedient, loving attitude toward the adult representatives of the parents of their childhood: toward God, priests, magicians, and fortunetellers. From clinical experience, however, as well as from direct observation, we know that the attitude of a small child to his parents is an ambivalent one. It includes angry, rebellious, even murderous and castrative wishes, as well as loving and obedient ones. Sometimes the former are the more obvious, sometimes the latter, as in the examples just given. We shall consider now some familiar aspects of adult life in which hostile wishes are the more apparent ones. In these adult activities, conscious attitudes and behavior derive in large part from antagonistic and rebellious wishes from childhood that are still present in adult life, although unconscious.

It is a commonplace of political life that each new generation finds itself more or less in conflict with the older one. In fact, the terms "conflict of generations," or "generation gap," are commonly used to refer to the many aspects of this familiar phenomenon. In our own day, when political power is vested, at least in theory, in large groups of people, the conflict of generations is a mass phenomenon. At other times it has primarily involved individuals, or small groups of individuals. Even today the phrase is applied outside the political arena to situations of struggle or dispute in individual families between parents and their adolescent or grown offspring. It has only been since the discovery and the application of the psychoanalytic method that it has become apparent that the first occasion for serious conflict between the generations is not in adolescence, but in early childhood, usually in the oedipal phase of development. Later conflicts are a second or third version of the original. Something is new, but much is the same. The important point is that so much of what is a repetition of the past is unconscious in adult life. The adult behavior seems to an observer to be irrational, inexplicable, unrelated to the facts of the situation, and so it is. It can be understood only in terms of the unconscious legacy of childhood which supplies so important a part of the motivation for both of the generations involved. In the case of the younger generation one can see again and again evidence that the conscious reasons which are advanced for criticizing and attacking the older generation don't account at all for the sharpness and vehemence which are displayed by the younger one. Something else must be involved to account for the passion which is so evident in the attack.

What psychoanalytic experience indicates is that it is not merely the impetuosity of youth or the rashness of immaturity, or some similar general quality of "the young" that is involved. It is specifically the jealous and murderous wishes which had their beginnings in early childhood and which persist unconsciously in later life, wishes which are unique for each individual, to be sure, but which are similar enough in all to account for the appearance of uniformity that permits one to recognize "a conflict of generations" as a repetitive, more or less universal phenomenon.

Those of the older generation, for their part, are likewise motivated by their unconscious wishes, which stem from their own childhood, instinctual wishes. For example, the older generation may be unconsciously identified with their own parents, whom they still unconsciously believe to be omnipotent and to threaten with destruction or castration all who would dare to rebel against their authority. Or a member of the older generation may unconsciously equate the younger generation (his "children") with his own parents, who are now in reality aged or deceased, but who, in his unconscious fantasy, are reincarnated in the new generation. In any case, neither in political conflicts between the newly adult generation and its parents, nor in family ones are irrationality and seemingly inexplicable passion one sided. Both sides are human. Both are powerfully swayed by wishes from the past of which they are but dimly, if at all, aware, i.e., by unconscious instinctual wishes from childhood. Thus we can understand, on the one hand, the profound psychological truth behind Mark Twain's joke: "When I was seventeen, I was appalled at my father's ignorance. When I was twenty-one, I was amazed at how much he had learned in four short years." But, on the other hand, we can also agree with the intuitive shrewdness of the observation that one reason why national leaders have always been so ready to go to war is their eagerness to afford their sons an opportunity to become dead heroes.

Among the most violent conflicts to which human societies are liable are those that are called revolutions. They are of particular interest to us because we live in an age of revolution. Of course there were many instances of popular revolts against rulers before the French revolution. Never before, however, have there been as many such revolts as in the nearly 200 years since the French revolution. Never before were they as widespread. Never before have so many been successful in their immediate aim of overthrowing existing governments. What began in France and America has spread throughout the world. The revolutionary slogans and ideals of the eighteenth century are universally accepted: liberty, equality, fraternity, popular sovereignty, the rights of man, are written into every constitution in the world today; they are proclaimed as true and binding by every political leader, whereas 200 years ago they were accepted by almost nobody. At that time most people, and certainly all rulers, considered them to be either dangerous, pernicious heresy or mere poppycock, or some mixture of the two.

One thing that has impressed many observers of the political events in this age of revolution has been the frequency with which revolutionaries, once they have themselves achieved political power, become just like those against whom they revolted. Yesterday's foe of tyranny becomes today's tyrant. Nearly a hundred years ago Bernard Shaw observed with his customary wit that all that any revolution ever accomplishes is to shift the burden of oppression from one set of shoulders to another. And be it noted that Shaw was no defender of the establishment of his or any other day. On the contrary, he was a confirmed and active socialist. He was merely expressing his distrust of revolution as the means of achieving socialism.

One must also note that successful revolutionaries themselves are, generally speaking, unaware that they have undergone any such transformation as the one we have described. They and their followers consider such an assessment to be wholly false. On the contrary, they believe themselves to be as true to their original ideals as ever: still champions of liberty, equality, and the rights of man; still implacable foes of tyranny and of tyrants such as those whom they overthrew. In their opinion, anyone who says that they have become like their former rulers is a malicious slanderer who is probably a secret counterrevolutionist.

It often happens, as in this case, that an individual shows by his behavior that he has motives which are readily apparent to others, but of which he himself is wholly unaware. On the contrary, he strenuously denies them when the evidence for them is brought to his attention. The reader may recall that instances of this sort are mentioned in Chapter I as evidence of the correctness of the psychoanalytic hypothesis concerning unconscious mental functioning. It seems, therefore, that the revolutionaries we are discussing are motivated by an *unconscious* wish to become like the very rulers they consciously detest, to occupy the same position, to exercise the same prerogatives, the same power, and to enjoy the same authority.

What can be the origin of such an unconscious wish in the mind of a sincere revolutionary, who is consciously convinced that if he is successful, he will be the very antithesis of those he wishes to overthrow? Knowing what we do about unconscious mental life, the most likely answer is that in this case, too, wishes are involved which had their origin in the instinctual conflicts of childhood. Little children admire their parents, envy them their authority, and wish to get rid of one or the other of them in order to become themselves a parent. As time goes on, these rebellious, parricidal wishes become unconscious to avoid the anxiety and guilt associated with them, and in later life they are, as we have noted, an unconscious part of the motivation for rebellion against authority in general, and for violent revolution in particular. The revolutionary, who is consciously motivated by concern for the common good and by a desire to democratize the social order, is unconsciously motivated by admiration and envy of the tyrants he opposes and by a wish to seize for himself the power they now exercise. Thus, when he is successful, he is likely to become just like his former rulers, though he has not the least conscious desire to do so—indeed, quite the contrary. It is probably true, as the British historian, Acton, said, that power corrupts those who have it. What psychoanalysis can add is that it is one's own unconscious instinctual wishes that play a considerable, probably a principal, role in causing one to betray one's own conscious reformist ideals when one has achieved the power one sought as a revolutionary. Human beings tend to be conservative in their political behavior, whether they are aware of their conservatism or not. They also tend to be irrational in their political behavior, however hotly they deny it and however successful they are in proving to their own satisfaction, i.e., in rationalizing, their irrational beliefs and actions. Psychoanalysis suggests that both the conservatism and the irrationality which characterize politics derive from the same unconscious source; that both are a heritage of the instinctual conflicts of childhood.

It should be emphasized that we have been discussing only one of the many aspects of revolutionary psychology, namely, the fact that rebels unconsciously identify more or less strongly with their rulers, as do rebellious children with their parents. We can safely assume that this psychological fact plays an important part in revolutions. Thus, the French revolution produced an emperor, Napoleon, and a new aristocracy. The Russian revolution produced Stalin, who, as a ruler, was very like the tsars who preceded him. In China there is a new occupant of the royal palace who is not in the least inferior to any of his imperial predecessors in the power he wields or the reverence accorded him, even though he is called Chairman, rather than Son of Heaven.

Not every revolution follows this pattern, however. The American revolution did not give rise to a new regime which repeated the essentials of the old one with only the trappings changed. Psychoanalysis suggests that there is a problem here which warrants more attention than it has received. Why did the American colonies not become a kingdom? The political pamphlets of the day make it clear that the thought was in everyone's mind. Washington was constantly accused of planning to become king, yet neither he nor any of the major figures in the revolution tried to do so. The few who aimed in that direction, like Burr, never got far. In fact, centralization of political power in America proceeded quite slowly after the American revolution, even though America had been subject to royal rule before it rebelled. The explanation for this fact must be interesting in itself. It might be of practical value in the future as well. In any case, psychoanalysis points to it as something out of the ordinary that deserves special study by historians, perhaps with the help of psychoanalysts.

There is another area of human activity in which psychological factors are clearly of great importance. This area is of much less practical significance to most people than are the grim ones of revolution, the generation gap, and politics in general. Still it is important enough to warrant attention, especially since psychoanalysis has some things to say about it that are both substantial and new. This is the field of art.

What is the role of unconscious mental life in the psychology of art? What part do unconscious mental processes play, first, in the process of artistic creation or performance, and, second, in the process of artistic appreciation; that is, in the activity of the artist on the one hand, and in the activity of the artist's audience on the other? To answer these questions with truly scientific rigor one should apply the psychoanalytic method itself to both artist and audience. It is often possible to do this to a member of the audience who happens to be in a therapeutic analysis, even though a patient's reaction to a work of art is not usually in the center of analytic attention, so to speak. An analyst is often in the position of obtaining frequent glimpses of connections between the unconscious mental life of his patients and their conscious artistic experiences. He less often has the opportunity for a systematic or thorough scrutiny of the relation between the two. One is even less often in the position of analyzing an artist. When the opportunity to do so does present itself, considerations of professional discretion nearly always prevent one from communicating one's findings. It is usually easy for a physician to preserve his patient's anonymity when reporting a case of some physical illness in the professional literature. It is much more difficult to preserve a patient's anonymity in a psychoanalytic case report. If the patient is himself well known, the difficulties are magnified. If the case report is chiefly concerned with the very activities on which the patient's fame rests, the task is an impossible one. It is for this reason that the psychoanalytic literature is so unsatisfactory with respect to the part played in artistic activity by unconscious mental processes. Most authors have limited themselves to the discussion of artists who were never analyzed, basing their conclusions concerning unconscious factors on available biographical and other historical evidence, as Freud did in his pioneer essays on Leonardo da Vinci (1910) and on Goethe (1917b). Other authors have published conclusions which are presumably based in part, at least, on clinical experience with artists, without being able to present the evidence on which their conclusions are based.

Despite these many difficulties, there are some generalizations which have emerged in the course of the years which seem to be both significant and valid. Let us consider first those which have to do with the artist. Of the many fields of art, we shall start with literature.

The relationship between fantasy and literary production is obvious. It was well known, and often remarked on long before the beginnings of psychoanalysis. When psychoanalysis did emerge, one of its early objects of scrutiny was fantasy life, since it appeared that neurotic symptoms are related to fantasy. The attention of psychoanalysts was therefore drawn both to nocturnal fantasies, i.e., to dreams, and to daytime ones, i.e., daydreams. It is the latter which are of particular interest to us at the moment, for it is they which are so obviously related to literary productions.

Because both neurosis and creative writing are related to daydreaming, Freud (1908a) attempted to exploit the connection to throw some light on certain aspects of creative writing. Since his pioneer work it has become abundantly evident that the same unconscious, instinctual wishes and conflicts that play so large a part in the production of dreams and daydreams are equally responsible for literary production. That is to say, a writer fashions his daydreams, his fantasy, into a form which he hopes will be interesting—in the broadest sense, enjoyable—to other people. Daydreaming, in general, is for oneself. Writing, in general, is for an audience. The devices a writer uses to make a story, poem, play, etc., attractive to his audience constitute the craft of the trade, just as skill with brush and chisel are the craft of the painter and sculptor. Such devices vary according to the medium in which he is working (spoken word, written word, etc.), and according to his cultural milieu. Whatever the devices an author may use to adapt a daydream he has to the audience he wishes to reach, the nucleus of his literary production, its starting point and principal content, is his daydream. Whatever one can say about the nature and function of daydreams, whatever has been learned about their psychology, should be important to an understanding of literary production as well.

Daydreams are usually concerned with unfulfilled wishes. A lover daydreams of making love. A child daydreams of being an adult: handsome, accomplished, and successful. A hungry man daydreams of eating a delicious meal, a thirsty one of drinking, a tired one of rest. Examples can easily be multiplied by observing oneself or by questioning others, and no knowledge of psychoanalysis is necessary. If one wants something very much, and if one has the time for reverie, one will daydream that one's wants are satisfied, that one's wishes are fulfilled. Exceptions are not rare in the sense that there are also unpleasant daydreams, even frightening ones, but, in the great majority of daydreams, conscious wishes are consciously gratified. This fact is well known, and, as we have said, is easily confirmed. What psychoanalysis has to add is this. Unconscious wishes are also an important source of daydreams. Whenever, in the course of psychoanalytic treatment, one has an opportunity to analyze a daydream of a patient by applying to the task the psychoanalytic method, one observes that unconscious wishes have played an important part in its formation. Many of the instinctual wishes of childhood remain forever more or less unsatisfied, forever impelling every individual more or less urgently to seek to gratify them, even though the individual himself is unaware of their existence, is ignorant of what it is that he wishes to achieve and to satisfy. Daydreaming is one way of achieving some degree of gratification.

A few examples from clinical practice may be useful. At the beginning of an analytic session an adult, male patient reported a daydream which had occurred a few minutes before, as he was walking toward his analyst's office. He imagined turning the corner and seeing police cars and an ambulance in front of the office entrance. There had been a terrible accident. A patient had become violent and had shot the analyst, who was lying on the floor in a pool of blood. At this point, the daydreamer revised his fantasy. He was in the office himself, grappled with the insane assailant, and was successful in disarming him before he could use his gun.

The daydreamer's associations began with a film he had

seen the night before which was filled with scenes of violence and murder. The film had also contained frankly erotic scenes which had been sexually stimulating to the patient. In one of the scenes a man seduced the widow of someone he himself had murdered. This had been both horrifying and fascinating to the patient. Later he mentioned that one of the characters, an older man, had reminded him of his father. Not that he really looked like him. Just the glasses he wore were like the ones his father had. The patient then went on to speak of how reliable his father had been—how he could always count on him—and from there to his annoyance with his analyst because of disappointment about a change in the schedule of his daily appointments with him.

In this case the daydream expressed the patient's consciously ambivalent feelings for his analyst. He was annoyed at having to change his daily schedule to suit his analyst and felt like telling him to go to hell. At the same time he was ashamed of himself for feeling angry, since he was appreciative of the help he felt he was getting and was generally well disposed toward his analyst. In his daydream, these conscious attitudes were expressed in a form which had obviously been influenced by the film he had seen the night before. That is to say, he gratified his anger by having someone kill his analyst, and his friendly feelings by saving him from death. Guilt over his angry feelings was presumably responsible for the fact that the murder was committed by another patient, rather than by himself, as well as for his exposing himself to danger, in fantasy, by grappling with the assailant.

These motives were all conscious. The patient was readily aware of them. However, they were by no means the whole story. The patient's father had been shot to death in his office by an employee who was mentally ill, at a time when the patient was in early adolescence. He had missed his father very much after the latter's death and had often imagined scenes in which he had been in his father's office, had disarmed his assailant, and had saved his father's life. It seems, therefore, that the patient expressed his unconscious murderous and loving wishes about his father in his daydream, as well as his currently conscious, ambivalent wishes about his analyst. One might say that he unconsciously had identified his analyst with his father, and had transferred to the former some of the feelings and wishes he still harbored unconsciously toward the latter. Moreover, his associations indicate that his transferred wishes were oedipal in origin: a stimulus for the daydream was provided by the sexually exciting scenes of the film he had seen the night before, in which a man murdered another man and later seduced his widow, something which was connected in the patient's mind with thoughts of his own father. In other words, the patient's sexual jealousy of his father, his murderous rage toward him, as well as his remorse, all of them legacies of his childhood, oedipal period, were consciously satisfied in the daydream he had as he walked toward his analyst's office.

The conscious wishes of everyday life vary with everyday circumstances, with daily needs, impressions, and interests. The instinctual wishes of childhood persist essentially unchanged throughout one's life, even though largely unconsciously. The result is that while one's daydreams constantly vary, as one's conscious wishes do, they also remain the same, since they reflect the various facets of unconscious instinctual wishes and conflicts. Thus, the patient referred to above had repeated daydreams, during adolescence, of saving his father's life. His reveries were regularly concerned with parricide. Another patient, during childhood, had recurrent fantasies of being in the army and operating a machine gun. In his daydreams he killed thousands of his imaginary enemies. He also had a "buddy," a beloved comrade, in each daydream, who was always nearly fatally wounded, but rescued by the patient in a heroic, self-sacrificing way. In this case, the military setting was determined by external events: World War II. The patient consciously wished to be grown up and a manly soldier. The unconscious determinants were both more complex and more important. The patient's playmate in real life, his "buddy," was a sister four years younger than himself, who was his mother's darling. His jealous rage encompassed the entire family, but could never be expressed openly. Instead, it found an outlet in fantasies of patriotic slaughter, as well as in various symptoms and inhibitions of competitive activity. It also resulted in his wishing that he himself were a girl. In his childish mind, becoming a girl meant losing his penis, a prospect which caused him intense anxiety. Thus, in his repeated daydreams, it was not he who was a girl, but his sister who had become a man. Moreover, he had a large machine gun in his hands as a further reassurance—a symbolic one—that he had not lost his penis. Finally, to deny most emphatically that he hated his sister and wished her dead, he rescued her in every daydream at the risk of his own life, and tended her wounds with loving care.

How can we apply our knowledge of patients' daydreams to the psychology of artistic literary productions? What conclusions can we draw that are likely to be valid? For one thing, we can be sure that writers are no different from other people with respect to the relationship between their daydreams and their unconscious wishes. Their daydreams, too, must be motivated at least in part by childhood instinctual wishes which are still active in their minds, though they themselves are unaware of them. Because their daydreams are the raw material, so to speak, of what they write, it should be possible, at least in many cases, to infer something of the content of a particular author's childhood wishes, and of his conflicts about them, by reviewing his writings. If one can see not only his published works, but his sketches, notebooks, and preliminary drafts, all the better, for they are even closer to the raw material, to his daydreams themselves.

Sometimes an author's preoccupation with a particular theme, or themes, is so intense that one cannot fail to notice it, and to draw the proper conclusions, once one has learned of the connection of such themes with the unconscious residue of childhood instinctual life. Hemingway, for example, was constantly preoccupied with the theme of virility. Toughness and masculinity characterize his style as well as his plots. From clinical experience we know that when daydreams emphasize virility so insistently, the unconscious fantasies behind them often deal with the danger of castration. Could this have been so for Hemingway? Our guess that it was is at least supported by the fact that in one of his novels the hero had lost part or all of his genitals in battle. For another example, Dostoievsky was constantly occupied with the themes of guilt, remorse, and punishment. Crime and punishment could have been the title for his collected works, as it was, in fact, for one of his greatest novels. One can understand at least part of the reason for his lifelong concern with this theme when one learns that as a boy he witnessed his own father's murder.

Other writers are not as closely bound to a single theme as the ones just mentioned. Their daydreams range over a wider variety of unconscious themes, judging from the writings which derive from them. What is striking, however, is that the basic themes of adult literary art are the same as those we discussed earlier in connection with myths and fairy tales. They derive from the instinctual wishes and conflicts of childhood. However artfully he may disguise the fact, however sophisticatedly he may express himself, and, above all, whatever he himself may consciously believe the purpose of his work to be, a writer is always concerned with presenting to his readers his reactions to his own unconscious wishes, i.e., his daydreams. As a human being he can do nothing else.

The connection between daydreams and artistic productions is as close in other fields of art as in literature, but it is more difficult to identify and to be sure of, as a general thing, when words are not involved in an art form than when they are. If one cannot psychoanalyze the artist himself, one must usually remain in doubt concerning the unconscious determinants of his daydreams. The conscious determinants may be fairly accessible. It is the unconscious ones that are usually hard to get to with any degree of certainty. For that reason the psychoanalytic literature contains many more studies of literary works and literary artists than of those of other art forms.

Those who make up the artists' audiences far outnumber the artists. For this reason alone the unconscious motivations of the audience are more often accessible to direct study by the psychoanalytic method than are those of the artist. It is true, as we said earlier, that a patient's reaction to an artistic production is not usually the principal focus of his associations. Nevertheless, his reaction to a book, film, play, or other performance comes to a patient's mind often enough to justify certain conclusions. For a literary work to have a strong, or, even more, a lasting appeal, its plot must arouse and gratify some important aspect of the unconscious oedipal wishes of the members of its audience. If the work is what we call a tragedy, its plot also conforms to the unconscious fears and self-punitive trends which are so intimately associated with such unconscious instinctual wishes.

The importance of the themes of childhood sexuality in literature was recognized very early by psychoanalysts (Rank, 1912) and has often been confirmed since (Beres, 1951; Wangh, 1968). To be sure, it is only one among the many conditions which are necessary for a literary work to achieve greatness. It does not by any means suffice in itself. Yet it must be met if the work is to have a strong and lasting appeal. Mastery of language, skill in plot construction, portrayal of character, drama, descriptive ability, an ear for dialogue, relevance to the current scene, originality, are all important, but they must be accompanied by a plot that unconsciously gratifies the violent and passionate wishes of childhood if enduring greatness is to be attained.

In some cases one can confirm the correctness of this statement quite simply by reviewing the plot of a great literary work. In Hamlet, one brother murders another and marries his wife, a sexual relationship which the poet explicitly calls incestuous. The murdered brother's son takes revenge by killing his uncle and mother, and is killed himself by his uncle. In Tolstoy's *Anna Karenina*, the heroine leaves her only son and her husband, a man old enough to be her father, in order to live with a young lover. She then ruins her own happiness, drives her lover from her by her behavior, and kills herself. In *The Brothers Karamazov*, the major element of Dostoievsky's plot is punishment for parricide. It seems quite clear that throughout man's life the themes of incest and parricide have an unconscious fascination for him, however he may consciously disguise the fact or even vehemently deny it.

Character traits, identifications, hobbies, choice of vocation, choice of sexual partner, fairy tales, myths, legends, religion, morality, politics, magic, superstition, the conflict between generations, revolution, art—these constitute a broad sample of normal mental functioning. We have attempted to show that in each a considerable part is played by unconscious mental processes which stem from the instinctual wishes of childhood, by the fears, the remorse, and the self-punitive tendencies to which these wishes give rise, and by the psychic conflicts which result from the clash between wish and fear. Hopefully this sample discussion will give an adequate indication of the power, the pervasiveness, and the lasting impact of the instinctual life of early childhood. The wishes themselves persist unconsciously as long as life continues. The conflicts to which they gave rise are acted out over and over again in every area of mental functioning, whether normal or pathological, until life itself comes to an end.

SUGGESTED READING

FREUD, S., Civilization And Its Discontents. *Standard Edition*, 21: 57–145.

KRIS, E., *Psychoanalytic Explorations In Art*. New York: International Universities Press, 1952.

LANGER, W. L., The Next Assignment. Chapter 22 in *Explorations In Crisis*. Schorske, C. E., & Schorske, E., eds. Cambridge, Mass.: Harvard University Press, 1969.

CHAPTER X

PSYCHOANALYSIS TODAY

This final chapter is partly a survey, partly a summary, partly a glance at the future. It may serve to stimulate in the reader some thoughts concerning the place of psychoanalysis in the world today, to give an idea of its contribution to the scene which we think of as "the present." It is also intended to convey some indication of the possible role to be played by psychoanalysis in the future. As such, it is to a greater extent than any of the previous chapters an expression of the personal bias of the author. It necessarily reflects more of his individual experience and his personal outlook than do any of the others.

Every scientific discovery changes the world. Some change it more, some less, but the world is never quite the same after a scientific advance as it was before. Sometimes the effect of a discovery is a practical one, like the invention of an efficient steam engine, which made possible the industrial revolution of the nineteenth century. Sometimes the effect is rather on the world of ideas, on man's view of himself and of the universe, rather than on his material surroundings. In the case of psychoanalysis, the effect has been significant in both respects: practically, as a method of therapy, and, in addition, as a source of information to man "about what concerns human beings most of all—about their own nature" (Freud, 1933, pp. 156–157).

Even earlier, in commenting on the effect of psychoanalysis on the world of ideas, Freud (1917b) had compared the discovery of psychoanalysis to the introduction of the theories of Copernicus and of Darwin, whose *Origin of Species*, incidentally, was published in the year that Freud was born. The heliocentric theory of Copernicus showed that our world is not the center of creation, but is merely one of several planets which revolve about the sun. The theory of evolution similarly puts us in our proper place, biologically speaking. We were not created specially to rule the world, as the Bible maintains. We are one among the millions of species that have evolved since the first protein molecules were somehow formed several hundred million years ago. Psychoanalysis, as Freud put it, tells us that we are not even masters in our own minds. We are swayed, even directed, by unconscious mental processes, by wishes, by fears, by conflicts, and by fantasies whose very existence was not even suspected before psychoanalysis was discovered.

It is common knowledge that any such major challenge to accepted belief tends to make most people uneasy. The majority of mankind are not happy to have the ideas with which they are comfortable so rudely upset. They fight against changes for that reason. As we would expect from what has been said earlier, they defend themselves against new ideas in order to avoid or to minimize the mental discomfort, the unpleasure associated with the prospect of change. It would be interesting to speculate concerning the unconscious fears which are associated with such changes, but this is not the place for such a discussion. Freud himself, in the work referred to above, emphasized the role of narcissism. When one's feeling of importance is wounded or threatened, he said, unpleasure results. Unconscious feelings of inferiority and helplessness dating from childhood are stirred up, with all the conflicts to which they give rise.

By now, however, psychoanalysis is no longer so new. The novelty is wearing off, as has long since happened with respect to evolution and to the nature of the solar system.

When one grows up accepting the validity of the ideas of Darwin and Copernicus, they become possible sources of pleasure rather than of unpleasure, as they were when they were first proposed. To learn something of the origin of species, something of the nature and size of the universe, is exciting and gratifying for most individuals, as witness the wide appeal of popular scientific books and articles. Again one may speculate concerning the unconscious wishes which are being gratified, and about their origins in childhood. Once more, however, we must content ourselves with alluding to the problems involved and forego discussing them.

The point we wish to make here is that a knowledge of psychoanalysis such as this book has attempted to convey results in the same sort of broadened horizon as does a similar understanding of the fundamentally important theories of the physical and biological sciences. The latter open our minds to the nature of the world about us. The world is never the same to us once we have studied chemistry or physics or biology or astronomy or geology. The tides on a beach, the ice on a pond, the earth and rocks under our feet, as well as the Milky Way above our heads, are all new and different afterward from what they were before. In the same way psychoanalysis enables us to understand more about the people around us than we could before. It gives us a new dimension in our view of the world of human beings like ourselves.

By its discoveries, psychoanalysis enables us to have a more accurate, a fuller, a more rounded picture of man's mental life and behavior—of man as a person. From physics we know that no physical object is what it seems to be to our unaided senses. We know that even our own bodies are not continuous solid structures, but, like all other solid objects, are a discontinuous conglomerate of countless millions of molecules, each in turn made up of atoms, electrons, and nuclear particles, all in constant, rapid motion. In just the same way we know from psychoanalysis that every thought and every action is far more complexly determined than anyone imagined them to be before Freud devised the psychoanalytic method of investigation. We know that whatever we do or think is shaped in part by the forces of the id, i.e., by the legacy of the instinctual wishes of childhood, in part by defenses against those wishes (the ego), in part by moral demands (superego), and in part by the exigencies imposed by our current external circumstances, as well as by the opportunities for gratification which they offer. With a knowledge of psychoanalysis one can see how great is the role played in human motivation by the drives and by the conflicts to which they give rise. Kris (1947) wrote that psychoanalysis is human behavior viewed as conflict—a thoroughly psychoanalytic epigram which expresses a profound insight into man's nature. Man is a creature whose animal appetites, shaped by the experiences of childhood, constitute the main motivations that drive him to action throughout his life. The drives, the ego functions which act as their executants or as defenses against them, anxiety, guilt, conflict, and the great role played by unconscious processes in mental life, are all parts of the psychoanalytic perspective on man. It is a perspective which is incomparably the most comprehensive one available at present. What the future may bring in the way of new means of study of human psychology is something at which one can only guess. So far, the method of psychoanalysis has been the best one available. The results it has yielded leave many questions unanswered and many others in doubt, it is true, yet its application has thrown much light on areas of human psychology that were previously wholly obscure. It has made the first substantial beginning toward a better understanding of the problems of psychology which are of major importance to man himself. We know a good deal more about ourselves and our fellow men now than we did before Freud's psychological researches began.

What are the future prospects for psychoanalysis? What areas are still unexplored, or currently in dispute among psychoanalysts themselves? What are the currently active areas of investigation by psychoanalysts?

It is always risky to forecast future prospects in a field of science. At the moment one is writing, some new development, some unexpected discovery may be under way that is to influence the whole course of events in a wholly unexpected and unpredictable way. Such a possibility is inherent in the very nature of scientific endeavor. Its horizons are constantly expanding. Most scientists believe that they always will, that science is an endless quest, a ceaseless exploration. Perhaps they are right in their belief, though the words "endless" and "ceaseless" imply infinity, a concept which is very difficult indeed to come to grips with in any sort of personal way. One thing is very likely, however. The end of new discoveries in science won't come for a very long time. As yet, man's efforts have but scratched the surface of the world he is part of, the world in which he lives and which includes himself. It is most unlikely that his quest to understand it will be completed soon.

Bearing in mind then the risk involved in attempting to make any prediction, what can one suggest with regard to the future of psychoanalysis?

At present, interest in psychoanalysis is expanding. In the United States, for example, there are ten times as many trained psychoanalysts as there were in 1940; twenty times as many as in 1930. Still, the total number is small. The roster of the American Psychoanalytic Association in 1971 listed 1,332 members, not a large number for a country with more than two hundred-million inhabitants. The fact is that in 1930 there were but a handful of psychoanalysts in the entire world, and most of those were in Vienna, Berlin, New York, and London. Today there are a growing number of psychoanalysts who are practising professionally in most countries of Latin America and Western Europe, as well as in Canada, the United States, Australia, Israel, India, and Japan. There are important centers of psychoanalytic education, practice and research from Tel Aviv to Oslo and from Buenos Aires to Montreal. It seems likely that the current interest in psychoanalysis on the part of psychiatrists and associated workers in the field of mental health will continue to grow for some time. A knowledge of the fundamentals of psychoanalysis is essential to the rational practice of any form of psychotherapy. Without it, one is working in the dark on a hit or miss basis. In addition, if a person is to practice psychotherapy, he is well advised to learn as much as possible about his own psychic conflicts. Without a thorough knowledge of himself, without a satisfactory resolution of his own principal mental conflicts, he is liable to react to his patients' conflicts, to their unconscious wishes and fears, in ways that are difficult or impossible for him to control and that may at times be detrimental to his patients. What this means is that in most cases persons who wish to practice psychotherapy should themselves be psychoanalyzed. A personal psychoanalysis is always a valuable addition to one's training. Often it is an essential one.

In the recent past there has been growing awareness of the importance of psychotherapy as a method of treatment with a corresponding growth in its application. If this trend continues, one may feel safe in predicting a continuing growth in the teaching and practice of psychoanalysis as well. As long as any form of psychotherapy is widely practiced, psychoanalysis will play an important role, both as therapy and as source of knowledge.

The importance of psychoanalysis extends much farther than the field of mental illness, however. As we attempted to show in some detail in the previous chapter, psychoanalysis has much to say about many aspects of normal mental life as well. The fact is that psychoanalysis can supply to those whose interest lies in any of the social or behavioral sciences, as well as to specialists in law and students of art or literature, a more accurate knowledge of the mind of man than is available from any other source—a knowledge of his needs, his fears, his conflicts, and his motives as they develop in the course of childhood and as they function in maturity. This knowledge is understandably valuable to professionals in any of the fields just mentioned, although its value is only beginning to be recognized by them. Those who have begun to apply the findings of psychoanalysis to their own related fields of interest are still pioneers. One can anticipate a very considerable increase in this direction. Hopefully the time will come when a knowledge of psychoanalysis will be recognized to be a proper part of the education of a professional in any field that deals with man and his works.

These are the prospects for the future course of the development of psychoanalysis, as far as one can judge at present. It is interesting that psychoanalysis has found little acceptance in the Soviet Union or in those countries allied to it. It is not easy to understand completely why this should be so. It is true that Freud himself once wrote a few words expressing some scepticism concerning the likelihood that communism would be successful in altering human nature so that men would become less competitive with and hostile to one another. Those sentences seem unlikely to be the real basis, however, for the fact that the countries in question have officially adopted an attitude of indifference or outright hostility to psychoanalysis. In fact Freud was never openly hostile to the political and economic ideas of Marx, and many psychoanalysts in the 1920's were active Marxists. Neither does it seem likely that the antagonism to psychology of any sort which was such a special personal characteristic of the great Russian neurophysiologist, Pavlov, could have had such a lasting, widespread effect. In the absence of any satisfactory explanatory data, one can only recall that about

1950, Soviet politicians considered themselves competent to decide between theories of genetics and ended up by endorsing those of Lysenko. A number of years later the error was repaired, but only after the political leadership of the country had moved to other hands. Perhaps something similarly unfortunate has taken place with respect to psychoanalysis. If so, the error has yet to be repaired.

Now for a few words about current areas of particular interest within the field of psychoanalysis itself. The principal areas of interest continue to be clinical practice and psychoanalytic education, i.e., the training of analysts for clinical practice. The great majority of psychoanalysts are principally concerned in improving their own skill in the application of the psychoanalytic method itself and in making more precise the formulations concerning mental functioning and mental development which derive principally from the data of clinical observations. Their chief interest is how to better understand and to better treat those who come to them for help. Their secondary, closely related interest, is to assist those who wish to practice analysis themselves in acquiring the knowledge and experience which is necessary for them to be able to do so.

In addition to these major areas of interest there are other areas which deserve mention. Increasing attention is being paid to the psychoanalytic education of professionals in fields related to psychoanalysis, particularly by the institutes for psychoanalytic education in the United States and in the German Federal Republic. As yet, however, such programs are still in an early stage of development. As indicated earlier, this is an area of activity which one may expect to increase considerably in the future.

Another area which has occupied the energies of a small group of psychoanalysts in recent years and which has attracted the interest of many more is that of child development. Psychoanalysts engaged in observing the behavior of small children in specially developed nurseries have made substantial contributions to knowledge of the psychology of the early years of life. Some of these contributions have already had an influence on the psychoanalytic treatment both of children and of adults. The centers for work of this sort are in London and in a few cities in the United States. It is work that is extremely time consuming, since it so often involves observing a child and its family over a period of many years.

Closely related to the interest of analysts in child development is the increasing attention which psychoanalysts have paid in recent years to the role played in a child's mental development by the treatment it receives during the first two years of its life by the adults responsible for its care. Our knowledge on this subject is as yet not extensive enough to justify any sort of final formulations. It seems likely that as knowledge does accumulate it will throw considerable light on some vexing problems which are still obscure. For example, we know that the oedipal phase (roughly two-and-a-half to six years) is a time of difficulty and turmoil for every child. It is a crucially important time in his psychological development. What happens to a child in those years affects its later development, both normal and pathological, and persists throughout all the years that follow. Why is it that oedipal conflicts, though present in every child, are so much more unfavorable in their consequences for some children than for others? Why do they leave some children psychological cripples for the rest of their lives, while others are affected only to the degree that we consider to be normal?

Often the answer to this question seems to be furnished by the events of the oedipal period itself, by sexual experiences, by frightening events, by death or desertion, by physical illness, and so on. This is not always the case, however, and very early in his work Freud pointed to the importance of factors which he termed constitutional, as distinguished from experiential factors such as those just mentioned. In addition to such constitutional factors, it seems likely that what has happened in a child's life during the first two years plays an important role in determining how he will react to the stressful events of the next three or four. It may be that as evidence accumulates concerning the role which is played during the earliest years of life by the way the adults who care for it treat a child—by the "quality of mothering" the child receives—it will be possible to understand better the reasons why one child is affected so much more unfavorably than another by the psychological stresses of the oedipal period.

No doubt other valuable contributions will be made by current and future psychoanalytic studies of the first two years of life, contributions which will be useful in practical ways to those directly concerned with child care.

Every psychoanalysis is, among other things, a study of the life history of an individual. It is a search for the chief events of that life, of their connections with one another, and of both their psychological causes and their psychological consequences. The history that emerges from an individual psychoanalysis bears little resemblance, it is true, to the type of personal history we call a literary biography, and even less to an obituary or panegyric. It deals less with the parts of a life most visible to the world at large than do biographies and obituaries. Its main concern is rather with those parts of his life which every man keeps concealed, not only from those about him, but from himself as well. It is the story of the hidden forces and events which underlie the visible circumstances of every man's life, which determine them, and which give them the shape and the sequence that we recognize as human.

Their very profession, therefore, makes historians of psychoanalysts and, to some extent at least, of all who become acquainted with what psychoanalysis has to say of the mind and behavior of man. In this chapter we have tried, as historians often do, to predict the future from what we know of the past and of the present. Interesting as such predictions may be, however, they can never match the fascination of seeing what really happens, of watching the future itself unfold as it becomes the present, and of learning from it more of the past than we could know or guess when it was itself the present.

REFERENCES

ARLOW, J. A. (1949), Anal sensations and feelings of persecution. *Psychoanal. Quart.*, Vol. 18, pp. 79–84.

—— and BRENNER, C. (1964), *Psychoanalytic Concepts and the Structural Theory.* New York: International Universities Press.

BERES, D. (1951), A dream, a vision, and a poem: a psychoanalytic study of *The Rime of the Ancient Mariner. Internat. J. Psycho-Anal.*, Vol. 32, pp. 97–116.

—— and OBERS, S. J. (1950), The effects of extreme deprivation in infancy on psychic structure in adolescence: a study in ego development. *The Psychoanalytic Study of the Child*, Vol. 5, pp. 212–235. New York: International Universities Press.

BIBRING, E. (1941), The development and problems of the theory of the instincts. *Internat. J. Psycho-Anal.*, Vol. 22, pp. 102–131.

BLAU, A. (1952), In support of Freud's syndrome of anxiety (actual) neurosis. *Internat. J. Psycho-Anal.*, Vol. 33, pp. 363–372.

BREUER, J. & FREUD, S. (1895), Studies on Hysteria. *The Standard Edition of the Complete Psychological Works of Sigmund Freud*, Vol. 2, pp. 1–305. London: Hogarth Press, 1955.

DEUTSCH, H. (1933), *Psychoanalysis of the Neuroses.* New York: Anglo-books, 1952.

—— (1934), "*Über einen Typus der Pseudoaffektivität—als ob.*" *Internationale Zeitschrift für Psychoanalyse*, Vol. 20, pp. 323–335.

—— (1942), Some forms of emotional disturbances and their relationship to schizophrenia. In: *Yearbook of Psychoanalysis*, Vol. 1, pp. 121–136. Edited by S. Lorand. New York: International Universities Press.

EIDELBERG, L. (1948), *Studies in Psychoanalysis.* New York: International Universities Press, 1952, Chap. 14 & 15.

FENICHEL, O. (1939), *Problems of Psychoanalytic Technique.* New York: The Psychoanalytic Quarterly, Inc., 1941, p. 67.

—— (1945), *The Psychoanalytic Theory of the Neuroses.* New York: Norton.

FREUD, A. (1936), *The Ego and the Mechanisms of Defense. The Writings of Anna Freud*, Vol. 2. New York: International Universities Press, 1966.

—— (1954a), Problems of infantile neurosis. *Ibid.*, Vol. 4, pp. 327–355. New York: International Universities Press, 1968.

—— (1945b), The widening scope of indications for psycho-analysis. *Ibid.*, pp. 356–376.

—— (1965), *Normality and Pathology in Childhood. Ibid.*, Vol. 6, pp. 100–107. New York: International Universities Press.

FREUD, S. (1894), The neuro-psychoses of defence.* Vol. 3, pp. 43–61, 1962.

—— (1895), On the grounds for detaching a particular syndrome from neurasthenia under the description "anxiety neurosis." *Ibid.*, pp. 87–117.

—— (1896), Further remarks on the neuro-psychoses of defence. *Ibid.*, pp. 159–185.

—— (1898), Sexuality in the aetiology of the neuroses. *Ibid.*, pp. 261–285.

—— (1900), The interpretation of dreams. Vols. 4 & 5, 1953.

—— (1904), The psychopathology of everyday life. Vol. 6, 1960.

—— (1905a), Jokes and their relation to the theory of the unconscious. Vol. 8, 1960.

—— (1905b), Three essays on the theory of sexuality. Vol. 7, pp. 125–243, 1953.

—— (1905c), Fragment of an analysis of a case of hysteria. *Ibid.*, pp. 3–122.

—— (1906), My views on the part played by sexuality in the aetiology of the neuroses. *Ibid.*, pp. 269–279.

—— (1908a), Character and anal erotism. Vol. 9, pp. 168–175, 1959.

—— (1908b), Creative writers and day-dreaming. *Ibid.*, pp. 141–153.

—— (1910), Leonardo da Vinci and a memory of his childhood. Vol. 11, pp. 59–137, 1957.

—— (1911), Formulations on the two principles of mental functioning. Vol. 12, pp. 215–226, 1958.

—— (1913), A note on the unconscious in psycho-analysis. *Ibid.*, pp. 257–266.

—— (1914), On narcissism: an introduction. Vol. 14, pp. 69–102, 1957.

—— (1915a), Instincts and their vicissitudes. *Ibid.*, pp. 111–140.

—— (1915b), Repression. *Ibid.*, pp. 143–158.

—— (1915c), The unconscious. *Ibid.*, pp. 161–215.

—— (1916a), Mourning and melancholia. *Ibid.*, pp. 239–258.

—— (1916b), A metapsychological supplement to the theory of dreams. *Ibid.*, pp. 219–235.

—— (1916c), Some character-types met with in psycho-analytic work, *Ibid.*, pp. 310–333.

* All references to Sigmund Freud are to *The Standard Edition of the Complete Psychological Works of Sigmund Freud*, Volumes I–XXIII. London: Hogarth Press.

——— (1917a), Introductory lectures on psycho-analysis. Vols. 15 & 16, 1963.

——— (1917b), A difficulty in the path of psycho-analysis. Vol. 17, pp. 137–144, 1955.

——— (1917c), A childhood recollection from *Dichtung und Wahrheit. Ibid.*, pp. 146–156.

——— (1920), Beyond the pleasure principle. Vol. 18, pp. 3–64, 1955.

——— (1921), Group psychology and the analysis of the ego. *Ibid.*, pp. 67–143.

——— (1923), The ego and the id. Vol. 19, pp. 3–66, 1961.

——— (1924a), The passing of the Oedipus-complex. *Ibid.*, pp. 172–179.

——— (1924b), The loss of reality in neurosis and psychosis. *Ibid.*, pp. 183–187.

——— (1924c), The economic problem of masochism. *Ibid.*, pp. 157–170.

——— (1924d), Neurosis and psychosis. *Ibid.*, pp. 148–153.

——— (1925), An autobiographical study. Vol. 20. pp. 3–74, 1959.

——— (1926), Inhibition, symptoms and anxiety. *Ibid.*, pp. 77–174.

——— (1933), New introductory lectures on psychoanalysis. Vol. 22, pp. 3–182, 1964.

——— (1937), Analysis terminable and interminable. Vol. 23, pp. 211–253, 1964.

——— (1954), *The Origins of Psychoanalysis.* Edited by M. Bonaparte, A. Freud, & E. Kris. New York: Basic Books.

FRIES, M. E. & WOOLF, P. J. (1953), Some hypotheses on the role of the congenital activity type in personality development. *The Psychoanalytic Study of the Child*, Vol. 8, pp. 48–62. New York: International Universities Press.

HARTMANN, H. (1948), Comments on the psychoanalytic theory of instinctual drives. In: *Essays on Ego Psychology*, New York: International Universities Press, 1964, pp. 69–89.

——— (1953a), The metapsychology of schizophrenia. In: *Ibid.*, pp. 182–206.

——— (1953b), Remarks in discussion. Meeting of the New York Psychoanalytic Society.

——— & KRIS, E. (1945), The genetic approach in psychoanalysis. *The Psychoanalytic Study of the Child*, Vol. 1, pp. 11–30. New York: International Universities Press.

——— ———, & LOEWENSTEIN, R. M. (1946), Comments on the formation of psychic structure. *Ibid.*, Vol. 2, pp. 11–38.

——— ———, (1949), Notes on the theory of aggression. *Ibid.*, Vol. 3/4, pp. 9–36.

HOFFER, W. (1950), Development of the body ego. *Ibid.*, Vol. 5, pp. 18–23.

ISAKOWER, O. (1954), Spoken words in dreams. *Psychoanal. Quart.*, Vol. 23, pp. 1–6.

JACOBSON, E. (1953), The affects and their pleasure-unpleasure qualities in relation to the psychic discharge processes. In: *Drives, Affects, and Behavior*, Vol. 1. pp. 38–66. Edited by R. M. Loewenstein. New York: International Universities Press.

JONES, E. (1931), *On the Nightmare*. New York: Liveright, 1951.

KRIS, E. (1947), The nature of psychoanalytic propositions and their validation. In: *Psychological Theory*, edited by M. H. Marx. New York: Macmillan, 1951.

―――― (1952), *Psychoanalytic Explorations in Art*. New York: International Universities Press, Chap. 14.

―――― (1954), *The Origins of Psychoanalysis*. New York: Basic Books, pp. 3–47.

RANK, O., (1912), *Das Inzest-Motiv in Dichtung und Sage*. Leipzig, Vienna: Deuticke, 1926.

―――― (1924), *The Trauma of Birth*. New York: Robert Brunner, 1952.

RAPAPORT, D., ed. (1951), *Organization and Pathology of Thought*. New York: Columbia University Press.

RÓHEIM, G. (1950), *Psychoanalysis and Anthropology*. New York: International Universities Press, 1970.

SACHS, H. (1942), *The Creative Unconscious*. Cambridge, Mass.: Sci-Art Publishers, 1942.

SPITZ, R. A. (1945), Hospitalism. *The Psychoanalytic Study of the Child*, Vol. 1, pp. 53–74. New York: International Universities Press.

STÄRCKE, A. (1920), The reversal of the libido sign in delusions of persecution. *Internat. J. Psycho-Anal.*, Vol. 1, pp. 231–234.

VON OPHUIJSEN, J. H. W. (1920), On the origin of feelings of persecution. *Ibid.*, pp. 235–239.

WANGH, M. (1968), A psychoanalytic commentary on Shakespeare's "The Tragedie of the Second" King Richard. *Psychoanal. Quart.*, Vol. 36, pp. 212–238.

INDEX

Accident, *see* Parapraxes
Addiction, 209
Affect
  as ego function, 42, 73, 79
  in dreams, 178 ff.
  isolation, 96 ff.
Aggression, 22
  see also Drive, aggressive, Energy,
    aggressive
Alcohol
  addiction, 209
  intoxication, 89
Alexander the Great, 233
Ambivalence, 110 ff.
  and reaction formation, 92
Anality, *see* Drives; Object relations
Animism, 237
Anxiety, 72, 75 ff.
  and dreams, 178 ff.
  and parapraxes, 140
  and symptoms, 203 ff.
Apparatus, psychic, Chapters III, IV,
  V.
Arlow, Jacob A., 38, 101, 184, 271
Art, 248-249; 254-257
  see Daydreams
"As if" personality, 111
Astrology, 241-242
Atheism, 232
Autoerotism, 30, 121
  see also Masturbation
Autonomy, *see* Ego, autonomy
Avocation, 216-217

Beres, David, 111, 256, 271
Bernheim, H. M., 8
Bibring, Edward, 20, 271
Birth
  and anxiety, 78
  as trauma, 78
Bisexuality, 125
Blau, A., 271

Body, *see* Autoerotism; Ego and body
Brenner, Charles, 38, 184
Breuer, Joseph, 7 ff., 186, 190, 271

Castration
  anxiety, 84, 118 ff., 124
  in parapraxis, 146 ff.
Cathexis, 19 ff.
  and countercathexis, 88 ff.
  and identification, 47
  and narcissism, 107 ff.
  and secondary process, 51
  mobility and primary process, 50
  see also Discharge; Fixation
Causality, psychic, *see* Determinism,
  psychic
Character neurosis, 200 ff.
  see also Psychopathology
Character traits, 211-215
Charcot, Jean-Martin, 7
Christian Science, 6
Compromise formation
  in dreams, 176 ff.
  in symptoms, 201 ff.
Condensation, 56
  in dreams, 173
Conflict
  and ambivalence, 110
  and instinctualization, 60
  and neutralization, 60
  and psychopathology, 190 ff., 195,
    201 ff.
  between ego and id, 41, 68 ff., 140,
    201 ff.
  between ego and superego, 135 ff.,
    140
Conscience, *see* Superego
Conscious as mental system, 36
Consciousness, 1
Continuity, psychic, 2
Control, motor, as ego function, 42,
  62

Copernicus, N., 260-261
Countercathexis, 88 ff.
  and parapraxis, 140
  and wit, 160 ff.

Danger and anxiety, 78 ff., 81 ff.
Darwin, C., 260-261
Daydreams, 249-254
  see Art
Delirium, 89
Defense, 87 ff.
  see also Defense mechanisms
Defense mechanisms, 87 ff., 190
  against superego, 134 ff., 140
  and Oedipus complex, 119
  and superego, 130 ff.
  in dreams, 174 ff., 82 ff.
Defense neuropsychoses, 190
Dementia praecox, see Psychopathology
Deneutralization, 60
Denial, 103 ff.
Depression
  and identification with lost object, 48
  see also Psychopathology
Destrudo, 22
Determinism, psychic, Chapter I; 33
Deutsch, Helene, 111, 271
Discharge
  and neutralization, 57
  and primary process, 49 ff.
  and secondary process, 51
  and wit, 158 ff.
  control by ego, 66 ff.
  in dreams, 170, 173
  in symptoms, 202
  see also Cathexis; Energy, psychic; Gratification
Discontinuity, psychic, 2
Displacement, 56 ff.
Dostoievsky, F., 257
Dream work, 163
Dreams, Chapter VII
  and psychic determinism, 3
  and psychoneurosis, 194
  and repression, 88
  and unconscious mental processes, 11
Drive, aggressive
  and pleasure, 31 ff.

and narcissism, 108
  see also Drives
Drive, self-preservative, 20-21
Drive, sexual
  and narcissism, 107 ff.
  and pleasure, 31-32
  see also Drives; Libido
Drives, Chapter II
  and automatic anxiety, 79 ff.
  and object relations, 112-113
  and psychopathology, 196-197
  control, 196
  see also Id

Ego
  acquisition of energy from id, 69 ff.
  acquisition of energy by neutralization, 57 ff., 70
  and affects, 73, 79
  and anxiety, 79 ff.
  and body, 43 ff.
  and dreams, 165, 174 ff., 183
  and narcissism, 108
  and parapraxes, 152-153
  and primary process, 49-50
  and secondary process, 49-50
  and sublimation, 104-105
  and superego, 124-125, 140
  and symptoms, 201 ff.
  and wit, 160-161
  autonomy, 60
  boundaries, 65
  conflict with id, 41, 67 ff., 140, 201 ff.
  defense mechanisms, 87 ff., 200 ff.
  defense operations, 86, 200 ff.
  depletion by repression, 90 ff.
  executant for drives, 41, 66
  factors in development, 42 ff., 195 ff., 197
  functions, 41 ff., 62
  inhibition, 197 ff., 201
  integrative functions, 152 ff.
  regression, 55-56
  relations to environment, 40 ff., 62 ff.
  time of development, 39
Eidelberg, Ludwig, 271
Emotion, see Affect
Energy, aggressive, 22
  and severity of superego, 127 ff.

Energy, psychic, 18 ff.
  and primary process, 49 ff.
  and secondary process, 49 ff.
  at puberty, 89
  available to ego, 58
  distribution between ego and id, 70 ff.
  expenditure in repression, 91
  neutralization, 58
  nomenclature, 22
Energy, sexual, *see* Libido
Environment, *see* Ego, relation to environment
Erb, W. H., 7
Erotism, *see* Drives
Exhibitionism, 27

Fairy tales, 222-224
Fantasy
  and denial, 98
  and dreams, 168 ff.
  and gratification, 71
  and identification, 47, 102
  and parapraxes, 150
  and psychoneurosis, 194, 203 ff.
  and reaction formation, 92-93
  and reality testing, 65
  and repression, 88, 91
  and signal anxiety, 83
  and superego, 133
  and wit, 158
  masturbatory, 121
  oedipal, 115 ff.
Feeling, *see* Affect
Fenichel, Otto, 136, 189, 209, 271
Fixation
  ego, 198 ff.
  libidinal, 28 ff., 85 ff., 198 ff.
Forgetting
  and defense, 96
  and repression, 88
  see also Parapraxes
Fortune telling, 241-242
Freud, Anna, 30, 67, 87, 96, 98, 99, 105, 117, 271
Freud, Sigmund, *passim*
Fries, Margaret E., 192, 273
Frustration
  and failure of repression, 89
  and reality testing, 64
  excessive, 196

Galileo, 8, 231
Generations, conflict of, 243-244
  see also Revolution
Generation gap, *see* Generations, conflict of
Genital phase, *see* Drives
God; Gods, *see* Religion, Myths
Goethe, 249
Gratification
  and discharge of psychic energy, 74 ff.
  and ego control, 67
  and infantile ego, 40 ff.
  and object relations, 108 ff.
  and primary process, 50
  and sublimation, 104
  by fantasy, 71
  defensive, 87, 208
  dependence on parents, 69, 78-79
  excessive, 196
  in dreams, 170
Group psychology, 136
Guilt
  and anxiety, 84-85
  and parapraxes, 140
  and symptoms, 202 ff.

Hallucinations, 66, 182
Hamlet, 257
Hartmann, Heinz, 17, 32, 39n, 42, 51, 58, 59, 60, 111, 273
Hate
  and reaction formation, 92
  in early object relations, 110
  oedipal, 114 ff.
Hemingway, Ernest, 255
Hering-Breuer reflex, 7
Hoffer, Willi, 43, 273
Homeopathy, 6
Huxley, Aldous, 6
Hypnosis, 7-8, 186
Hysteria, 186 ff., 190, 191

Id, 38 ff.
  accretion by repression, 90 ff.
  and anxiety, 79 ff.
  and character structure, 199
  and dreams, 165 ff., 169
  and parapraxes, 140 ff.
  and primary process, 49
  and superego, 126 ff.

Id (*continued*)
 and symptoms, 206
 conflict with ego, 41
 loss of energy to ego, 69
 see also Drives
Identification, 44 ff.
 and ego development, 71 ff., 196,
  201
 and reaction formation, 95
 and superego formation, 124 ff.
 and turning against self, 101
 as defense, 102 ff.
 postoedipal, 130, 136-137
 with libidinally cathected objects,
  110, 215-217
Incest, 224, 226
 see also Oedipus complex
Incorporation, 102 ff.
Inferiority feelings, 131
Inhibition, *see* Ego, inhibition
Instincts, *see* Drives, esp. 17
Instinctualization, 60
Introjection, 102 ff.
Isakower, Otto, 125, 274
Isolation, 96

Jacobson, Edith, 75, 274
Jones, Ernest, 179, 274

Klein, Melanie, 39 n
Kris, Ernst, 30, 32, 39 n, 42, 58, 59, 60,
 156, 273, 274

Langer, W. L., 258
Language
 and identification, 45
 and neutralization, 59
 and primary process, 55
 and superego, 125
Latent dream, 163 ff.
Leonardo da Vinci, 249
Lex talionis, 132 ff.
Libido, 22
 detachment, 28-29
 fixation, 29 ff., 85 ff., 199 ff.
 regression, 29 ff.
 transformation into anxiety, 75 ff.,
  81-82
 usage, 32
Loewenstein, Rudolph M., 32, 39 n,
 58, 59, 60, 273

Love
 and anxiety, 84-85
 and reaction formation, 92
 in early object relations, 110
 loss, 84 ff.
 oedipal, 114 ff.

Magic, 235-237
 see also Thought, magical
Manifest dream, 163 ff.
Masturbation
 and neurasthenia, 187
 oedipal, 121
Marxism, 265
Maturation
 and ego development, 42 ff.
 and reality testing, 63
Memory
 and repression, 88
 and signal anxiety, 83
 as ego function, 42 ff.
Mental illness, *see* Psychopathology
Morality
 and religion, 229-231
Myths, 224-228

Narcissism, 106 ff.
 and scientific discoveries, 260-261
 and superego formation, 126 ff., 129
Naturopathy, 6
Neurasthenia, 187
Neurosis
 actual, 80 ff., 189 ff.
 anxiety, 80 ff., 187 ff.
 traumatic, 81 ff.
 see also Psychoneurosis
Neutralization, 58 ff.

Obers, Samuel J., 111, 271
Object (relations), 106 ff.
 cathexis and identification, 46 ff.
 loss and anxiety, 84
 loss and identification, 48 ff.
Object choice, adult, 219-221
Obsession
 and isolation, 96 ff.
 and undoing, 97 ff.
 as psychoneurosis, 188, 190
 etiology, 191, 192

Oedipus
  myth of, 224-225
Oedipus complex, 114 ff., 224-225,
  Chapter IX *passim*
  and dreams, 166, 176, 179
  and psychoneuroses, 202
  in parapraxes, 150
Orality, *see* Drives; Object
Omens, 241-242
Omnipotence
  of thought, 236
  parental, 227

Parapraxes, Chapter VI
  and psychic determinism, 2
  and unconscious mental processes,
    12 ff.
Parenticide, *see* Oedipus complex
Parricide, Chapter IX *passim*
Partner, sexual, *see* Object choice,
  adult
Pasteur, Louis, 8
Pavlov, I., 265
Penis envy, 119
Perception, sensory
  and latent dream, 164 ff.
  and signal anxiety, 83
  as ego function, 42, 61
Perversions, sexual, 25, 193 ff., 208
Phallic phase, *see* Drives; Oedipus
  complex
Play
  and denial, 99
  and sublimation, 104
Pleasure principle, 72 ff.
  and signal anxiety, 83
Politics, 232-235; *see also* Revolution
  and atheism, 232
Preconscious, 9, 35 ff.
Pregenital, 112
  see also Drives; Object
Preoedipal, *see* Drives; Object; Oed-
  ipus complex
Prephallic, *see* Drives; Object
Primary gain, 205
Primary process, 49 ff.
  and dreams, 171 ff.
  and parapraxes, 145
  and pleasure principle, 72 ff.
  and wit, 154
Projection, 99 ff.

Psychoanalysis, 263-265
  current developments in, 266-268
  future of, Chapter X, *passim*
Psychoneurosis, 188, 189 ff., 201 ff.
Psychopathology, Chapter VIII
  and anxiety, 75 ff., 85
  and dreams, 163, 182
  and early object relations, 111
  and failure of defense, 91
  and oedipus complex, 114 ff.
  and primary process thinking, 53 ff.
  and psychic determinism, 3
  and reality testing, 66
  and unconscious mental processes,
    3, 14
Puberty, 89 ff.

Rank, Otto, 78, 256
Rapaport, David, 42, 61, 214
Reaction formation, 92 ff.
Reality, sense of, *see* Reality testing
Reality testing, 62 ff.
  and denial, 100
  and dreams, 183
  and object relations, 111
  and projection, 101
Regression
  and instinctualization, 60
  as defense, 103, 199 ff., 201, 207
  ego, 55
  libidinal, 29 ff.
Re-instinctualization, 60
Religion, 226-235
Repression, 88 ff.
  and dreams, 163, 167, 179 ff.
  and oedipus complex. 118
  and parapraxes, 139 ff.
  escape from, 150 ff., 179 ff.
  failure, 193 ff., 201 ff.
Revolution, 244-248
Ritual, 98
Róheim, Géza, 115, 274

Schizophrenia, *see* Psychopathology
Secondary elaboration, 53, 181
Secondary gain, 206
Secondary process, 49 ff.
  and neutralization, 58
  and sublimation, 105
  and wit, 154, 156
Seduction, 120, 191

Sexuality, infantile, 24 ff., 192
Spitz, René A., 111, 196, 274
Stärcke, August, 101, 274
Structural hypothesis, 38
Sublimation, 104 ff., 198, 201
Suggestion, posthypnotic, 10 ff., 36 ff.
Superego, 38 ff., 122 ff., 199
  and anxiety, 85
  and dreams, 179
  and parapraxes, 140, 150 ff.
  and psychopathology, 197, 198
Superstition, 237-242
Suppression, 91
Symbol, 57 ff.
Symptom, (psycho) neurotic, 201 ff.

Technique, psychoanalytic
  and psychoneuroses, 189 ff.
  and study of unconscious mental
    processes, 15, 141, 143 ff., 154
  development, 6
  influence on psychiatry and psy-
    chotherapy, 8
Thinking, see Thought
Thought
  and delay in discharge, 42
  and signal anxiety, 82
  as ego function, 42
  magical, 66, 98, 133
  omnipotence of, 236

primary process, 52 ff., 145 ff.,
  154 ff.
secondary process, 52 ff., 155, 156
Time, 54 ff.
Tolstoy, Leo, 6, 257
Topographic hypothesis, 38
Trauma
  and anxiety, 77 ff.
  and hysteria, 191 ff.
  birth, 78
Traumatic neuroses, 80

Unconscious, as mental system, 36 ff.
Unconscious mental process, Chapter
  I, et passim
Undoing, 97 ff.
  example, 204
Unpleasure, 72 ff.

van Ophuijsen, J. H. W., 101, 274
Vocation, professional, 217-219
Voyeurism, 27

Wangh, M., 256, 274
Wish, see Drives; Fantasy, Gratifica-
  tion; Object; Oedipus complex;
  Wish fulfillment
Wish fulfillment, 169
Wit, Chapter VI
Woolf, P. J., 273